TRAVELER'S GUIDE TO

CAMPING MEXICO'S BAJA

Explore Baja and Puerto Peñasco With Your RV Or Tent

Third Edition

Mike and Terri
Church

D0556316

ROLLING HOMES PRESS

Published by
Rolling Homes Press
161 Rainbow Dr., #6157
Livingston, TX 77399-1061
www.rollinghomes.com

Printed in the United States of America
First Printing 2006

Publisher's Cataloging in Publication

Church, Mike.
Traveler's guide to camping Mexico's Baja : explore Baja
    and Puerto Peñasco with your RV or tent / Mike and Terri Church–Third
    Edition
    p.cm.
    Includes index.
    Library of Congress Control Number: 2006933877
    ISBN 0-9749471-5-6

    1. Baja California (Mexico : State)–Guidebooks. 2. Recreational vehicles–Mexico–Baja California (State)–Guidebooks. 3. Camp sites, facilities, etc.–Mexico–Baja California (State)–Guidebooks. 4. Recreation areas–Mexico–Baja California (State)–Guidebooks. I. Church, Terri. II. Title.

F1246.2.C48 2006   2006 933877
917.2'204836–dc21

*This book is dedicated
to four very good friends*

**Sophie, Giovanni, Sarah, and Mark
Aoki-Fordham**

Other Books by Mike and Terri Church
and
Rolling Homes Press

Traveler's Guide To
Mexican Camping

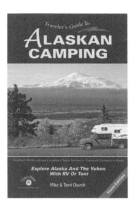

Traveler's Guide To
Alaskan Camping

Pacific Northwest
Camping Destinations

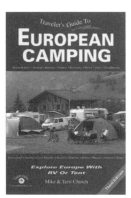

Traveler's Guide To
European Camping

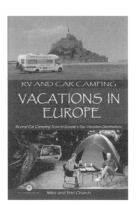

RV and Car Camping
Vacations in Europe

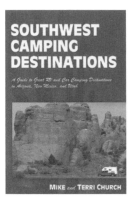

Southwest
Camping Destinations

A brief summary of the above books is provided on pages 254 and 255

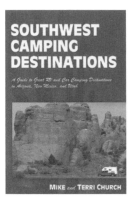

Updates Online

www.rollinghomes.com

When traveling by RV the most complete and up-to-date information on RV parks is always important. To provide our readers with the most current and accurate information available we maintain a website which lists all known updates and changes to information listed in our books. Just go to our website at www.rollinghomes.com and click on the *Book Additions and Corrections* button to review the most current information.

Warning, Disclosure, and Communication
With The Authors and Publishers

Half the fun of travel is the unexpected, and self-guided camping travel can produce much in the way of unexpected pleasures, and also complications and problems. This book is designed to increase the pleasures of Baja camping and reduce the number of unexpected problems you may encounter. You can help ensure a smooth trip by doing additional advance research, planning ahead, and exercising caution when appropriate. There can be no guarantee that your trip will be trouble free.

Although the authors and publisher have done their best to ensure that the information presented in this book was correct at the time of publication they do not assume and hereby disclaim any liability to any party for any loss or damage caused by errors, omissions, or any other cause.

In a book like this it is inevitable that there will be omissions or mistakes, especially as things do change over time. If you find inaccuracies we would like to hear about them so that they can be corrected in future editions. We would also like to hear about your enjoyable experiences. If you come upon an outstanding campground or destination please let us know, those kinds of things may also find their way to future versions of the guide or to our internet site. You can reach us by mail at:

Rolling Homes Press
161 Rainbow Dr., #6157
Livingston, TX 77399-1061

You can also communicate with us by sending an email through our website at:

www.rollinghomes.com

Chapter 4
South to Ensenada

Chapter 11
San Felipe

Chapter 12
Puerto Peñasco, Golfo, and Algodones

Chapter 5
Southern Northwest Coast

Chapter 6
Central Baja

Chapter 7
Central Gulf of California Coast

Chapter 8
South to La Paz

Chapter 9
Southern Loop

Chapter 10
Los Cabos

USA

MEXICO

Tecate

Tijuana

Rosarito

1D

Ensenada

3

2D

Mexicali

Algodones

San Luis Río Colorado

5

40

2

Golfo de
Santa Clara

8

Sonoyta

USA

MEXICO

3

San Felipe

Puerto
Peñasco

1

San
Quintín

El Rosario

1

Cataviña

Bahía de
los Angeles

Guerrero
Negro

1

San Ignacio

Santa Rosalía

Mulegé

Bahía
Concepción

Loreto

Puerto
Escondido

Ciudad
Constitución

San
Carlos

1

La Paz

La
Ventana

Todos
Santos

Los
Barriles

1

Cabo
San Lucas

San José
del Cabo

TABLE OF CONTENTS

INTRODUCTION 11

CHAPTER 1
WHY CAMP THE BAJA PENINSULA? 13

CHAPTER 2
DETAILS, DETAILS, DETAILS 18

CHAPTER 3
HOW TO USE THE DESTINATION CHAPTERS 42

CHAPTER 4
SOUTH TO ENSENADA 49
Introduction 49
    Highlights 49
    Roads and Fuel Availability 49
    Sightseeing 50
    Golf 51
    Beaches and Water Sports 51
    Fishing 51
    Backroad Adventures 51
The Routes, Towns, and Campgrounds
    Tijuana 52
    Tijuana to Rosarito 54
    Rosarito 56
    Rosarito to Ensenada 57
    Ensenada 64
    Tecate 72
    Tecate to Ensenada 75

CHAPTER 5
SOUTHERN NORTHWEST COAST 79
Introduction 79
    Highlights 79
    Roads and Fuel Availability 80
    Sightseeing 81
    Beaches and Water Sports 81

Fishing 81
Backroad Adventures 82
The Routes, Towns, and Campgrounds
Ensenada to San Quintín 83
San Quintín 89
San Quintín to El Rosario 93
El Rosario 94

CHAPTER 6

CENTRAL BAJA 97

Introduction 97
Highlights 97
Roads and Fuel Availability 98
Sightseeing 98
Beaches and Water Sports 99
Fishing 100
Backroad Adventures 101
The Routes, Towns, and Campgrounds
El Rosario to Cataviña 102
Cataviña 104
Cataviña to Guerrero Negro 106
Guerrero Negro 108
Side Trip to Bahía de los Angeles 112
Bahía de los Angeles 112
Guerrero Negro to San Ignacio 117
San Ignacio 119

CHAPTER 7

CENTRAL GULF OF CALIFORNIA COAST 123

Introduction 123
Highlights 123
Roads and Fuel Availability 123
Sightseeing 124
Golf 124
Beaches and Water Sports 124
Fishing 125
Backroad Adventures 125
The Routes, Towns, and Campgrounds
San Ignacio to Santa Rosalía 126
Santa Rosalía 127
Santa Rosalía to Mulegé 129
Mulegé 132
Mulegé to Bahía Concepción 136
Bahía Concepción 136
Bahía Concepción to Loreto 142
Loreto 143
Loreto to Puerto Escondido 146
Puerto Escondido 148

CHAPTER 8
SOUTH TO LA PAZ 151
Introduction 151
Highlights 151
Roads and Fuel Availability 151
Sightseeing 152
Beaches and Water Sports 152
Fishing...153
Backroad Adventures 153
The Routes, Towns, and Campgrounds
Puerto Escondido to Ciudad Constitución 154
Ciudad Constitución..155
Side Trip to San Juanico..157
San Juanico..158
Side Trip to Lopez Mateos 159
Lopez Mateos 159
Side Trip to Puerto San Carlos 160
Puerto San Carlos 161
Ciudad Constitución to La Paz.....................................162
La Paz..163
Side Trip to La Ventana 169
La Ventana...169

CHAPTER 9
SOUTHERN LOOP 173
Introduction 173
Highlights 173
Roads and Fuel Availability 173
Sightseeing 174
Beaches and Water Sports 174
Fishing...175
Backroad Adventures 175
The Routes, Towns, and Campgrounds
La Paz to Todos Santos..176
Todos Santos..177
Todos Santos to Cabo San Lucas 178
La Paz to Los Barriles 180
Los Barriles 182
Los Barriles to San José del Cabo................................185

CHAPTER 10
LOS CABOS 189
Introduction 189
Highlights 190
Roads and Fuel Availability 190
Sightseeing 190
Golf..191
Beaches and Water Sports 191

Fishing...192
Backroad Adventures 192
The Routes, Towns, and Campgrounds
Cabo San Lucas...193
Cabo San Lucas to San José del Cabo.........................195
San José del Cabo...199

CHAPTER 11
SAN FELIPE **203**
Introduction 203
Highlights..203
Roads and Fuel Availability 203
Beaches and Water Sports 204
Fishing...204
Backroad Adventures 204
The Routes, Towns, and Campgrounds
Mexicali...205
Mexicali to San Felipe.....................................206
San Felipe...209

CHAPTER 12
PUERTO PEÑASCO, GOLFO DE SANTA CLARA, AND ALGODONES **223**
Introduction 223
Highlights..223
Roads and Fuel Availability 224
Sightseeing 225
Golf...225
Beaches and Water Sports 225
Fishing...225
Backroad Adventures 225
The Routes, Towns, and Campgrounds
Sonoyta, Sonora and Lukeville, Arizona......................226
Lukeville/Sonoyta Crossing to Puerto Peñasco............227
Puerto Peñasco 230
San Luis Río Colorado, Sonora and San
Luis, Arizona...239
San Luis Río Colorado to Golfo de Santa Clara 239
Golfo de Santa Clara 240
Algodones...242

APPENDIX - ROAD SIGNS...**244**

INDEX **246**

ABOUT THE AUTHORS **253**

OTHER BOOKS **254**

ORDER FORM...**256**

Introduction

Traveler's Guide to Camping Mexico's Baja is one of seven guidebooks we write for campers. The titles of the others are *Traveler's Guide to European Camping, Traveler's Guide to Alaskan Camping, Traveler's Guide to Mexican Camping, Pacific Northwest Camping Destinations, Southwest Camping Destinations,* and *RV and Car Camping Vacations in Europe.*

Like all of our books this one is a guidebook written specifically for camping travelers. As a camper you don't need the same information that a fly-in visitor does. You don't care much about hotels, restaurants, and airline schedules, but you need to know what campgrounds are near, how to drive right to them without making wrong turns, and where to buy supplies. We want our book to be the one that you keep up front where it's handy, the one you refer to over and over because it contains what you need to know in a convenient format.

This is the third edition of *Traveler's Guide to Camping Mexico's Baja.* It's been only two years since we completed the last edition. We love to travel the Baja and doing the research to update this book is a great excuse to do it. You'll find several new campgrounds here, and if you're familiar with the Baja you'll find that a few have disappeared, particularly in the San Felipe area.

This book builds on the information included in *Traveler's Guide to Mexican Camping.* While that book covered the campgrounds of the Baja pretty thoroughly, it seemed to us that many travelers to the peninsula didn't really need the mainland information that makes up the greatest part of that book. Not only do they not need it, but they probably would rather not pay for it! It seemed to make sense to publish a Baja book and offer it for a much lower price. So that's pretty much what we have done. All of the Baja campgrounds that are included in *Traveler's Guide to Mexican Camping* are also included in this book as are many additional ones. We've also added over a hundred pages of Baja-specific information to this book.

This book also includes information about two destinations in northwest Sonora. The reason we've included this information is that these two locations offer many of the same attractions to RVers that the Baja does. They're just to the east of the Baja, close to the border, have great weather, and offer lots of outdoor attractions. If you haven't yet traveled to Mexico as a camper we recommend that you give Puerto Peñasco or Golfo de Santa Clara a try. Once you get your feet wet you might opt for a trip down the Baja or even one to mainland Mexico.

Updating the information and expanding the book has been a lot of fun. The Baja is one of our favorite camping destinations, we enjoy it more each time we visit. The peninsula is a Mexican jewel that is easily enjoyed by anyone with an RV or a tent and a sense of adventure. We hope to see you there!

BAJA

SUNRISE AT PLAYA SANTISPAC

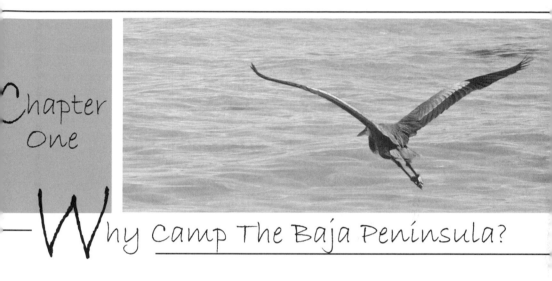

Chapter One

Why Camp The Baja Peninsula?

The border between the U.S. and Mexico's Baja Peninsula is like no other border on earth. It divides two countries with huge contrasts in culture, language, wealth, lifestyle, political systems, topography, and climate. Mexico is a fascinating place to visit and we think that driving your own rig and staying in campgrounds is the best way to do it. We hope that with this book in hand you will think so too.

People from north of the border have been exploring the Baja for years. The trip became much easier in 1973 when the paved Transpeninsular highway was built. Today this paved two-lane road leads to unparalleled camping opportunities.

Probably the largest number of folks who visit the Baja do so as fly-in tourists bound for the Los Cabos area at the end of the peninsula. There they find huge hotels, beaches, golf, fishing, and a bit of Mexican culture. That may be the easiest way to visit, it certainly is the most expensive. You can visit Los Cabos too, but as a camping traveler you'll also see the rest of the peninsula as you drive south, and you'll probably find you like it better.

While not really on the road to Los Cabos, Puerto Peñasco and San Felipe offer an easy introduction to Mexico. Both have easy to use border stations and good roads leading to seaside resorts that cater to the RV crowd. These are small, friendly towns that are easy to get around. There is a tradeoff, of course. Neither has great fishing and the new golf courses are just getting started. They do have great winter weather, decent prices, campsites along the beach, miles of back roads to explore with your four-wheeler, grocery stores, restaurants, and crafts markets. If you have any doubts about heading into Mexico these two towns can help you get your feet wet.

The west coast of the Baja near the California border, from Rosarito Beach south to Ensenada, is more of a weekend destination for folks from California than a long-term RVing destination. That's a simplification, many people have permanently-located RVs in this area. Others bring their rigs south for a month or two. The attractions here are bigger Mexican cities; lots of top-quality shopping, restaurants, and entertainment; golf; and decent fishing. You should be aware that unlike the rest of the Baja, this area is more popular as a summer destination than a winter one because winter weather is cool.

For those interested in desert flora and fauna the Baja between El Rosario and Santa Rosalía is a fascinating place. For over 300 miles (480 km) the road winds its way through a variety of desert terrain with a wealth of cactus species and rock gardens perfect for photography. There's even a sight offered nowhere else on earth - desert whales! During January through March you can visit the California gray whale nursery lagoons and actually closely approach the whales with government-supervised small boat tour operators. Another unusual attraction of the area is the cave paintings left by ancient Baja inhabitants.

If your real dream is to boondock in your RV on a quiet beach next to tropical waters there are many places you can go on the Baja. Many great camping beaches are located along the Gulf of California between Santa Rosalía and Puerto Escondido. Lots of people go no farther south, they're perfectly satisfied to stay on one beautiful beach for the entire season.

Fishermen love the Baja. Both coasts offer great fishing. Some places require heavy open-water boats so you either have to bring a big boat from north of the border or charter. In other places a small car-top aluminum boat or an inflatable will give you access to plenty of fish. Or you can fish right off the beach. There are many places to go if you want to find excellent fishing, some favorites are the East Cape near Los Barriles, the Loreto area, and Los Cabos.

Are you looking for a winter destination offering a comfortable full-hookup campground with the services of a larger city, lots to do, and great weather? Consider La Paz. It has a population of about 180,000, large supermarkets, airline service, and four campgrounds with full hookups, many with swimming pools. Los Cabos is only a day trip from La Paz. For a smaller town to use as a winter base try Los Barriles. It offers excellent fishing as well as good RV parks, good restaurants, and interesting nearby destinations.

A Possible Itinerary

Probably the best way to actually show you what Baja has to offer is to outline a tour down the peninsula. This is a seventeen day tour, that's the bare minimum, better would be a month.

The 1,060 mile (1,731 km) long Mex 1 stretches the entire length of the Baja Peninsula, from Tijuana in the north to Cabo San Lucas at the far southern cape. The two-lane highway gives access to some of the most remote and interesting country in the world including lots of desert and miles and miles of deserted beaches.

This proposed itinerary takes 17 days and allows you to see the entire length of the peninsula. There are layover days at Guerrero Negro, Bahía Concepción, La Paz, and Cabo San Lucas. Many travel days require only a morning of driving leaving lots of time to relax and explore.

The most tempting modification to this itinerary will be to spend more time at each stop. There are also many additional stopover points along this route, just take a look through this book. Finally, it is possible to take a ferry from either La Paz or Santa Rosalía to the Mexican west coast where you can head north for home or head south for more fun. If you plan to do that don't forget to take our book *Traveler's Guide to Mexican Camping* along.

🚐 **Day 1 - Tijuana to Ensenada, 67 miles (108 km), 1.5 hours driving time** - This first day you cross the border at Tijuana. You'll have to stop at the border to pick up a tourist card unless you've already taken care of this important bit of paperwork. There's a four-lane toll road that follows the coast all the way to Ensenada. You completed the drive to Ensenada before noon so there's plenty of time to look around town and pick up some groceries at one of the large modern supermarkets. Instead of spending the night at a campground in town you decide to stay at the beautiful Estero Beach Hotel/Resort campground beside the ocean a few miles south of Ensenada. You can celebrate your arrival in Mexico by having dinner at the excellent hotel restaurant.

🚐 **Day 2 - Ensenada to San Quintín, 122 miles (197 km), 4 hours driving time** - This will be another short day so there's really no hurry to get started. Once on the road you pass through rolling hills with the countryside getting dryer as you head south. At San Quintín you have a choice of campgrounds, try the Posada don Diego in Vicente

Guerrero if you want full hookups and a restaurant or maybe the El Pabellón to sample a simple ejido-run campground with miles of windswept beach out front.

🚐 **Day 3 - San Quintín to Bahía de los Angeles, 219 miles (353 km), 6.25 hours driving time** - This is a longer day's drive so get a fairly early start. You'll want to stop and explore the cactus and rock fields in the Cataviña area before leaving Mex 1 and driving east on a beautifully paved highway to Bahía de los Angeles for your first glimpse of the Gulf of California. There's not a lot to the town itself, perhaps this is a good opportunity to head north of town to a no-hookup campground along the water. If you have a small boat you might give the fishing a try. This is also great kayaking water.

Day 4 - Bahía de los Angeles to Guerrero Negro, 121 miles (195 km), 3.75 hours driving time - Today's destination is back on the other side of the peninsula, the salt-producing company town of Guerrero Negro. You'll spend two nights here because you want to visit the California gray whale nursery lagoon (Scammon's Lagoon) south of town. Spend the first night at the Malarrimo RV Park and visit their well-known restaurant. The second night you can spend at the primitive camping area right next to the lagoon after a day on the water with the whales.

Day 6 - Guerrero Negro to San Ignacio, 89 miles (144 km), 2.25 hours driving time - San Ignacio is a true date-palm oasis in the middle of desert country. There's a good campground here, the Rice and Beans Oasis. It has an excellent restaurant. Don't forget to visit the plaza at the center of town to visit the cave art museum and the old mission church.

Day 7 - San Ignacio to Bahía Concepción, 95 miles (153 km), 2.5 hours driving time - Today, once again, you return to the Gulf of California side of the peninsula. You'll pass two interesting towns en route, Santa Rosalía and Mulegé. Neither has much room for big rigs so don't drive into either of these little towns. At Santa Rosalía you might leave your rig along the highway and take a stroll to see the Eiffel-designed metal-framed church. You'll probably have a chance to explore Mulegé later since it is quite close to the evening's destination at Bahía Concepción. Many people decide to end their journey at this point and go no further since the ocean-side camping along beautiful Bahía Concepción is a camping paradise. We'll assume you'll be strong and only stay for two nights.

Day 9 - Bahía Concepción to La Paz, 291 miles (469 km), 8.25 hours driving time - Since you are all rested up after that time along the bahía you decide to get an early start and blast on through all the way to La Paz. Don't forget to drive into Loreto for a quick look around, this was the first permanent Spanish settlement on the peninsula. You'll have to ignore the golf course too, even though you'll see people teeing off as you pass.

You will find your progress along the coast to be quite scenic but slow, especially as you climb up and over the Sierra de la Giganta, but later for a long stretch on the plains to the west the roads are flat and straight allowing you to make good time. A late arrival in La Paz is not a problem because there are lots of campgrounds to choose from, but it's best to arrive before dark. You can take it easy the next day and explore the city.

Day 11- La Paz to Cabo San Lucas, 104 miles (168 km), 2.5 hours driving time - Today you will arrive in the true tourist's Baja. Take the short route to the Cape area by following Mex 19 around the west side of the Sierra de la Laguna. Stop to do a little shopping or perhaps have lunch in Todos Santos. You'll have made reservations at one of the campgrounds near Cabo San Lucas to ensure a place to base yourself.

Day 13 - Cabo San Lucas to Los Barriles, 68 miles (110 km), 1.5 hours

driving time - A short drive east to San José del Cabo and then north on Mex 1 will bring you to Los Barriles. There are a selection of reasonably-priced campgrounds in this interesting region. This is an excellent place to spend several weeks to gather yourself for the trip north.

Day 14 through 17 - Los Barriles to Tijuana, 974 miles (1,571 km), 26 hours driving time - You really have two choices for the return to the border. Many folks catch a ferry from La Paz to Topolobampo near Los Mochis and then drive north on four-lane Mex 15 to cross the border at Nogales near Tucson, Arizona. Others simply drive back the way they've come. By putting in decently long days of driving you could make the trip in four days with overnight stops at Ciudad Constitución (194 miles or 313 km), San Ignacio (255 miles or 411 km), and El Rosario (305 miles or 492 km). The final day to the border in Tecate is 220 miles (355 km).

How This Book Is Arranged

Chapter 2 - Details, Details, Details is filled with essential background information. It tells you how to prepare your rig, how to cross the border, and how to deal with unfamiliar things while you are in Mexico.

Chapter 3 - How to Use the Destination Chapters gives a brief guide to using the information making up the bulk of the book.

Chapters 4 through 12 - These are the meat of the book. They describe the route down the Baja and also San Felipe and Puerto Peñasco. Along the way we provide a location map and description of virtually every formal campground on the Baja. You'll also find information about places to explore and things to do along the way.

Have Fun!

Chapter Two

Details, Details, Details

Backroad Driving

It is hard to think of any other location in North America with such a wealth of back-road driving opportunities. While this is not a guidebook to Baja's backroad destinations we have tried to give readers some idea of what is available.

It seems that every guide to the Baja uses some system to rate the quality of the back roads. This is necessary, since they vary from wide graded roads to rocky tracks really only suitable for a burro. We've tried to skip the burro routes, but you should bear in mind that all back roads in this part of Mexico are very changeable. A winter storm can make even the best of them impassable for months and it's hard to predict when someone will run a grader along a road improving it in a major way. When you drive the back roads you must be prepared for the unexpected. Check road conditions with the locals, travel in groups of at least two rigs, and bring along equipment for getting out of trouble as well as for enduring several days in the hot dry desert. Some of the roads are very remote, you may have to save yourself if you have a problem.

We grade the roads into three types, the classifications depend upon the type of rig that is suitable:

Type 1 - An unpaved road usually suitable for motorhomes to 35 feet, and trailers that are not large or heavily loaded. Logic rules out big bus-type motorhomes, large fifth- wheels, and large trailers for travel off the pavement. These roads are occasionally graded but may have miles of washboard surfaces forcing you to creep along at very low speeds.

Type 2 - An unpaved road suitable for smaller RVs but not trailers. Our definition of smaller RVs requires good ground clearance, a maximum length of about 22 feet with no long or low rear overhangs, the ability to make steep climbs, and sturdy construction. The most common vehicle of this type is pickups with slide-in campers.

Type 3 - Requires four-wheel drive, lightly loaded, lots of clearance, and drivers with rugged constitutions and off-road experience.

We've rated roads based upon their normal condition but the roads do change and the ratings may become outdated. Check with someone who has recently driven the backroad route you are considering to see if conditions have changed.

Distances

As you plan your Baja trip and as you drive the highways you'll find the nearby Distance Table to be very helpful. We like to limit our driving days to no more than 200 miles on the Baja. Driving fast on Baja's roads is a good way to have an accident.

Campgrounds

Mexican campgrounds vary immensely, especially on the Baja. They range from full-service campgrounds near the border comparable to anything in the U.S. to places that are boondocking sites where nothing is provided except perhaps an outhouse.

Bathroom facilities in Mexican campgrounds are often not up to the standards of Canadian and U.S. private campgrounds. Cleanliness and condition vary widely, each of our campground descriptions tries to cover this important subject. Campers in larger RVs probably won't care since they carry their own bathrooms along with them. Other campers might keep in mind that many of the campgrounds they frequent in the U.S. and Canada, especially in national, state, or provincial parks, have pit toilets and no shower facilities just like many of the places on the Baja.

In rural Mexico it is usually not acceptable to put used toilet tissue in the toilet bowl, a waste-paper basket is usually provided. Toilet tissue creates problems for marginal plumbing and septic systems, it plugs them up. Travelers who have visited other third-world countries have probably run into this custom before.

Many Baja campgrounds have hookups for electricity, water, and sewer. The condition of the outlets, faucets, and sewer connections may not be of the same quality that you are accustomed to in the U.S. We find that in many campgrounds the hardware wasn't great when installed, and maintenance doesn't get done unless absolutely necessary. It is often a good idea to take a look at the connections on a parking pad before pulling in, you may want to move to another one.

Mexico uses the same 110-volt service that we use in the U.S. and Canada so your RV won't have to be modified for Mexico. Many campgrounds only have 15-amp household-type sockets so be sure that you have an adapter that lets you use these smaller sockets. Many sockets do not have a ground, either because the plug is the two-slot variety without the ground slot, or because the ground slot is not wired. It is a good idea to make yourself an adapter with a wire and alligator clip so you can provide your own ground.

When we identify a hook-up as 15 amp it usually just means that there is a normal

DISTANCE TABLE

Miles

Kilometers

Distance table (triangular matrix) with the following locations along the diagonal: Bahía Concepción, Bahía de Los Ángeles/Cabo San Lucas, Catavina, Ciudad Constitución, El Rosario, Ensenada, Golfo de Santa Clara, Guerrero Negro, La Paz, La Ventana, Loreto, Los Barriles, Mexicali, Mulegé, Puerto Escondido, Puerto Peñasco, Rosarito, San Carlos, San Felipe, San José/San José del Cabo, San Luis Río Colorado, San Quintín, Santa Rosalía, Tecate, Tijuana, Todos Santos.

two prong household-style outlet. Often it is impossible to determine the actually breaker setting, sometimes one breaker serves many sites and it is even possible that there is no breaker. You'll see many burnt-out or blackened sockets in Mexico because much more than the designed load has been pulled through the outlet.

It is a good idea to test the electricity at your site before plugging in. You can buy a tester at your camping supply store before heading south that will quickly indicate the voltage and any faults of the outlet. This is cheap insurance.

Air conditioner use is something of a problem in Mexico. Heavy air conditioner use can cause voltage drops because most campgrounds do not have adequately sized transformers. Our understanding is that service of less than 105 volts can damage your air conditioner, so keep an eye on voltage.

Water connections are common, but you may not want to trust the quality of the water even if the campground manager assures you that it is good. See the *Drinking Water* section of this chapter for details on how to cope with this.

Sewer connections in Mexican campgrounds are often located at the rear of the site. You should make sure that you have enough hose to reach several feet past the rear of your RV before you come south. You will find it difficult to buy sewer hose south of the border.

There are two references you may see in our campground write-ups that need a little explanation. We sometimes make reference to "government campgrounds". When the Transpeninsular was built the government put in many campgrounds for travelers. These soon deteriorated, generators stopped working and most were abandoned, at least for a time. Now many are in operation again as virtual boondocking sites run by individuals or ejidos.

You will also see references to ejidos or ejido campgrounds. Ejidos are a unique Mexican social enterprise. Space does not allow explanation of the whole idea here, but among gringos on the Baja the phrase ejido generally refers to a farming village while an ejido campground is one owned or operated by a Mexican village or family.

Caravans

An excellent way to get your introduction to Mexico is to take an escorted caravan tour. Many companies offer these tours, you'll see lots of caravans on the Baja. These range from luxury tours costing over $100 per day to months-long escort-only arrangements that are much less expensive.

A typical caravan tour on the Baja is composed of approximately 25 RVs. The price paid includes a knowledgeable caravan leader in his own RV, a tail-gunner or ca-boose RV with an experienced mechanic, campground fees, many meals and tours at stops along the way, and lots of camaraderie. Many people love RV tours because someone else does all the planning, there is security in numbers, and a good caravan can be a very memorable experience. Others hate caravans, and do so for just about the same reasons.

Remember that there will we a lot of costs in addition to those covered by the fee paid to the caravan company including fuel, insurance, maintenance, tolls, and groceries. We hear lots of good things about caravans, but also many complaints. Common problems include caravans that do not spend enough time at interesting places, delays due to mechanical problems with other rigs in the caravan, and poor caravan leaders who do not really know the territory or speak the language. A badly run caravan can be a disaster.

We've given the names, addresses and phone numbers below of some of the leading caravan companies. Give them a call or write a letter to get information about the tours they will be offering for the coming year. Once you have received the information do not hesitate to call back and ask questions. Ask for the names and phone numbers of people who have recently taken tours with the same caravan leader who will be in charge of the tour you are considering. Call these references and find out what they liked and what they didn't like. They are likely to have some strong feelings about these things.

Adventure Caravans, 125 Promise Lane, Livingston, TX 77351 (800 872-7897 or 936 327-3428).

Baja and Back, #138-5751 Cedarbridge Way, Richmond, BC, Canada V6X 2A8 (866 782-2252).

Baja Winters Travel Club, 315 S Hwy 101, #U, PMB 78, Encenitas, CA 92024 (866 771-9064).

Fantasy RV Tours, 111 Camino Del Rio, Gunnison, CO 81230 (800 952-8496).

Good Sam Caraventures, PO Box 6852, Englewood, CO 80155-6852 (800 664-9145).

Tracks to Adventure, 2811 Jackson Ave., Suite K, El Paso, TX 79930 (800 351-6053).

Vagabundos del Mar Boat and Travel Club, Adventure Tours, 190 Main St., Rio Vista, CA 94571 (800 474-2252).

Individual campers often do not like to stay in campgrounds that cater to caravans. When a campground fills with the RVs of a caravan the services usually deteriorate. The restrooms, hookups, and other facilities become strained. Also, campgrounds that accept caravans will often force short-term individual campers to leave when a caravan is scheduled. From about the 15th of January to the end of March the campgrounds of the southern Baja are full of caravans, they really affect individual campers. For this reason we have tried to indicate the locations that specialize in caravans.

Cash and Credit Cards

Mexico, of course, has its own currency, called the peso. As we go to press the exchange rate is about 10.9 pesos per US dollar. The currency has been relatively stable with a slow devaluation against the US dollar since a large devaluation in 1994. Some visitors, particularly on the Baja Peninsula, never seem to have any pesos and use dollars for most purchases. They pay for the privilege, prices in dollars are sometimes higher than if you pay in pesos.

Cash machines are now widespread in Mexico and represent the best way to obtain cash. If you don't already have a bank card you should take the trouble to get one before heading south, make sure it has a four-digit international number. Both Cirrus (Visa) and Plus (Master Card) networks are in place, not all machines accept both. Don't be surprised if a machine inexplicably refuses your card, bank operations and phone lines are both subject to unexpected interruptions. If you can't get the card to work try a machine belonging to another bank or just go directly to a teller inside the bank. You should consider bringing a back-up card in case the electronic strip stops working on the one you normally use or in case the machine eats your card. This last is infrequent but does happen. Most cards have a maximum daily withdrawal limit, usually about $400 U.S. In Mexico the limit is sometimes lower than in the U.S.

There are cash machines in Tijuana, Rosarito, Ensenada, Tecate, San Quintín, Guerrero Negro, Santa Rosalía, Loreto, Ciudad Constitución, La Paz, Los Barriles, Todos Santos, Cabo San Lucas, San José del Cabo, Mexicali, San Felipe, and Puerto Peñasco.

Traveler's checks are a decent way to carry money for emergencies. You never know when your debit card will inexplicably stop working. You'll probably be required to produce a passport for identification.

Visa and MasterCard credit cards are useful on the Baja. Restaurants and shops, particularly in tourist areas, accept them. Outside metropolitan and tourist areas their acceptance is limited. Pemex stations accept only cash but large supermarkets in Ensenada, Ciudad Constitución, La Paz, Cabo San Lucas, Mexicali and Puerto Pe-

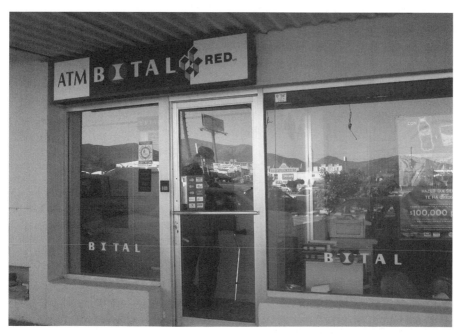

ATM MACHINES ARE AVAILABLE AT MANY BAJA CITIES

ñasco usually do accept them. It is also possible to get cash advances against these credit cards in Mexican banks but the fees tend to be high and passports are required for identification.

Crossing the Border
(Insurance, Tourist Cards, Fishing Licenses, Crossings)

One of the reasons campers choose the Baja over mainland Mexico is that it is easier to cross the border because less paperwork is required. Unlike the mainland, Baja does not require temporary vehicle permits.

While you are not required at this time to have a passport to travel to Mexico, you should know that the U.S. government has just announced new rules. Beginning December 31, 2007 all people crossing the border into the U.S. will be required to have a passport, that includes both U.S. and Canadian citizens. If you don't have a passport now you're going to need one then, you might as well go ahead and bite the bullet and get one. Those new passport application lines could get pretty long in the fall of 2007.

You must have a **tourist card** if you are going to travel on the Baja except in Puerto Peñasco, Golfo de Santa Clara, or San Felipe, see below. These are obtained at the Migración office at the border or from agents in the US, notably Discover Baja or Vagabundos del Mar (see insurance broker list below). To get your card you must present identification in the form of a passport or certified copy of your birth certificate and a picture I.D. like a drivers license. The card is issued for a set length of time, you should be asked how long you plan to be in Mexico. Make sure to get a card giving you enough time even for unexpected extensions. There is a fee of 210 pesos (about $19 U.S.) per person for the card. If you are getting the card at the border the money is not collected at the Migración office. Instead you take it to a bank and pay there. Sometimes there is a bank right at the crossing, at other times you'll have to visit a bank in town. The card is validated by a stamp at the bank. If you are buying your card from an agent in the US you pay when you get it, but you still must get the card stamped when you cross the border at the Migración office there.

Note that if you are in Mexico for less than 7 days you do not have to pay for the tourist card. Note also that you are required to turn the card when you cross the border heading north.

A word of warning is in order. The border crossings are very crowded and it can be difficult to find a place to park while you go inside to get your tourist cards. Many people find it easier to spend the night near the border the day before going into Mexico. They walk across the border from the US, get their cards, and then come back into the US. That way they can just drive on across the next day with no stop. It is no longer possible to get cards in Ensenada or at the border between Baja California and Baja California Sur near Guerrero Negro as in prior years. However, you will be checked to make sure you have one at the checkpoint at that location.

The towns of **Puerto Peñasco** and **Golfo de Santa Clara** fall within the Sonora free zone. Neither tourist cards nor vehicle permits are required for visiting these places. Cards and permits are not required for travel to **San Felipe** either.

If you plan to take a ferry from Santa Rosalía or La Paz to the mainland you will have to get your **temporary vehicle permits** before you will be allowed on the ferry. It is possible to do this in both Santa Rosalia and La Paz. In both they are issued at the ferry ticket offices at the ports. To get a vehicle permit you will need a driver's license for each motorized vehicle (in other words, you need two drivers to bring two motorized vehicles); a Visa, MasterCard, or American Express Card in the name of the vehicle driver; and your registration or title. If the vehicle is not registered in your name you need a notarized letter from the owner stating that you can take it into Mexico. A fee of about 320 pesos (approximately $30) will be charged on the card for each vehicle, you will be given a packet of paperwork, and a sticker will be placed on the inside of your front window in the upper middle. When you return to the U.S. you must stop at the Mexican border station and have them remove the sticker. They must do it, not you. If you do not have one of the credit cards mentioned above you must post a bond which is more complicated and expensive.

Your **automobile insurance** from home will not cover you in Mexico. Insurance is not required in Mexico, but you are very foolish to drive in Mexico without it. If you have an accident and have no insurance it is possible that you might be detained (in jail) for a considerable time.

Don't believe the old saw that all Mexican insurance costs the same, this is not true. Get several quotes and compare coverage. People who go into Mexico for just a short time usually buy daily coverage. This is extremely expensive, if you are planning to be in Mexico for over three weeks a six-month or one-year policy makes more sense. Some people get short-term coverage for the week or so it takes to get to their favorite campground. Once there they park the vehicle and don't use it until they buy more short term coverage for the drive home.

Longer term coverage, for six months or a year, is much cheaper. It is comparable with the cost of insurance in the U.S. Here are names and phone numbers for a few of the companies that offer Mexican insurance:

ADA Vis Global Enterprises, Inc., 38790 Sky Canyon Dr., Murrieta, CA 92563; (800) 909-4457; Website: www.adavisglobal.com.

Caravan Insurance Services, 127 Promise Lane, Livingston, TX 77351; (800) 489-0083 or (936) 327-5831; Website: www.caravaninsuranceservices.net.

Discover Baja Travel Club, 3089 Clairemont Dr., San Diego, CA 92117; (800) 727-2252 or (619) 275-4225; Website: www.discoverbaja.com.

Lewis and Lewis Insurance Agency, 8929 Wilshire Blvd., Suite 220, Beverley Hills, CA 90211; (800) 966-6830 or (310) 657-1112; Website: www.mexicanautoinsurance.com.

Miller Insurance Agency, Inc., 5805 SW Willow Lane, Lake Oswego, OR 97035; (800) 622-6347; Website: www.MillerRVInsurance.com.

Point South Insurance, 11313 Edmonson Ave., Moreno Valley, CA 92555; (888) 421-1394; Website: www.mexican-insurance.com.

Sanborn's Mexico Auto Insurance, 2009 S. 10th (SH-336), PO Box 310, McAllen, TX 78505-0310; (800) 222-0158; Website: www.sanbornsinsurance.com.

Vagabundos del Mar Boat and Travel Club, Adventure Tours, 190 Main St., Rio Vista, CA 94571; (800) 474-2252; Website: www.vagabundos.com.

Some of these are travel clubs requiring that you join, others are not. Additionally, most caravan companies (listed under *Caravans* in this chapter) also offer Mexican insurance, even to people not taking one of their caravans.

We recommend that you use the phone to compare costs and coverage long before you hit the road toward the Baja.

If you are going to take a boat in to Mexico for fishing you must have a boat permit and fishing permits for each person who will be in the boat. These boat and fishing permits are available from Mexican travel clubs like Discover Baja Travel Club (800 727-BAJA) and Vagabundos del Mar (800 474-BAJA). You will need your vehicle registration form for the boat to get the boat permit. You can also directly contact the Mexican Department of Fisheries in San Diego by calling (619) 233-6956. They will fax or mail you an application for boat and fishing permits so that you can do everything by mail. Their address is 2550 5th Ave., Suite 101, San Diego, CA 92103.

An important note about fishing and boat permits. You do not need a license to fish from shore, you also don't need a boat permit if you are not going to fish. However, if there is any fishing equipment in your boat at all, even a hook, you are required to have a permits for the boat and licenses for everyone on board. Additionally, even if you are only fishing from shore it is a good idea to have a fishing license since not all local police understand the rules. It's easier to have the license than to argue about a ticket.

Now, what can you bring in to Mexico? Campers tend to bring more things along with them when they visit Mexico than most people. When you cross the border you may be stopped and your things quickly checked. You are actually allowed to bring only certain specified items into Mexico duty free and most RVers probably have more things along with them than they should. Fortunately Mexican border authorities seldom are hard-nosed, in fact they usually don't do much looking around at all. Lately we have heard that people bringing large quantities of food sometimes have problems getting it across the border. Now that Mexico has such good supermarkets there is really little need to bring in food.

What can't you bring in to Mexico? Guns and illegal drugs. Either of these things will certainly get you in big trouble. If you travel much on Mexican highways you'll eventually be stopped and searched. Guns and drugs are exactly what they will be looking for. It is illegal for any non-Mexican to have a firearm of any type without a special Mexican permit. These are for hunters and must be obtained through licensed Mexican hunting guides.

There are a limited number of **border crossings** for visiting the Baja and northwest Sonora. Here are the details.

Tijuana has two crossings: San Ysidro and Otay Mesa. Of the two we prefer San

Ysidro even though it is closer to the center of town. When you are heading south the route to the toll road is straight forward and not difficult, we have included a driving log in the section *Tijuana to Rosarito* of Chapter 4 detailing the route. Heading north there can be terrible waits at both crossings, we prefer Tecate. San Ysidro is open 24 hours a day, Otay Mesa is open from 6 a.m. to 10 p.m.

The **Tecate** crossing is small and usually not crowded. The disadvantage of the crossing is that it is a little out of the way on both sides of the border. Crossing northwards Tecate usually has much shorter waits than either San Ysidro or Otay Mesa. This crossing is open from 6 a.m. to 11 p.m.

Mexicali has an in-town crossing and one about 7 miles east of town. We prefer the one east of town as it allows you to avoid driving through the center of town. The in-town crossing is open 24 hours, the east-of-town crossing is open from 6 a.m. to 10 p.m. We have included a driving log to reach the highway south from the crossing east of town in the *Mexico to San Felipe* section of Chapter 11.

Algodones is a crossing just east of Yuma, Arizona. We do not recommend crossing here unless you are just going to Algodones (there is a campground). The officials on the Mexico side have a bad reputation with RVers and connection to the road system is not as good as in nearby San Luis Río Colorado. The crossing is open 6 a.m. to 8 p.m.

The **San Luis Río Colorado** crossing is about 26 miles (42 km) south of Yuma, Arizona. It is usually not extremely busy, crosses into a small easy-to-navigate Mexican town, and is open 24-hours a day.

Finally, the **Sonoyta** crossing north of Puerto Peñasco is in a small town in the middle of nowhere. People crossing here are almost all headed for Puerto Peñasco. The crossing can be very busy on weekends and holidays, but otherwise is pretty quiet. It is open 24 hours a day.

Coming back into the U.S. you will need to be concerned about what you can bring back without duty. You are allowed $400 in purchases, 50 pounds of food, 200 cigarettes, 100 cigars, and 1 liter of alcohol per person.

Some Mexican-produced food is not allowed into the U.S. Customs agents know RVs have refrigerators and they will probably search yours and restrict importation of certain fruits and vegetables. All fruits are prohibited except bananas, blackberries, cactus fruits, dates, dewberries, grapes, lemons, limes (sour, the little ones), lychees, melons, papayas, pineapples, and strawberries. Avocados are prohibited but are allowed if you remove the seed, but not into California. All vegetables are allowed except potatoes, (Irish, sweet, and yams) and sometimes okra. Cooked potatoes, however, are allowed. Nuts are prohibited except acorns, almonds, cocoa beans, chestnuts, coconuts (without husks or milk), peanuts, pecans, piñon seeds (pine nuts), tamarind beans, walnuts, and waternuts. Eggs are prohibited if not cooked. Pork, raw, cooked, or processed is prohibited except some shelf-stable canned pork and hard cooked pork skins (cracklings). Poultry is prohibited if it is raw, thoroughly cooked poultry is allowed. Beef may not be allowed under the mad cow rules. Further information about customs allowances is available on the internet at www.customs.ustreas.gov/.

Drinking Water and Vegetables

Don't take a chance when it comes to drinking Mexican water. Even water considered potable by the locals is likely to cause problems for you. It is no fun to be sick, especially when you are far from the border in an unfamiliar environment. There are several strategies for handling the water question. Many people drink nothing but bottled water. Others filter or purify it in various ways.

We use a simple system. We purify all of the water that goes into our RV's storage tank with common bleach. Then we use a filter to remove the bleach taste, the microorganisms in the water have already been killed by the bleach. This means that we never hook up permanently to the local water supply, we always use the stored water in our rig. The advantage of this system is that you do not need to keep a separate supply of drinking water underfoot. The proof is in the results. We are almost never sick, and if we are it is usually possible to trace the problem to something we ate or drank while away from the RV. The filter we use is commonly offered as standard equipment on many RVs, it is manufactured by Everpure. Other charcoal filters probably work equally well to remove the taste of bleach.

The system we use is called superclorination. Add 1/6 ounce (1 teaspoon) of bleach (sodium hypochlorite) per each 10 gallons of water. The easiest way to do this is to measure it into the same end of your fill hose that will attach to or into your RV. That way you purify the hose too. Check the bleach bottle to make sure it has no additives, Clorox and Purex sold in Mexico are usually OK. You can tell because they have instructions for water purification right on the label.

If you don't want to bleach your water the best alternative is to drink bottled water. Everywhere in Mexico you can buy large 19 liter (approximately five-gallon) bottles of water. They are available at supermarkets, purified water shops, or from vendors who visit campgrounds. These are very inexpensive, you can either keep one of the large bottles by paying a small deposit or actually empty them into your own water tank.

Occasionally, even if you bleach your water and use a filter, you will pick up a load of water that doesn't taste too good. This is usually because it contains salt. This is a common problem on the Baja. A filter won't take this out. You can avoid the problem by asking other RVers at the campground about water quality before filling up.

Another source of potential stomach problems is fruit and vegetables. It is essential that you peel all fruit and vegetables or soak them in a purification solution before eating them. Bleach can also be used for this, the directions are right on the label of most bleach sold in Mexico. You can also purchase special drops to add to water for this purpose, the drops are stocked in the fruit and vegetable department of most supermarkets in Mexico.

Drugs, Guns, and Roadblocks

Visitors to Mexico are not allowed to possess either non-prescription narcotics or guns (except those properly imported for hunting). Do not take either in to Mexico, they can result in big problems and probably time spent in a Mexican jail.

Roadblocks and vehicle checks are common in Mexico. Often the roadblocks are staffed by military personnel. These stops can be a little intimidating, the soldiers

A MILITARY CHECKPOINT

carry automatic weapons and bring them right in to your RV when doing an inspection. English, other than a few words, is usually not spoken at the checkpoints but not much communication is really necessary, we have never had a problem. In general you will probably be asked where you came from (today), where are you going, do you have drugs or guns, and perhaps why you are in Mexico. It seems like every third RV or so gets inspected so don't get paranoid if yours is chosen. Accompany the person inspecting the rig as they walk through to answer any questions they might have, sometimes they have trouble figuring out how to open unfamiliar cabinets and storage areas. We generally discourage offering a beverage or anything else to officials at checkpoints, this might be considered a suspicious bribe, or might get the inspecting soldier in trouble with his superiors. It can also create expectations by the guards that later RVers will have to deal with.

Ferries

The ferry situation on Baja has changed completely in the last few years. There are now no fewer than three companies servicing La Paz and another servicing Santa Rosalía. It's much easier to use the ferries too, there are now offices to obtain your necessary vehicle documentation right at the ferry offices at the terminals in both places.

In La Paz there are three choices, one daily to Topolobampo near Los Mochis and two daily or semiweekly to Mazatlán. Note that all of these companies are likely to change their schedules and offerings frequently and on short notice. Also note that you should make reservations in advance with these companies. Many people make a reservation when they arrive in La Paz on the way south and then come back to take the ferry in a week or two.

The ferry company offering daily service to Topolobampo is Baja Ferries. They have the most modern ship, it makes the run in six hours. The old Sematur boat took ten hours. Their office is out at the Pichilingue terminal. The telephone numbers are (800) 122-1414 and (612) 125-7474, their website is www.bajaferries.com.

A new company making daily runs to Mazatlán is Transportación Maritima de California. This is a longer run, perhaps as much as 16 hours. We've heard that this company will let you stay in your RV while en route. You may have to request a special boat or parking location for this so be sure to check. This company also has an office at the Pichilingue terminal but it's a little hard to find, ask at the gate when you arrive. Their telephone number is (800) 744-5050 or (612) 121-4521 and their website is www.ferrytmc.com.

The original company, Sematur Transbordadores, continues to run a ferry to Mazatlán from La Paz but it no longer runs a ferry from La Paz to Topolabampo near Los Mochis. This company has a reputation for old ships and poor service. They have a ticket office at the Pichilinge terminal too. Their phone number is (800) 696-9600 or (612) 125-4440 and their website is www.sematur.com.mx.

From Santa Rosalía to Guaymas the company is Ferry Santa Rosalía. They have a very small ship but it will transport RVs. They run twice a week. Their telephone number is (615) 152-1246 and their website is www.ferrysantarosalia.com.

Fishing

Fishing is one of the most popular activities on the Baja. Today there are not as many fish as during the glory years of the 40's and 50's, but the fishing is still good. You can fish from shore, kayaks and canoes, car-top aluminum boats, trailer boats, or charter pangas or cruisers. They all can give you access to excellent fishing in the appropriate places and at the appropriate times.

Like fishing anywhere it helps to know the ins and outs of fishing on the Baja. Charter operators provide this as part of the package but if you are a do-it-yourselfer we suggest some research before you head south. See the *Internet* and *Travel Library* sections of this chapter.

Be sure to have the proper paperwork if you are going to fish or are on a boat with anyone fishing. See the *Crossing the Border* section above for details.

Fuel and Gas Stations

Choosing the brand of gas you're going to buy is easy in Mexico. All of the gas stations are Pemex stations. Pemex is the national oil company, it is responsible for everything from exploring for oil to pumping it into your car. Gas is sold for cash, no credit cards. There are often two grades of gasoline. Magna Sin in green pumps has an octane rating of about 87. A new higher octane unleaded called Premium is in the red pumps. Diesel is carried at many but not all stations.

On the Baja there are two price regions. Very near the border, for about 15 miles or so, where people come across from the US to fill up, prices are usually closer to the

U.S. price than farther south. Once you pass this border area prices are the same at every station, all the way to the tip of the peninsula. The only exception to this is very small stations in very remote places. Gas in these establishments is often pumped out of drums and can cost much more than the Pemex price. With proper planning you won't ever use one of these places.

Fuel prices in US dollars per gallon in May of 2006 were: Magna Sin $2.21, Premium $2.61, diesel $1.81. In Mexico there are seldom large increases in price. Instead, the price increases a few centavos per liter each month. For this reason Mexican prices are sometimes lower and sometime higher than U.S. prices.

Gas stations are not as common in Mexico as they are in the U.S. and Canada. On the Baja you should always be aware of how much fuel you have. One particularly bad spot is the "Baja gas gap" between El Rosario and Guerrero Negro. See Chapter 6 for more information about this.

Almost everyone you meet in Mexico has stories about how a gas station attendant cheated them. These stories are true. The attendants don't make much money and tourists are easy prey. You can avoid problems if you know what to expect.

The reason that the attendants are able to cheat people is that there are no cash registers or central cashiers in most of these stations. Each attendant carries a big wad of cash and collects what is displayed on the pump. Don't expect a receipt unless you ask. Until the stations install a control system with a separate cashier there will continue to be lots of opportunities for attendants to make money off unwary customers.

The favorite ploy is to start pumping gas without zeroing the pump. This way you have to pay for the gas that the previous customer received in addition to your own. The attendant pockets the double payment. The practice is so widespread that at many stations attendants will point to the zeroed pump before they start pumping. Signs at most stations tell you to check this yourself.

There are several things you can do to avoid this problem. First, get a locking gas cap. That way the attendant can't start pumping until you get out of the RV and unlock the cap. Second, check the zeroed meter carefully. Do not get distracted. If several people try to talk to you they are probably trying to distract you. They'll ask questions about the rig or point out some imaginary problem. Meanwhile the pump doesn't get zeroed properly.

While the gas is being pumped stand right there and pay attention. Another trick is to "accidentally" zero the pump and then try to collect for an inflated reading. If you watch carefully you will know the true reading and won't fall for this. Sometimes the pump gets zeroed before the tank is full, so don't just assume that you can chat because you have a big tank.

The process of making change presents big opportunities to confuse you. If you are paying in dollars, which is common on the Baja, have your own calculator handy and make sure you know the exchange rate before the gas is pumped. When paying do not just give the attendant your money. He'll fold it onto his big wad of bills and then you'll never be able to prove how much you gave him. We've also seen attendants quickly turn their backs and stuff bills in a pocket. Hold out the money or lay it out on the pump, don't let him have it until you can see your change and know that it is the correct amount.

All attendants will not try to cheat you of course. You'll probably feel bad about watching like a hawk every time you fill up with gas. The problem is that when you let down your guard someone will eventually take advantage of you, probably soon and not later. It is also customary to tip attendants a few pesos, particularly if they don't try to rip you off.

Green Angels

The Mexican government maintains a large fleet of green pickups that patrol all major highways searching for motorists with mechanical problems. Usually there are two men in the truck, they have radios to call for help, limited supplies, and quite a bit of mechanical aptitude. Most of them speak at least limited English. In Baja they only patrol the main highway and along most of Mex 1 pass by two times a day, once in the morning going out from their base and once in the afternoon coming back. The service is free except for a charge for the cost of supplies used. If they help you it is normal practice to give them a tip.

Groceries

Don't load your RV with groceries when you head south across the border. There is no longer any point in doing so. Some Mexican border stations are checking RVs to see that they don't bring in more than a reasonable amount of food. Also, at the border crossing between Baja California and Baja California Sur near Guerrero Negro officials are not allowing passage of citrus fruits, apples, potatoes, or avocados. Bananas and small limes are OK. Modern supermarkets in all of the large and medium-sized Mexican cities have almost anything you are looking for, often in familiar brand names. You can supplement your purchases in the supermarkets with shopping in markets and in small stores called *abarrotes, panaderías, tortillarías,* and *carnecerías* (canned goods stores, bakeries, tortilla shops, and butcher shops). There are now big supermarkets in the following towns: Tijuana, Rosarito, Ensenada, Ciudad Constitución, La Paz, Cabo San Lucas, Mexicali, and Puerto Peñasco.

Internet

The internet has become a wonderful tool for research. There are a great number of web sites with information about Mexico. Rather than trying to list them all here we have set up our own web site: **www.rollinghomes.com.** On it you will find current links to other web sites with good information about Mexico.

We have another use for our web site. As a small publisher we can only afford to update our travel guides on a two to four year cycle. In order to keep the books more current we publish updated information on the web. Our site has pages for each of our books with updates referenced by page number. We gather information for these updates ourselves and also depend upon information sent in by our readers. You can contact us through our web site or by mail with update information. This update information is only posted until we begin researching a new edition (generally about 6 months before publication), after that we only post updates for the new book.

Pets

You can take your dog or cat into Mexico. Virtually all Mexican RV parks allow dogs and cats although most do require that they be kept on a leash. Birds and other pets are subject to additional border restrictions, taking them to Mexico is not practical. We've not heard of anyone taking a pet into Mexico who has run into problems going south, a rabies vaccination certificate is officially required but seldom checked. The rules you need to be concerned about are the ones for bringing the animal back into the U.S. The U.S. Department of Health and Human Services web site says that dogs coming back into the U.S. require a rabies vaccination certificate that is at least 30 days old with an expiration date that is not expired. Your vet should have the proper form to certify this. Your dog or cat may also be examined at the border to see if it seems to be sick, if there is a question you may be required to have it examined by a vet before it will be admitted to the U.S.

Propane

Either propane or butane is available near most larger town or cities. The LP Gas storage yards are usually outside the central area of town. Ask at your campground for the best way to get a fill-up, in many locations trucks will deliver to the campground. We've also seen people stop a truck on the street and get a fill-up.

We're accustomed to seeing only propane in much of the U.S. and Canada because butane won't work at low temperatures, it freezes. In parts of the southern U.S. and the warmer areas in Mexico butane is common and propane not available. This probably won't be a problem, most propane appliances in RVs will also run on butane. Make sure you use all the butane before you take your RV back into the cold country, however.

The fact is that you may never need to fill up with LP Gas at all. We find that if we fill up before crossing the border we have no problem getting our gas to last two months because we only use it for cooking. Some people run their refrigerators only on gas because the modern electronic control boards can be damaged by the fluctuating electrical voltage common to Mexican campgrounds, particularly if the batteries in the circuit are not in good charged-up condition.

Roads and Driving in Mexico

If there were only one thing that could be impressed upon the traveler heading south to drive in Mexico for the first time it would be "drive slowly and carefully". The last thing you want in Mexico is an accident or a breakdown, driving slowly and carefully is the best way to avoid both of these undesirable experiences.

Baja's roads are getting better. The last time we drove Mex 1 long stretches had just been resurfaced and were beautiful. On the other hand, travelers who had driven this same road just a month before reported terrible potholes. Conditions change and you can't count on great roads. Cautious driving will mean fewer flat tires and broken springs.

One concern many travelers have about the Transpeninsular is that much of it is only nineteen feet wide (9.5 foot lanes) with no shoulders. That is indeed narrow, wide-body RVs are eight and a half feet wide not counting the mirrors. RVer usually adjust

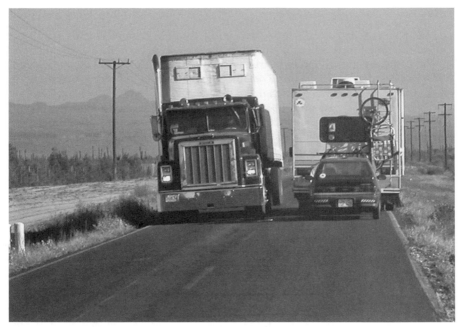

MEX 1 CAN SEEM A LITTLE NARROW

their left-side rear-view mirror to be as close to the side of the RV as possible while still being useable. Marking the front face of the left outside mirror with high-visibility tape also helps. The best strategy to follow is to drive slowly and carefully. When you see traffic approaching; especially if it is a truck, bus, or RV; slow even more so that you have complete control of your rig, and get over as far as you safely can. The good news is that there is very little traffic on most of the Transpeninsular.

Do not drive at night. There are several reasons for this. Animals are common on roads in Mexico, even in daylight hours you'll find cows, horses, burros, goats, pigs and sheep on the road. At night there are even more of them, they're attracted by the warm road surface and they don't have reflectors. Truckers like to travel at night because they can make good time in the light traffic. Some of these guys are maniacs, in the morning you'll often see a fleet of tow trucks lined up along the edge of a highway trying to retrieve one from a gully. Truckers also often leave rocks on the road at night, this is done to keep someone from hitting them when they break down, or to block the wheels when stopped on a hill. Often these rocks aren't removed, they're very difficult to see in time at night. Finally, driving at night means that if you have a breakdown you're going to be in an unsafe position. Mexican roads are good places to avoid after dark.

No discussion of driving in Mexico is complete without a discussion of traffic cops and bribes. Traffic cops (and many other government functionaries) are underpaid, they make up for it by collecting from those who break the law. This is not condoned by the government, but it is a fact of life. Norteamericanos usually feel uncomfortable with this custom and as a result they are difficult targets for cops with a *mordida* habit. Unfortunately some cops do not yet know this.

The best way to avoid the *mordida* trap is to scrupulously follow all traffic laws. Even if everyone around you is breaking the law you should follow it. If only one person in a line of cars gets arrested for not stopping at a railroad crossing you can be sure that it will be the gringo in the fancy RV (we know this from personal experience). Obey all speed limits, especially easy to miss are those at schools and small towns along a highway. Stop at the stop sign at railroad crossings even though no one else will. Wear your seat belt too, this is the law in Mexico and probably the largest source of tickets.

In the event that you do get stopped we recommend against offering a bribe. It is possible that you might get yourself in even worse trouble than you are already in. If you can't talk your way out of a fine the normal practice is to accompany the officer back to his headquarters (bringing your vehicle) to pay the fine. Most fines are quite reasonable by Norteamericano standards and if you've really done something wrong it's best to go ahead and pay.

Occasionally a police officer will suggest that such a trip can be avoided by paying a reasonable fee to him on the spot, let your conscience be your guide. There are no hard and fast rules or sure-fire ways to deal with the police. We find that the best strategy is to be very polite, appear to be relaxed, speak little or no Spanish, and be prepared to follow the officer to the police station if it becomes necessary. A dishonest officer doesn't really want to spend a lot of time and effort conspicuously dealing with a gringo in a huge and hard to miss vehicle. If you haven't really done anything wrong you'll usually end up being told to "go with god".

Recently we've heard several reports of RVers stopped by police who have paid large bribes. The unfamiliar situation and fear of foreign laws is no doubt the reason. Don't do this – it makes it harder on everyone who follows behind.

Everyone's least favorite thing is to get involved in an accident. In Mexico there are special rules. First and most important is that you had better have Mexican insurance. Your insurance carrier will give you written instructions about the procedure to follow if you get into an accident. Take a look at it before you cross the border to make sure you understand exactly how to handle an accident before it happens. Usually you must report an accident of any kind before leaving Mexico to receive reimbursement. See the *Crossing the Border* section above for the names of some Mexican insurance brokers.

Road signs in Mexico are usually not hard to understand. International-style signs are used for stops, parking, one way roads, and may other things. However, we often meet folks with questions about one or another sign they have been seeing during their travels. In the appendix at the back of this book you'll find our signpost forest, pictures of signs you're likely to see along the road along with their meaning in English.

Safety and Security

Mexico would be full of camping visitors from the U.S. and Canada if there was no security issue. Fear is the factor that crowds RVers into campgrounds just north of the border but leaves those a hundred miles south pleasantly uncrowded. People in those border campgrounds will warn you not to cross into Mexico because there are banditos, dishonest cops, terrible roads, and language and water problems. The one thing you can be sure of when you get one of these warnings is that that person has not tried Mexican camping him/herself.

First-time camping visitors are almost always amazed at how trouble-free Mexican camping is. Few ever meet a bandito or get sick from the water. The general feeling is that Mexico is safer than much of the U.S., especially U.S. urban areas. After you've been in Mexico a few years you will hear about the occasional problem, just as you do north of the border. Most problems could have been easily avoided if the person involved had just observed a few common-sense safety precautions. Here are the ones we follow and feel comfortable with.

Never drive at night. Night driving is dangerous because Mexican roads are completely different at night. There are unexpected and hard-to-avoid road hazards, there are aggressive truck drivers, and there is little in the way of formal security patrols. If there are really any banditos in the area they are most likely to be active after dark.

Don't boondock alone except in a place you are very sure of. Individual free campers are uniquely vulnerable. Many folks don't follow this rule and have no problems, it is up to you.

Don't open the door to a knock after dark. First crack a window to find out who is knocking. Why take chances?

Don't leave your rig unguarded on the street if you can avoid it. Any petty crook knows your RV is full of good stuff, it is a great target. We like to leave ours in the campground while we explore. Use public transportation, it's lots of fun.

There are a couple of security precautions that you can take before leaving home, you probably have already taken them if you do much traveling in your RV. Add a deadbolt to your entrance door, some insurance policies in the States actually require this. If possible install an alarm in your vehicle, it can take a load off your mind when you must leave it on the street.

Spanish Language

You certainly don't need to be able to speak Spanish to get along just fine in Mexico. All of the people working in campgrounds, gas stations and stores are accustomed to dealing with non-Spanish speakers. Even if you can't really talk to them you'll be able to transact business.

Telephones

Telephone service is rapidly improving in Mexico but is still expensive. Almost all towns along the highway now have phones on the street that you can use to call home for a reasonable fee, if you know how. If a town does not yet have the street-side phones it usually has a phone office. You go in and the operator will dial for you and send you to a booth. When you are finished she'll get the charge and you pay her with cash.

Mexican phone numbers now have a three digit area code and then seven digits, just like in the U.S. and Canada. The exception is cell phones. In some areas they have a prefix, 044. When you are in the local area you dial that prefix, outside the local area you leave out the prefix and just dial normally, as explained below.

To call into Mexico from the U.S. or Canada you must first dial a 011 for international access, then the Mexico country code which is 52, then the Mexican area code and number. Often businesses will advertise in the U.S. with a number which includes some or all of these prefixes. Now that you know what they are you should have no problems dialing a Mexican number.

In recent years phones in kiosks or booths, usually labeled Ladatel or Telmex have appeared along the streets in more and more Mexican towns. To use them you buy a phone card, usually at pharmacies. These are computerized smart cards charged with 10, 20, 30, 50, or 100 pesos. When you insert them into the phone the amount of money left on the card appears on a readout on the phone. As you talk the time left counts down on the readout.

To dial an international call to the U.S. or Canada you dial 00 + 1 + area code + the local number.

To place a collect call you dial 09 + 1 + area code + local number.

To dial a Mexican long distance number you dial 01 + area code + the local number.

To dial a local number you generally just dial the local number without the area code.

The latest scourge to hit the telephone-starved traveler to Mexico is credit card-accepting phones placed conveniently in many tourist areas. Many Mexican businesses have allowed these things to be installed as a convenience to their customers since a normal phone is difficult to obtain. Unfortunately they are a real problem, the rate charged is often in excess of $10 per minute for calls to numbers outside Mexico. We have talked to several unsuspecting users who found charges of several hundred dollars on their credit card statements when they returned home. You can pick up any of these phones and ask the English-speaking operator for the name of the company providing the service as well as the initial and per-minute fee. If the service is not being provided by Telmex you should be extremely cautious. Hopefully these rates will go down as people wise up and learn to ask.

Travel Library

Don't go to Mexico without a general tourist guide with information about the places you'll visit. Even if you're on the Baja for the sun and fun you'll have questions that no one seems to be able to answer. One of the best of the guides for our money is *Moon Handbooks: Baja* by Joe Cummings (Moon Publications Inc., Chico, CA, 2004, ISBN 1-56691-606-2).

A cult favorite in the travel guide genre is *The People's Guide to Mexico* by Carl Franz (John Muir Publications, Santa Fe, NM, ISBN 1-56691-711-5). This book has been around since 1972, it's frequently updated, and it's filled with an encyclopedic mix of information about pretty much everything Mexican that you will wonder about during your visit. It's also so well written that it is hard to put down.

A book that is very helpful in understanding the Mexican culture and people is *There's a Word for It in Mexico: The Complete Guide to Mexican Thought and Culture* by Boyé Lafayette De Mente (NTC Publishing Group; Lincolnwood, Illinois, ISBN 0-8442-7251-5).

Maps are very useful on the Baja, particularly if you are traveling back roads. There's an atlas of the peninsula called *Baja California Almanac: Mexico's Land of Adventure* (Baja Almanac Publishers, Inc.; Las Vegas, NV; ISBN 0-9658663-2-7). The same publishers also offer a great folding map called Baja California Peninsula: Mexico's Land of Adventure (ISBN 0-9658663-3-5).

There are a wealth of books available about the Baja. Some of the following are out of print but if they are you can probably find them on Amazon.com or E-Bay. Don't read Walt Peterson's *The Baja Adventure Book* (Wilderness Press, Berkeley, CA, 1999, ISBN 0-89997-231-4) if you're not sure you really want to visit the Baja because after reading it you won't be able to stay away. *The Magnificent Peninsula: The Comprehensive Guidebook to Mexico's Baja California* by Jack Williams (H.J. Williams Publications, Redding, CA, 1998, ISBN 1-891275-00-3) is just what the title says. It has lots of information about camping spots on the peninsula, and lots of other things too. A book using satellite maps of the peninsula is *The Baja Book IV: The Guide to Today's Baja California* by Ginger Potter (Baja Source, Inc., El Cajon, CA, 1996, ISBN 0-9644066-0-8). To get some good background try reading *Into a Desert Place: A 3000-Mile Walk Around the Coast of Baja California* by Graham Machintosh (W.W. Norton & Co., New York, NY, 1990, ISBN 0-393-31289-5). Fishermen will find *The Baja Catch* by Neil Kelly and Gene Kira (Apples and Oranges, Inc., Valley Center, CA, 1997, ISBN 0-929637-04-6) to be absolutely essential. Surfers may find **The Surfer's Guide to Baja** by Mike Parise (SurfPress Publishing, California, 2003, ISBN 0-9679100-1-3) to be worth parting with the change. Kayakers will love *Adventure Kayaking Baja* by Andromeda Romano-Lax (Wilderness Press, Berkeley, California, 2001, ISBN 0-89997-247-0). For information about the landforms and plants along the highway bring along *Roadside Geology and Biology of Baja California* by John, Edwin, and Jason Minch (John Minch and Associates, Inc., Mission Viejo, CA, 1998, ISBN 0-9631090-1-4). Also lots of fun if you can find them are some old books about exploring the Baja back country by Perry Mason detective novel author Erle Stanley Gardner: *Mexico's Magic Square, Off the Beaten Track in Baja, The Hidden Heart of Baja, Hovering over Baja*, and *Hunting the Desert Whale*. Try libraries and used book stores for these classics.

A visit to Mexico is a great way to study Spanish. Make sure to bring along a good Spanish-English dictionary. If you want to study while on your trip we recommend **Living Language's Spanish Complete Course: Basic-Intermediate, Compact Disc Edition,** ISBN 140002031X. It comes with CDs, great for studying while on the road.

Most of these books can be purchased at Amazon.com. You can follow links from our web site: www.rollinghomes.com.

Units of Measurement

Mexico is on the metric system. Most of the world has already learned to deal with this. For the rest of us it takes just a short time of working with the metric system, and there is no way to avoid it, to start to feel at home. Conversion tables and factors are available in most guidebooks but you will probably want to memorize a few critical conversion numbers as we have.

For converting miles to kilometer, divide the number of miles by .62. For converting kilometers to miles, multiply the kilometers by .62. Since kilometers are shorter than miles the number of kilometers after the conversion will always be more than the number of miles, if they aren't you divided when you should have multiplied.

For liquid measurement it is usually enough to know that a liter is about the same as a quart. When you need more accuracy, like when you are trying to make some sense out of your miles per gallon calculations, there are 3.79 liters in a U.S. gallon.

Weight measurement is important when you're trying to decide how much cheese or hamburger you need to make a meal. Since a kilogram is about 2.2 pounds we just round to two pounds. This makes a half pound equal to about 250 grams and a pound equal to 500 grams. It's not exact, but it certainly works in the grocery store, and we get a little more than we expected for dinner.

Temperature is our biggest conversion problem. The easiest method is to just carry around a conversion chart of some kind. If you don't have it with you just remember a few key temperatures and interpolate. Freezing, of course is 32 F and 0 C. Water boils at 212 F and 100 C. A nice 70 F day is 21 C. A cooler 50 F day is 10 C. A hot 90 F day is 32 C.

Here are a few useful conversion factors:

1 km = .62 mile	1mile = 1.61 km
1 meter = 3.28 feet	1 foot = .30 meters
1 liter = .26 U.S. gallon	1 U.S. gallon = 3.79 liters
1 kilogram = 2.21 pounds	1 pound = .45 kilograms

Convert from °C to °F by multiplying by 1.8 and adding 32
Convert from °F to °C by subtracting 32 and dividing by 1.8

Vehicle Preparation and Breakdowns

One of the favorite subjects whenever a group of Mexican campers gets together over cocktails is war stories about breakdowns and miraculous repairs performed by Mexican mechanics with almost no tools. Before visiting Mexico many people fear a breakdown above all else. Our experience and that of the people we talk to is that on the main roads help is generally readily available. Lots of other RVers are traveling the same route and they will stop to help.

While it is usually possible to find someone to work on the vehicle, it is often very hard to get parts. Ford, General Motors, Chrysler, Volkswagen and Nissan all manufacture cars and trucks in Mexico and have large, good dealers throughout the country. Toyota does not. These dealers are good places to go if you need emergency or maintenance work done on your vehicle. However, many of the models sold in the north are not manufactured in Mexico and the dealers may not have parts for your particular vehicle. They can order them but often this takes several weeks.

Often the quickest way to get a part is to go get it yourself. One of our acquaintances recently broke an axle in Villahermosa. His vehicle is common in Mexico, but the type of axle he needed was not used in the Mexican models. Rather than wait an indeterminate length of time for a new axle he went and picked one up himself. He climbed on a bus, traveled to Matamoros, walked across the border, caught a cab to a dealer, picked up a new axle and threw it over his shoulder, walked back across the border, caught another bus, and was back in Villahermosa within 48 hours. This works on the Baja too, there is a steady stream of busses traveling the Transpeninsular to and from Tijuana.

Avoid problems by making sure your vehicle is in good condition before entering Mexico. Get an oil change, a lube job, and a tune-up. Make sure that hoses, belts, filters, brake pads, shocks and tires are all good. Consider replacing them before you leave. Driving conditions in Mexico tend to be extreme. Your vehicle will be operating on rough roads, in very hot weather, with lots of climbs and descents.

Bring along a reasonable amount of spares. We like to carry replacement belts, hoses, and filters (and any special tools necessary to change them). Make sure you have a good spare tire.

RV drivers need to be prepared to make the required hookups in Mexican RV parks. RV supplies are difficult to find in Mexico so make sure that you have any RV supplies you need before crossing the border.

Electricity is often suspect at campgrounds in Mexico. It is a good idea to carry a tester that will tell you when voltages are incorrect, polarities reversed, and grounds lacking. Always carry adapters allowing you to use small 110V, two-pronged outlets. The best setup is one that lets you turn the plug over (to reverse polarity) and to connect a ground wire to a convenient pipe, conduit, or metal stake.

If you spend several weeks hooked up to high voltage Mexican electricity it is likely that your batteries will boil off a lot of water. It is absolutely essential to check your batteries much more frequently in Mexico than you do at home. Once a week is best. We're convinced that poorly serviced batteries are a major problem of damage to refrigerator circuit boards. Charged batteries provide a cushion effect, dead ones do not.

Sewer hookups in many Mexican campgrounds are located at the rear of the site. Make sure you have a long sewer hose, one that will reach all the way to the rear of your RV and then another couple of feet. You'll be glad you have it.

Water purity considerations (see the *Drinking Water* title in this chapter), mean that you may need a few items that you may not already have in your RV. Consider adding a charcoal water filter if you do not already have one installed. You should also have a simple filter for filtering water before it even enters your RV, this avoids sediment build-up in your fresh water tank. Of course you'll also need a hose, we have found a 20-foot length to be adequate in most cases.

It is extremely hard to find parts or knowledgeable mechanics to do systems-related work on camping vehicles. Before crossing the border make sure your propane system, all appliances, toilet, holding tanks, and water system are working well because you'll want them to last until you get home. Marginal or jury-rigged systems should be repaired. Consider bringing a spare fresh water pump, or at least a diaphragm set if yours isn't quite new. Make sure your refrigerator is working well, you'll need it and replacement parts are impossible to find. There is one repair center for refrigerators and some other RV systems in San José del Cabo. See that section in this book for more information.

Make sure you have all the tools necessary to change a tire on your rig, and a spare tire. Many large motorhomes no longer come with jacks, tire-changing tools, or even spares. The theory must be that it is too dangerous for an individual to change a tire on one of these huge heavy RVs. This may be true but you need to have the proper tools available so that you can find help and get the job done if you have a flat in a remote location. Mexican roads are rough and flat tires common. Even if you don't normally carry a spare you should have at least an unmounted tire that can be mounted if you destroy one on your RV, it can be difficult to find the right size tire for big RVs on the Baja.

If you do have a breakdown along the road what should you do? It is not a good idea to abandon your RV. RVs are a tempting target, one abandoned along the road invites a break-in. This is one good reason not to travel at night. Daytime drivers can usually find a way to get their broken-down RV off the road before night falls. If you are traveling with another rig you can send someone for help. If you are traveling by yourself you will probably find it easy to flag down a car or another RV. Ask the other driver to send a mechanic or *grúa* (tow truck) from the next town. Large tow trucks are common since there is heavy truck traffic on the Transpeninsular.

Weather and When To Go

The winter dry season is when most travelers visit the Baja. In a fortunate conjunction of factors the extremely pleasant warm dry season on the Baja occurs exactly when most northerners are more than ready to leave snow and cold temperatures behind. Comfortable temperatures occur beginning in November and last through May. The shoulder months of October and June may be uncomfortably warm for some people.

Be aware that August through October is the hurricane season on the Baja. Each year several hurricanes strike the southern end of the peninsula, some do a considerable amount of damage. When this happens flash floods are common and often cause loss of life, stay out of the washes during storms.

On the other hand, unlike the rest of Mexico the Baja is a popular summer RV destination too. The northern west coast of the peninsula is really a summer destination, winters can be pretty cool. Also, many people come to the Baja for the fishing, and the hot season is the best one for that.

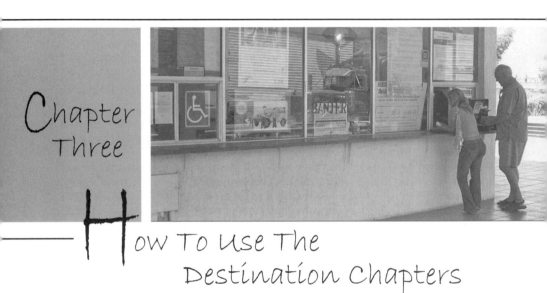

Chapter Three

How To Use The Destination Chapters

The focus of this book is on campgrounds, of course. A question we often hear is "Which campground on the Baja is your favorite?" Usually the person asking the question has a personal favorite in mind. Our answer is always the same – we like them all. No one campground is the best because everyone likes different things. Also, the personality of a campground depends upon the people staying there when you visit. People traveling on their own in an environment they are not used to tend to be very friendly, this is one of the best things about Mexican camping. We can't tell you exactly who will be staying in each of the campgrounds in this book when you decide to visit, but we will try to give you a good feel for what to expect in the way of campground features and amenities.

Chapter 4 through 12 contain information about the many camping destinations you may visit on the Baja and in northwest Sonora. The chapters are arranged somewhat arbitrarily into regions that fall naturally together for a discussion of their camping possibilities.

Introductory Map

Each of the campground chapters begins with a road map. The map shows a lot of information that will allow you to use it as an index to find campgrounds as you travel. The map shows the route covered in the chapter and also the most important towns. Dotted lines on the map show areas covered in maps later in the chapter, these later maps show the actual locations of the campgrounds. An index on the map page shows the names of all route and town descriptions in the chapter and the page number where each can be found.

Introductory Text

Each chapter starts with an introduction giving important information about the region covered in the chapter. Most of this information is important to a camping traveler and much of it is not necessarily included or easy to find in normal tourist guides. On the other hand, much information that is readily available in normal tourist guides will not be found in this book. Other books do a good job of covering things like currency information, hotels, restaurants, language, and tour details. This book is designed to be a supplement to normal tourist guides, not to replace them. It provides a framework, other guides must be used to fill it the details.

For Baja travelers the roads and fuel availability are especially important so there is a section in each chapter describing the major roads and giving the location of the gas stations. When appropriate we also include sections summarizing the details of sightseeing, golf, beaches and water sports, and fishing in the area. It is handy to have some idea what to expect.

We've also included a section titled *Backroad Adventures*. Paved roads other than the Transpeninsular are scarce, in remote areas of the peninsula you'll probably find yourself on some back roads. They are the only way to reach many of the best destinations on the Baja. You must be aware, however, that these roads are not appropriate for all vehicles, especially not for all RVs. Be sure to review the section titled *Backroad Driving* in the *Details, Details, Details* chapter. Very few of the formal campgrounds on the Baja are away from the paved highway system so don't be concerned if you don't have a rig that is appropriate for backroad driving.

Route and Town Descriptions

Following the introductory material in each chapter is ***The Routes, Towns, and Campgrounds*** section. You'll find campground overview maps showing the major roads and campground locations and text describing each route or town. There are descriptions of the driving routes and of the towns and recreational areas.

We have given population numbers for each major town. These are our estimates. Population figures are notoriously unreliable in Mexico, and the number of residents in an area can change rapidly.

We've also included many mileage figures and have used kilometer markers extensively. Almost all of the major roads on the Baja Peninsula are marked with kilometer posts. Be prepared for many missing ones, but overall they are a useful way to fix locations.

The users of this book are probably going to be folks from both the U.S. and Canada.

As everyone knows the U.S. uses miles and Canada uses kilometers. We've tried to give both numbers when we mention distances. Canadians will no doubt notice our bias - the mileage figures come first. Our excuse is that most Canadians are familiar with both systems while most of us from the states aren't quite comfortable yet with kilometers.

Campground Overview Maps

Each important city or town and each region between the towns has its own campground overview maps. These maps are designed to do two things: they quickly show you the lay of the land and the campgrounds that are available, and if you examine them more carefully they will help you drive right to the campground you have decided to use.

There are two different types of campground overview maps. The first is a city map. Each city map is associated with a written description of the city and a listing of the campgrounds in that city. The second type is an area map. These usually show the road between two cities and each is associated with a description of that road and also a listing of the campgrounds on that road.

In an effort to make our maps and descriptions more useful we have included Pemex stations, the types of fuel they stock, and their numbers. Each Pemex has a unique identification number which is almost always boldly stated on the sign out front. This number seldom changes, it seems like Pemexes are the most reliable reference point on Baja roads and they're often conveniently located near crucial intersections.

TYPICAL PEMEX
SIGN

Green - Unleaded Gas (m)

Red - Premium Unleaded Gas (p)

Black - Diesel (d)

Station Number

American Express Accepted (For a Fee)

Note: Fuel types shown on maps as m/p/d

While the maps are for the most part self-explanatory here is a key.

```
┌──────────────────────── MAP LEGEND ────────────────────────┐
│                                                              │
│  ══════   Major Freeway          🚐    Campground with       │
│                                        Text Write-up         │
│  ══════   Toll Road              ⌐⌐    Campground - no        │
│                                        Text Write-up         │
│  ──────   Other Paved            ┌─┐                         │
│           Roads                  │P│  Pemex Station           │
│  ─■─■─■   Unpaved Roads        #7420  Pemex Station Number    │
│                                 m/p/d Type of Fuel           │
│    U.S.A.                              m = magna             │
│   ·─··─·  Country or                   p = premium           │
│   MEXICO  State Border                 d = diesel            │
│                                                              │
│  ══□══    Freeway Off-ramp        ▲    Area of Interest       │
│                                                              │
│  ┌──────┐ Off-ramp -              ●    City, Town, or Village │
│  │ San  │ Name Indicated                                     │
│  │Antonio│                                                   │
│  └──────┘                         ✈    Airport               │
│  ┌──┐     Freeway or Road                                    │
│  │1D│     Number                                             │
│  └──┘                            ▓▓▓   City Center            │
│                                                              │
└──────────────────────────────────────────────────────────────┘
```

Campground Descriptions

Each campground description begins with address and telephone number, if available. While it is not generally necessary to obtain campground reservations in Mexico you may want to do so for some very popular campgrounds. If we think that reservations are necessary we say so in the campground description.

One thing you will not find in our campground descriptions is a rating with some kind of system of stars, checks, or tree icons. Hopefully we've included enough information in our campground descriptions to let you make your own analysis.

We've included limited information about campground prices. Generally you can expect that tent campers will pay the least. RV charges sometimes depend on the size of the rig but more often are based upon the number of people with a two-person minimum. If hookups are available and you are in an RV you should expect to pay for them, campground owners usually do not distinguish between those who hook up and those who don't. Some oceanside campgrounds have higher rates for spaces close to the water.

We've grouped the campground fees into the following categories in our campground descriptions:

FREE	Free	$ / $$$	Over $15 and up to $20
$	Up to $5 U.S.	$$ / $$$	Over $20 and up to $25
$$	Over $5 and up to $10	$$$ / $$$	Over $25
$$$	Over $10 and up to $15		

All of these prices are winter prices for an RV with 2 people using full hookups if available. The prices given are for normal sites, sometimes premium site like those along the water are more expensive. Some campgrounds, particularly near Ensenada, actually have higher rates in the summer, we've tried to indicate the summer prices in those campgrounds.

Campground icons can be useful for a quick overview of campground facilities or if you are quickly looking for a particular feature.

All of the campgrounds in this book accept RVs but not all accept tent campers. We've included the tent symbol for all campgrounds that do accept tents.

Hookups in Mexican campgrounds vary a great deal so we've included individual symbols for electricity, water, and sewer. For more information take a look at the written description section. Usually we include information about the type of electrical hookup and apparent amperage in the write-up. The water symbol means water is available, it may not be piped to the sites. If we show a dump icon it means that there are either drains at the sites, a dump station, or both. There's usually more information about this in the write-up.

Showers in Mexican campgrounds often have no provision for hot water so we give separate shower symbols for hot and cold water. If there is provision for hot water but it was cold when we visited we list it as providing cold water only. You may be luckier when you visit.

An on-site restaurant can provide a welcome change from home-cooked meals and a good way to meet people. In Mexico almost all restaurants also serve alcohol of some kind. Often campground restaurants are only open during certain periods during the year, sometimes only during the very busy Christmas and Semana Santa (Easter) holidays. Even if there is no restaurant at the campground we have found that in Mexico there is usually one not far away.

If we've given the campground a shopping basket icon then it has some groceries. This is usually just a few items in the reception area. Check the write-up for more information.

If we include a washing machine icon it means that there is a self-service washing machine. If laundry service is provided we talk about it in the write-up but there is no icon. If laundry service is provided make sure to ask the price before you turn over your laundry, this can be a pricey option.

A swimming icon means that the campground has swimming either on-site or nearby. This may be a pool or the beach at the ocean.

The telephone icon means that there is a telephone either in the campground or on the street nearby.

The internet icon indicates that internet service is available in the campground. In Mexico this usually means that they provide a machine for your use, a data port is unusual.

The Wi-Fi icon means that wireless internet is available. Sometimes service is only available near the office, but other places broadcast throughout the campground. The campground description usually tells more about this. We are finding more and more Wi-Fi service in Mexican campgrounds, often very good service.

Our big RV symbol means that there is room for coaches to 40 feet to enter the campground, maneuver, and park. Usually this means we've seen them do it. The driver we saw may have been better than most, exercise caution. If you drive a fifth wheel you'll have to use your own judgment of how your rig handles compared to a coach. If you drive an even larger 45-footer you can at least use our symbol as a starting point in making your campground decisions. There's often more in the write-up itself about this.

You'll find that this book has a much larger campground description than most guidebooks. We've tried to include detailed information about the campground itself so you know what to expect when you arrive. While most campgrounds described in this book have a map we've also included a paragraph giving even more details about finding the campground.

GPS (Global Positioning System) Coordinates

You will note that we have provided a GPS Location for each campground. GPS is a modern navigation tool that uses signals from satellites. For less than $150 you can now buy a hand-held receiver that will give you your latitude, longitude, and approximate altitude anywhere in the world. You can also enter the coordinates we have given for the campgrounds in this book into the receiver and it will tell you exactly where the campground lies in relation to your position. If our maps and descriptions just don't lead you to the campground you can fall back on the GPS information.

If you don't have a GPS receiver already you certainly don't need to go out and buy one to use this book. On the other hand, if you do have one bring it along. More and more drivers are using GPS mapping systems for navigation. In Mexico they'll find that the maps in these systems aren't particularly accurate, but if you're flexible they still offer some useful information. If you are finding that our readings are not entirely accurate you should check to see which Map Datum your machine is set to use. The coordinates in this book are based upon the World Geodetic System 1984 (WGS 84) datum. Also remember that GPS is only accurate to about 50 feet.

Tijuana, Baja California and Chula Vista, California

Chula Vista

Tecate

Tijuana

USA
MEXICO

Tijuana to Rosarito

Tecate

2D

2

2D

1D

2

Rosarito

Punta el Descanso

Rosarito

1

Tecate to Ensenada

Puerto Nuevo
Punta Mesquite

3

Parque Nacional Constitución de 1857

Laguna Hanson

1D

1

N

Punta San Miguel

Ensenada

Rosarito to Ensenada

Estero Beach

1

Ensenada

3

Punta Banda

Maneadero

To San Quintín

To San Felipe

CHAPTER INDEX

Highlights . . . . Page 49
Roads and Fuel Availability . . . . Page 49
Sightseeing . . . . Page 50
Golf . . . . Page 51
Beaches and Water Sports . . . . Page 51
Fishing . . . . Page 51
Backroad Adventures . . . . Page 51
Tijuana, Baja California and
  Chula Vista, California . . . . Page 52
Tijuana to Rosarito . . . . Page 54
Rosarito . . . . Page 56
Rosarito to Ensenada . . . . Page 57
Ensenada . . . . Page 64
Tecate . . . . Page 72
Tecate to Ensenada
  on Highway 3 . . . . Page 75

SOUTH TO ENSENADA

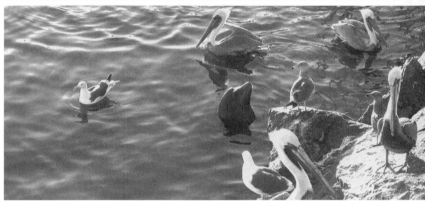

Chapter Four

South to Ensenada

INTRODUCTION

The Pacific Coast south to Ensenada is an extremely popular camping destination. So many people visit from the San Diego area across the border in southern California that it seems almost an extension of that state. In this chapter we also include the inland corridor from Tecate to Ensenada.

Highlights

Ensenada is a fun town to visit for a day or a week with lots to keep you occupied. There are many day trips to places like **La Bufadora**, **Puerto Nuevo**, the **Guadalupe Valley**, and **Laguna Hanson**. And don't forget a fishing trip on one of the many charter boats based in Ensenada.

Roads and Fuel Availability

Mex 1 begins in Tijuana. From Tijuana to Ensenada there are actually two different highways, one is the free road, Mex 1 Libre. The other is a toll road, Mex 1D. The toll road is by far the best road, it is four lanes wide and for most of its length a limited-access highway. Much of the road is extremely scenic with great views of cliffs and ocean. There are three toll booths along the 65-mile (105 km) road, an automobile or van was being charged about $7.50 U.S. for the entire distance during the late winter of 2005/2006 and double that for larger RVs. Both dollars and pesos are accepted as payment at the three toll booths on this highway.

This is the only section of toll road on all of Mex 1.

The free road, Mex 1 Libre, is much less direct than the toll road. It leaves Tijuana to the south and heads directly to Rosarito. After passing through the bustling streets of this beach town it parallels the toll road on the ocean side for 20 miles (33 kilometers) to the vicinity of La Misión. There it turns inland and climbs into the hills where after 20 miles (32 km) it rejoins Mex 1D just south of the southernmost toll booth and 5 miles (8 km) north of Ensenada. The road through the mountains is scenic and fine for carefully driven big RVs but only two lanes wide, few people drive it because it takes much longer than the toll road.

There is a good alternate to Mex 1 as far south as Ensenada. This is Mex 3 which runs from Tecate on the border to Ensenada. Actually this is a very useful highway if you are headed north since the Tecate border crossing has much shorter waiting lines to cross into the U.S. than the Tijuana crossings. Using Mex 3 the distance from Tecate to El Sauzal and then on to Ensenada on the free portion of Mex 1 is 65 miles (105 km).

Mex 3 also continues eastward from Ensenada to meet with Mex 5 about 31 miles (51 km) north of San Felipe on the Gulf of California. This 123 mile (201 km) two-lane paved highway offers an alternative to Mex 5 south from Mexicali for San Felipe-bound travelers.

Fuel, both gas and diesel, is readily available at Pemex stations at population centers throughout this section.

Sightseeing

This section of the Baja Peninsula offers a wealth of sightseeing opportunities. This is at least partly because there is such a large population within easy driving distance. Remember, Tijuana is Mexico's fourth largest city, and southern Californians can easily visit the entire region as day-trippers.

Tijuana gets most of the visitors, of course. The best way to visit is to walk across the border. Many sights are within walking distance of the San Ysidro crossing. To travel farther just use a taxi, or if you are more adventurous, catch a bus. See the *Tijuana* section below for specific destinations.

The town of **Rosarito** is best known for its beach. See *Rosarito* below for more details.

The small town of **Puerto Nuevo**, 9 miles (15 km) south of Rosarito, is famous for its restaurants. They specialize in lobster dinners. There are many of them, just pick one that looks good to you.

South of Rosarito Beach the toll highway travels along **spectacular cliffs** offering some great views. Watch for the viewpoints that have room to pull larger RVs off the highway to take a picture or two.

If you are following Mex 3 south from Tecate you will have the opportunity to visit a couple of **wineries in the Guadeloupe Valley**. This is Mexico's premier wine-growing area.

Ensenada is a popular destination for folks from north of the border. It offers shopping and restaurants and has a much more relaxed atmosphere than Tijuana. See the Ensenada section below for more information.

 ### Golf

If you enjoy golf there are a number of possibilities in this region.

In Tijuana there is the **Club Campestre Campo de Golf Tijuana**. It is an 18-hole course near central Tijuana and is located just off the Boulevard Agua Caliente.

As you drive south along Mex 1D watch for the **Real del Mar Golf Resort** near Km 19.5. It has 18 holes and is associated with a Marriott hotel.

Farther south along the same road, near Km 78, you'll find the **Bajamar Ocean Front Golf Resort**. There are three 9-hole courses here, as well as a hotel and housing development.

Just south of Ensenada is the **Baja Country Club** which has 18 holes.

Along the border again, and just south is Tecate, there is a new course being developed. This is the **Rancho Tecate Resort and Country Club** with 9 holes.

Finally, to the east near Mexicali is the **Club Campestre de Mexicali**. It has 18 holes and is located south of town.

Beaches and Water Sports

While there is some surfing on Rosarito Beach you'll find more surfers to the south from about Km 33 on Mex 1 Libre at Punta el Descanso south to Punta Mesquite. Off the campground at San Miguel is Punta San Miguel, one of the most popular surfing spots in Baja California.

People from Ensenada generally head for the beaches south of town at Estero Beach. Several campgrounds offer access to these beaches and are listed in the Ensenada section.

Fishing

Many people come to Ensenada for charter fishing trips. Big boats from Ensenada range far to the south along the Pacific Coast of the Baja Peninsula. They're after yellowtail and albacore tuna. Smaller boats also run out of Ensenada on day trips after bottom fish like rockfish and halibut.

Surf-casting is popular along many of the beaches along the upper northwest coast. One sandy beach where this is popular is the one in front of the Rancho Mal Paso and Baja Seasons campgrounds.

Backroad Adventures

See the ***Backroad Driving*** section of ***Chapter 2 - Details, Details, Details*** for essential information about driving off the main highway on the Baja and for a definition of road type classifications used below.

From Km 55 on Mex 3 between Ensenada and San Felipe - A national park, **Parque Nacional Constitución de 1857**, is accessible from Mex 3 east of Ensenada. A road goes north to the shallow **Laguna Hanson**, the distance to the lake is 22 miles

(36 km). There are primitive campsites at the lake and hiking trails. This is usually a Type 2 road. This lake is also accessible from Mex 2 to the north but that road is usually a Type 3. It meets Mex 2 between Tecate and Mexicali near Km 72.

THE ROUTES, TOWNS, AND CAMPGROUNDS

TIJUANA (TEE-HWAN-AH), BAJA CALIFORNIA AND CHULA VISTA, CALIFORNIA
Population 1,500,000

Tijuana is the fourth largest city in Mexico, and perhaps the fastest growing city in North America. That means that the atmosphere can be somewhat chaotic, particularly if you are driving an RV. It's a great city to visit, but not in your own vehicle.

We think that the best base for visiting Tijuana is actually on the north side of the border in the U.S. The **Tijuana Trolley**, a light rail line, runs from San Diego to a station right at the border. Several campgrounds are located near the line. From them you can board the trolley and travel effortlessly to the border, walk across, and then either walk or use taxis to visit the city's attractions.

The border crossing between San Ysidro and Tijuana (the main Tijuana-area garita or gate) is said to be the busiest border crossing anywhere in the world. This presents a challenge for automobile travelers, but pedestrians find the crossing pretty easy.

Once in Mexico you are within walking distance of the **La Reforma District**, also known as **Avenida Revolución**. Most visitors who walk across the border never get beyond this area. They bargain for souvenirs of their trip to Mexico and perhaps visit one of the restaurants or bars in the area. Many folks come to Tijuana to watch jai alai, the game is played at the **Frontón Palacio Jai Alai de Tijuana** which is located where Calle 7 crosses Avenida Revolución. The north-south street just west of Avenida Revolución is **Avenida Constitución**, the shopping along it is less tourist-oriented but worth a look. Prices on this street are usually marked and not negotiated.

About a mile east of the La Reforma district is the **Zona Río Tijuana**. This is an area of nicer restaurants, hotels, and large shopping centers. The **Centro Cultural Tijuana** has a good cultural museum covering all of Mexico, an Omnimax theater, a performing-arts theater where a Ballet Folklórico is often performed, and crafts shops.

Another area of interest is the **Agua Caliente District** which stretches down Blvd. Agua Caliente to the southeast from the south end of the La Reforma District. Here you'll find one of two bull rings in Tijuana as well as the **Caliente Greyhound Track**, the **Club Campestre Campo de Golf Tijuana** and several large hotels.

Tijuana Campgrounds

Tijuana actually has no campgrounds, but there is good access from campgrounds north of the border in Chula Vista and San Diego. These campgrounds double as excellent bases for preparation for your trip south of the border.

CHULA VISTA RV RESORT AND MARINA

Address:	460 Sandpiper Way, Chula Vista, CA 91910
Telephone:	(619) 422-0111 or (800) 770-2878
Fax:	(619) 422-8872
Website:	www.chulavistarv.com
Email:	info@chulavistarv.com
Open:	All Year

GPS Location: N 32° 37' 41", W 117° 06' 17"

This is a first class, very popular campground in an excellent location for preparing to enter Mexico. Chula Vista is a convenient small town with all the stores and facilities you'll need, and both San Diego and Tijuana are close by. Reservations are necessary.

This campground is located adjacent to and operated in conjunction with a marina. Prices range from approximately $40 to $65 depending upon season and size. There are 237 back-in and pull-through sites with 50-amp power and full hookups including TV. Parking is on paved drives with patios, sites are separated by shrubbery. Large RVs and slide-outs fit fine. The bathroom facilities are excellent and there is a nice warm pool as well as a spa, small store, and meeting rooms. The marina next door has two restaurants and a shuttle bus provides access to central Chula Vista, stores, and the local stop of the Tijuana Trolley. Paved walkways along the water are nice for that evening stroll.

Take the J Street Exit from Highway 5 which is approximately 7 miles north of the San Ysidro border crossing and about 8 miles south of central San Diego. Drive west on J Street for 2 blocks, turn right on Marina Parkway, and drive north to the first street from the left (about 1/4 mile) which is Sandpiper, turn left here and drive one block, then follow the street as it makes a 90 degree right-angle turn, the entrance will be on your left.

San Diego Metro KOA

Address:	111 North 2nd Ave, Chula Vista, CA 91910
Telephone:	(619) 427-3601
Reservations:	(800) KOA-9877
Website:	www.koa.com/where/ca/05112.htm
Email:	reservations@sandiegokoa.com
Open:	All Year

GPS Location: N 32° 39' 25", W 117° 04' 54"

This large campground in Chula Vista also make a good base for exploring Tijuana and San Diego. It has about 270 spaces. It's a well-equipped park with everything you would normally expect at a KOA including a pool, spa, playground, and store. There's a shuttle to the San Diego (Tijuana) Trolley. Many caravans to Mexico use this campground as a starting point. It is suitable for any size RV although not quite as good for really big RVs as the Chula Vista RV Resort above. Reservations are necessary, it is extremely popular.

To reach the campground take the E Street Exit from I-5 in Chula Vista. Travel east on E Street until you reach 2nd Ave. Turn left here on 2nd and proceed about .7 mile. The gate is on the right.

TIJUANA TO ROSARITO
17 Miles (27 Km), .5 Hour (From San Ysidro crossing via Mex 1D)

There are two roads south from Tijuana to Rosarito and points south. One is the toll road, Mex 1D. The other is a free road called Mex 1. The toll road is much easier to reach from the border crossing so it is usually the preferred route, especially among those with big rigs.

Mex 1D, the toll road, is accessed by heading westward from the San Ysidro border crossing along the fence that divides Mexico and the U.S. The following instructions were written to describe the route as it existed in the winter of 2005/2006. Tijuana is a fast-growing town and things do change so be alert. If you miss one of these turns you get to explore Tijuana.

As you cross the border zero your odometer. A new off-ramp makes getting on the road along the south side of the border fence a snap. Stay in the far right lane. Follow signs for "Scenic Road – Rosarito & Ensenada" and "Cuota". The new off-ramp goes right and connects to the westbound road just south of the border fence. At 2.5 miles (4.0 km) you start a long uphill grade. Then at 3.5 miles (5.6 km) you reach the top of the hill and start to descend. At 3.9 miles (6.3 km) at the bottom of the hill take the exit to the right for 1D and merge onto a 4-lane highway heading west. Get in the left lane within a mile. At 5.2 miles (8.4 km) the highway splits, take the left fork. You'll soon arrive at the first toll booth on Mex 1D. In another 12.6 miles (20.3 km) you'll reach the northern Rosarito exit. You can join the free road here and drive through Rosarito, or you can continue south on the toll road toward Ensenada.

The free road from Tijuana to Ensenada heads south from the Libramiento or ring road that circles the southern border of Tijuana. If you were following the directions given above for reaching the toll road you would be on the Libramiento if you had gone straight instead of turning onto the toll road after leaving the border fence. While the Libramiento is better than most surface streets in Tijuana it can still be a challenge, that's why the toll road is the preferred route.

The free road branches off the Libramiento (watch for signs for Rosarito or Mex 1 or "Libre") and from that point it is only a short 7.3 mile (11.8 km) drive until you cross over the toll road and enter Rosarito. The free road is the main drag through Rosarito, watch for the many stop signs, there are dozens of them.

Some folks like to cross the border at another crossing to the east of Tijuana called Otay Mesa. See *Crossing the Border* in the *Details, Details, Details* chapter for more information.

Tijuana to Rosarito Campgrounds

CENTURY BEACH RESORT

Address:	Km 25 Carretera Escénica Tijuana-Ensenada, Playas de Rosarito, B.C., México
Telephone:	(664) 631-3250 (Mex), (800) 818-3133 (Reservations)
Website:	www.centurybeachresort.com
Open:	All Year

GPS Location: N 32° 23' 48", W 117° 05' 19"

This resort has been here a while with several different names. Daily rates are higher in summer than winter, and weekend rates are higher than mid-week: summer weekends $49, mid-week $39, winter weekends $39, mid-week $29. The monthly rate is $500. Popular destinations in this part of the Baja have higher summer rates because that's when most people visit. You'll find that this is the first of several campgrounds north of and just south of Ensenada that have very high rates compared with the rest of Mexico.

There are about 60 back-in campsites available for visitors. Many others have fifth-wheels and trailers permanently installed that the hotel rents as rooms. Each slot has a paved parking area, a patio, 50-amp outlets, sewer, water, TV hookup, patio, and barbecue. The whole place is beautifully landscaped and fairly posh but needing some maintenance due to salt air and resulting corrosion. There are very nice restrooms with hot showers, several swimming pools including one with a geyser-like fountain in the middle, a spa next to the pool, a weight room and sauna with ocean view, a tennis court, a pool room, ping-pong, a putting course, a laundry, and nice restaurant. There is also a convention center for groups of up to 1,200, if you need one of those. The campground is next to the beach and has beach access. Security is tight and English is spoken. Don't be run off by this description, the place really isn't as big or threatening as it sounds.

You might expect that this would be a good stop for big RVs but that's not the case. Maximum RV length here is about 35 feet. Before accepting a campsite check it to

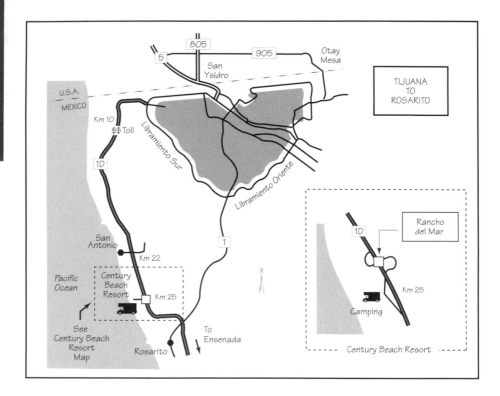

make sure that you can level your RV, many have an excessive slope. Make sure too that you can extend your slide-outs, some sites have trees that could interfere.

Heading south on the toll road Mex 1D the exit is marked with a RV pictogram just after the Rancho del Mar overpass, it is at Km 25 and is 8.3 miles (13.4 km) south of the new northernmost toll booth. Heading north there is also an exit, it is labeled Rancho del Mar.

ROSARITO (ROW-SAH-**REE**-TOE)
Population 60,000

The main attraction in Rosarito is a nice beach close to the U.S. and Tijuana. On school breaks and weekends, particularly during the summer, Rosarito is a busy place. At other times, particularly during the winter, the town is much more quiet. Virtually everything in town except the beach is right on Avenida Benito Juárez, the main road, so a drive through will give you a good introduction. Watch for the many stop signs!

Rosarito has a large supermarket so if you are not planning to go as far as Ensenada you may want to stop and do some shopping there. The town also has curio and Mexican crafts stores, just like Tijuana and Ensenada so you can do some shopping if you haven't yet had a chance.

The beach here is probably the main attraction. Unfortunately it is often polluted so swimming is not recommended.

For many years the top hotel in town has been the **Rosarito Beach Hotel**. It has been around since the 20s, and has grown over the years. Today a tour of the place is on most folk's itineraries.

ROSARITO TO ENSENADA
51 Miles (82 Km), 1 Hour

Mex 1 (Libre) meets the toll highway Mex 1D at the north end of Rosarito. The free highway runs through town while the toll road bypasses it, then they meet and run side by side for about 25 miles (41 km) south. There are lots of developments of various types along this double road. Just after leaving Rosarito off to the right you'll spot the **Fox Studios Baja** where Titanic was filmed. There's a theme park here called **Foxploration**, it's only open Monday, Thursday and Friday from nine to five-thirty. Another interesting attraction is **Puerto Nuevo**, about 13 miles (21 km) south of Rosarito. This has become the place to go to get a lobster dinner, there are about 30 restaurants in the small town, they cover the spectrum in price and quality.

For access to campgrounds immediately south of Rosarito we recommend that you stay on the free road. Otherwise stay on the toll road. Near La Misión the free road passes under the toll road and heads inland. From that point south all campgrounds are accessible from the toll road only. You'll have to get on the toll road at a point somewhat north of the point it passes under the freeway, the southernmost on-ramp is at Km 59 of the free road (and Km 66 of the toll road) and is called Los Alisitos.

Rosarito to Ensenada Campgrounds

POPOTLA DEL MAR TRAILER PARK

Address:	Km 34 Carr. Tijuana-Ensenada Libre, Rosarito, B.C. México
Reservations:	PO Box 431135, San Ysidro, CA 92143-1135
Telephone:	(661) 612-1501
Email:	popotla@telnor.net
Open:	All Year

GPS Location: N 32° 16' 49", W 117° 01' 48"

This is a large gated RV park mostly filled with permanent residents, but is has a very nice area set aside for short-term campers. We usually find these sites mostly empty, perhaps surprising considering the location next to the ocean, but probably reflecting the fact that we visit mostly during the winter.

There are about 37 spaces here for overnighters, all with ocean views. They are large back-in spaces suitable for large RVs with full hookups. Electrical outlets are 20 amp and all sites have parking pads. Some sites are set near the water near a small cove, others are above along the bluff. There are bathrooms with hot showers and a swimming pool. The campground is fenced and secure and there is a bar and restaurant on the grounds. Daily rates are $25 to $30 depending upon the parking area, monthly rates run from $420 to $680.

While the sites here are suitable for RVs up to 40 feet they are set at right angles to the access roads and maneuvering room is limited.

The campground is located near Km 34 on the free road about 7 km (4 miles) south of Rosarito.

ALISITOS K-58 SURF POINT CAMPING

Location:	Km 59 Carr. Tijuana-Ensenada Libre, B.C., México
Telephone:	(664) 155-0120
Open:	All Year

GPS Location: N 32° 07' 24", W 116° 53' 07"

This is primarily a surfing spot but also during weekends and holidays full of tent campers from Tijuana. There's a big red K58 painted on their water tank and visible from the highway. This is a basic no-frills place to park on a bluff above the ocean. There is a large open field with no hookups, plenty of room and easy access make it suitable for any size RV. There are flush toilets and cold showers available and the owners seem to make an effort to keep the place clean. A small tienda out front has basic supplies. Rates are $16.50 for tents, $18 for a trailer, and $22 for a motorhome. A paved access trail leads down to a long sandy beach.

The entrance is located near the Km 59 point of the free road south of Rosarito.

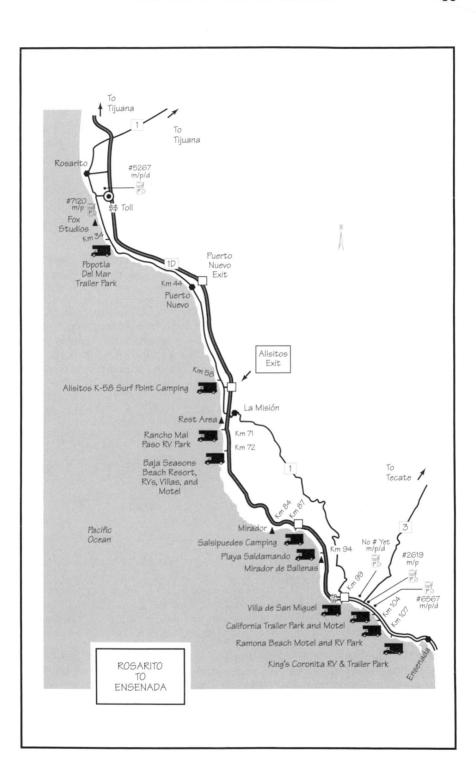

To Tijuana

1

To Tijuana

Rosarito

#5267 m/p/d

#7120 m/p

$$ Toll

Fox Studios

Km 34

Popotla Del Mar Trailer Park

1D

Km 44

Puerto Nuevo Exit

Puerto Nuevo

Alisitos Exit

Km 58

Alisitos K-58 Surf Point Camping

La Misión

Rest Area

Rancho Mal Paso RV Park

Km 71

Km 72

Baja Seasons Beach Resort, RVs, Villas, and Motel

N

To Tecate

Km 84 Km 87

1

Mirador

Salsipuedes Camping

Km 94

No # Yet m/p/d

3

Pacific Ocean

Playa Saldamando

Mirador de Ballenas

#2619 m/p

Km 99

Km 104

#6567 m/p/d

Villa de San Miguel

California Trailer Park and Motel

Km 107

Ramona Beach Motel and RV Park

King's Coronita RV & Trailer Park

Ensenada

ROSARITO TO ENSENADA

⛟ RANCHO MAL PASO RV PARK

Address:	La Salina Beach, Km 71 Carr. Tijuana-Ensenada, B.C., México
Open:	All Year

GPS Location: N32° 04' 30", W 116° 52' 45"

For many years this has been a primitive campground on the same beach as Baja Seasons which is located to the south. Now a modern new RV park is nearing completion.

The new park has at least 75 back-in paved sites off paved access roads. Utilities include 50/30/20 amp outlets at each site, also water and sewer. They're big sites suitable for RVs to 45 feet. There will be restroom buildings with hot showers and laundry facilities. Rates have not yet been determined but we assume they will be similar to those at the more expensive campgrounds along this coast.

The primitive camping will remain at the north end of the property. Camping there is on an area of solid fill. Sites are not delineated, RVs of any size park overlooking the beach. A new building is being built with flush toilets and hot showers.

Access to the campground is directly from the south-bound lanes of the toll road at the 71 Km marker. There's no access from the north-bound lanes, you'll have to drive north to the Alisitos exit and return to reach the campground. There is a walking overpass right beyond the exit so watch for it so you don't miss the turn. You'll drive into a small compound where you'll pay the fee and then drive on through to the beach or south to the new campground.

⛟ BAJA SEASONS BEACH RESORT, RVs, VILLAS, AND MOTEL

Address:	1177 Broadway #4, PMB 329, Chula Vista, CA 91911
Telephone:	(800) 754-4190 (U.S. Res.) or (646) 155-4015 (Mex)
Fax:	(619) 422-5923 (U.S.)
Website:	www.bajaseasons.com
Email:	bajaseasons@yahoo.com.mx
Open:	All Year

GPS Location: N 32° 03' 54", W 116° 52' 41"

The Baja Seasons is a large and very nice beachside RV park within reasonable driving distance of Ensenada. The drive into town is about 30 miles (50 km) on good four-lane highway, complicated only by a fascinating area where there seems to be an unending construction project to stabilize the road and keep it from sliding into the ocean. Prices are high, about $36 in winter and $48 in summer for a site away from the water, higher on holidays. Monthly rates run from $420 to $570.

The campground has about 140 very nice back-in camping spaces with electricity (some 50-amp, the rest 30-amp), sewer, water, TV, paved parking pad, patios and landscaping. The streets are paved, they even have curbs. We have seen tent campers here but it's not an ideal spot, sites are paved and there aren't good places to set up a tent. It's a very popular big-rig campground. There's a huge central complex with a restaurant and bar, swimming pool, spa, small store, tennis courts, sauna and steam baths, mini golf, game room, library and coin-op laundry. There are also restrooms with hot showers. The entire setup is on a wide, beautiful beach. Reservations are accepted.

The campground is right next to Mex 1D just south of the Km 72 marker. Going south watch the kilometer markers and turn directly off the highway. Going north you will see the campground on your left but cannot turn because of the central divider. Continue north 4.1 miles (6.6 km) to the Alisitos exit to return.

SALSIPUEDES CAMPING

    Location: Km 87 Carr. Escénica No. 1 Tijuana-Ensenada, B.C., México
    Open: All Year

GPS Location: N 31° 58' 51", W 116° 46' 58"

This campground offers primitive camping in an olive tree grove. It's popular with surfers who use a steep trail to the beach. The name of the campground suggests the problem for big RVs, Salsipuedes means "leave if you can" in Spanish. A very steep access road winds down about a half-mile from the highway far above. It is not suitable for RVs larger than vans. If it rains while you're here, good luck getting out.

After the initial descent you'll enter a compound where the managers live. They'll collect a fee for camping, then you drive down another steep section of road to a bluff above the beach. Back from the bluff there is an olive orchard. Campers set up on the bluff where they can watch the surfing or back in the orchard where there is some shade. There's lots of room. Facilities vary but usually include flush toilets, cold showers, and sometimes a small taco stand.

To find the campground watch for the Salsipuedes exit sign near Km 87 of the toll road. The entrance gate has a gatehouse next to it, we've always found it abandoned. The access road is very steep. Again, we think anything larger than a van or pickup would have problems with this road.

PLAYA SALDAMANDO

    Address: Km 94 Carr. Escénica No. 1 Tijuana-Ensenada, B.C., Mex.
    Telephone: (619) 857-9242 (U.S., for reservations)
    Website: www.playasaldamando.com
    Email: gsaldamando@cox.net
    Open: All Year

GPS Location: N 31° 55' 59", W116° 45' 16"

This campground, like Salsipuedes, has a steep access road. This one's not as bad, the owner says it's fine for RVs to 32 feet but maneuvering room is tight with narrow access roads. It would be tough for trailers. With prior arrangement he'll open another gate for larger RVs. The drop from the toll road to this campground is not nearly as great as the descent to Salsipuedes. In fact, it's not far at all compared to that one.

There are many camping sites spread along at least a half-mile of rocky coastline with a few small beaches. Roads and campsites are lined with white-painted rocks. Someone has put in a lot of time with a paintbrush. Most sites are pretty well separated from each other and sport picnic tables. Almost all have excellent view locations, you can watch the waves and surfers below. It's a great tenting campground and also

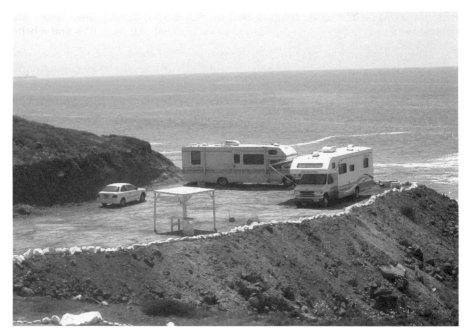

THE VIEWS FROM PLAYA SALDAMANDO ARE AWESOME

excellent for small RVs. There are no hookups, both pit toilets and flush toilets are available, as are cold water showers.

The access road to this campground is at Km 94 from the southbound lanes, just north of the Mirador de Ballenas. Be alert so you don't accidentally miss it. Going north you must use the Salsipuedes off-ramp about 3 miles to the north and return on the southbound lanes About 0.4 mile (0.6 km) down the hill is an attended entrance gate where the fee is collected.

VILLA DE SAN MIGUEL

Address:	Km 99 Carr. Tijuana-Ensenada, Apdo. 55, CP 22760 Ensenada, B.C., México
Telephone:	(646) 174-7948
Website:	www.villadesanmiguel.com
Email:	villadesanmiguel@yahoo.com
Open:	All Year

GPS Location: N 31° 54' 08", W 116° 43' 43"

This campground is very popular with surfers. The point just to the west is Punta San Miguel, this is one of the most popular surfing locations along the northern Baja coastline.

The campground itself is little more than a large gravel parking lot next to the beach. Many folks set up tents in front of the parking area on the beach. There are hookups, they form a line of about 30 pull-alongside or back-in sites at the back of the parking lot with 15-amp power outlets, water and sewer. There is a cement-block building with flush toilets and cold showers, it was dirty and in poor repair when we visited. Above the beach area are a large number of permanently-situated RVs and a better restroom building with hot showers, there's also a popular restaurant.

The campground is located off the four-lane coastal highway just south of the southernmost toll station. The exit is marked San Miguel and is near the Km 99 marker. There is an entrance gate where the fee is collected, then the road descends to the beach. The entrance road and campsite are suitable for the largest RVs.

CALIFORNIA TRAILER PARK AND MOTEL

Address:	Km 103-700 Carretera Tijuana-Ensenada, PO Box 262, Ensenada CP 02800 B.C., México
Telephone:	(646) 174-6033
Email:	qugo@telnor.net
Open:	All Year

GPS Location: N 31° 53' 04", W 116° 41' 12"

This is a small hotel with just a few campsites for RVs to about 30 feet. The sites are back-in, most with paved pads, there are about 8 of them. There are 15-amp power outlets, water and sewer hookups. The restrooms are small but offer flush toilets and cold showers.

The motel is located on the ocean side of the 4-lane highway north of Ensenada near the Km 104 marker. Reservations are accepted.

RAMONA BEACH MOTEL AND RV PARK

Address:	Carr. Transp. Km 104, Apdo. 513, Ensenada, B.C., México
Telephone:	(646) 174-6045
Open:	All Year

GPS Location: N 31° 52' 58", W 116° 41' 08"

The facilities at this campground are older and in poor repair. It is located just south of the Motel California. Driving by you might think it abandoned, often there seems to be no one around. However, usually the campground is open, the office is in the Ramona Beach Motel store just to the south.

Access is good and the 30 or so sites are suitable for large RVs. The campground is located next to the ocean with just a low bluff down to the water. If you decide to stay check for a site with working hookups. Most have 15-amp outlets, water, and sewer but many do not work. There are flush toilets and hot showers but they're hard to find. They're located just above the beach directly behind the motel office in a small white building.

KING'S CORONITA RV & TRAILER PARK

Address:	Hwy Tijuana-Ensenada Km 107, Ensenada CP 22860 B.C., México
Reservations:	PO Box 5515, Chula Vista, CA 91912
Telephone:	(646) 174-4540
Open:	All Year

GPS Location: N 31° 51' 58", W 116° 39' 50"

This is an older well-kept campground that is almost full of permanently located RVs. There are generally about 10 sites available for overnighters but you would do well to call ahead if you wish to stay here, particularly in the summer. The sites are being renovated and nice patios installed.

Campsites have full hookups with 15-amp outlets. Many sites are small although some would allow large RVs, access to the campground is not a problem for larger RVs. Restrooms are clean with flush toilets and hot showers. The campground is located on a bluff above a marina, but sites for overnight RVs would be back from the bluff and would not offer much in the way of views.

The campground is located off the four-lane coastal highway near Km 107.

ENSENADA (EHN-SEH-NAH-DAH)
Population 400,000

Ensenada is the Baja's third most populous town and one of the most pleasant to visit. It is an important port and is more than ready for the tourist hordes that make the short-and-easy 68 mile (109 km) drive south from the border crossing at Tijuana or disembark from the cruise ships that anchor in Todos Santos Bay. There are many, many restaurants and handicrafts stores in the central area of town, English is often spoken so this is not a bad place to get your feet wet if you have not visited a Mexican city before. Try walking along **Calle Primera**, also called Avenida López Mateos. It is lined with restaurants and shops and is located just one block inland from the coastal Blvd. Costero (also known as Blvd. Gral. Lázaro Cárdenas). There are also many supermarkets and Pemex stations so Ensenada is the place to stock up on supplies before heading down the peninsula. Many banks have ATM machines so you can easily acquire some pesos.

When you tire of shopping and eating Ensenada has a few other attractions. The best beach is at **Estero Beach** which also has several campgrounds, they are discussed below. The **fishing** in Ensenada is good, charters for yellowtail, albacore, sea bass, halibut and bonito can be arranged at the fishing piers. Ensenada has the largest fish market on the Baja, it is called the **Mercado Negro** (black market) and is located near the sport fishing piers. Nearby is a nice **Malecón** or waterfront walkway where you can take a good look at the fishing fleet and at a group of sea lions lined up in the water near the fish market. The waterspout at **La Bufadora**, located south near Punta Banda (see below) is a popular day trip. **Whale watching trips** are a possibility from December to March.

Important fiestas and busy times here are **Carnival**, spring break for colleges in the U.S. during late March, the Rosarito to Ensenada Bicycle Race and Newport to Ensenada Yacht Race in April, a wine festival in August, another Rosarito to Ensenada bicycle race in October, and the Baja 1000 off-road race in November.

The **Estero Beach** area is really a suburb of Ensenada. The road to Estero Beach leads west from near the Km 15 marker of Mex 1 about 7 miles (11 km) south of Ensenada. There's not much here other than beaches, the resorts, and vacation homes.

Punta Banda is another small area that is virtually a suburb of Ensenada. To get there follow the road west from near the center of Maneadero near the Km 21 marker, about 11 miles (18 km) south of Ensenada on Mex 1. It is then another 8 miles

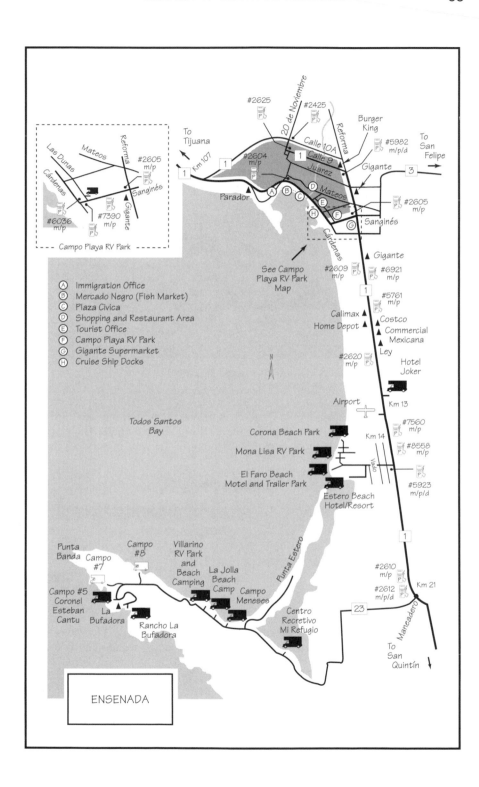

Campo Playa RV Park

To Tijuana

Km 107

#2625

#2425

20 de Noviembre

Reforma

Burger King

#5982 m/p/d

To San Felipe

Calle 10A
Calle 9
Juarez

#2604 m/p

1

Gigante

3

Parador

A B C D Mateos
E
H F
G Sanginés

Las Dunas
Mateos
Reforma
Cárdenas
#2605 m/p
Sanginés
Gigante
#7390 m/p
#6036 m/p

Cárdenas

Gigante

#2609 m/p

#6921 m/p

1

#5761

Calimax
Home Depot

Costco
Commercial Mexicana
Ley

#2620 m/p

Hotel Joker

Ⓐ Immigration Office
Ⓑ Mercado Negro (Fish Market)
Ⓒ Plaza Civica
Ⓓ Shopping and Restaurant Area
Ⓔ Tourist Office
Ⓕ Campo Playa RV Park
Ⓖ Gigante Supermarket
Ⓗ Cruise Ship Docks

See Campo Playa RV Park Map

N

Airport

Km 13

Km 14

#7560 m/p

#8558 m/p

Vado

Todos Santos Bay

Corona Beach Park

Mona Lisa RV Park

El Faro Beach Motel and Trailer Park

Estero Beach Hotel/Resort

#5923 m/p/d

1

Punta Banda

Campo #7

Campo #8

Villarino RV Park and Beach Camping

La Jolla Beach Camp

Campo Meneses

Punta Estero

#2610 m/p

Km 21

#2612 m/p/d

Campo #5
Coronel Esteban Cantu

La Bufadora

Rancho La Bufadora

Centro Recretivo Mi Refugio

23

Maneadero

To San Quintín

ENSENADA

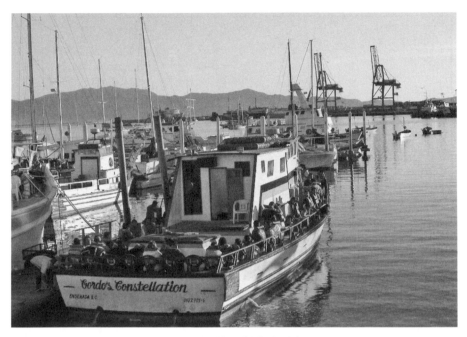

ENSENADA'S BOAT HARBOR

(13 km) out to Punta Banda. Punta Banda has grown up around the large RV parks here. A few miles beyond Punta Banda is the La Bufadora blowhole. There are several small campgrounds without hookups or much in the way of services near La Bufadora.

Ensenada Campgrounds

This section includes campgrounds in Ensenada itself and south to Maneadero. This includes Estero Beach and Punta Banda.

🚐 CAMPO PLAYA RV PARK

Address:	Blvd. Las Dunas No 570-300 & Calle
	Delante, CP 22880 Ensenada, B.C., México
Telephone:	(656) 176-2918
Email:	camplaya@telnor.net
Open:	All Year

GPS Location: N 31° 51' 01", W 116° 36' 50"

The Campo Playa is the only RV park actually in urban Ensenada and is the best place to stay if you want to explore the town. The downtown area is about 2 miles distant, the campground is right on the preferred route that you will probably be following through town, and there is a large Gigante supermarket just up the street. There are also an unusually large number of good restaurants nearby.

There are about 50 spaces in the park set under shade trees and palms. Most are pull-thrus that will accept big RVs with slide-outs. The spaces have 15-amp outlets, sewer, water and patios. There are also some smaller spaces, some with only partial utility availability. The restrooms are showing their age but are clean and have hot showers. The campground is fenced but the urban location suggests that belongings not be left unattended. The monthly rate here is $300.

The campground lies right on the old route through Ensenada. Entering town from the north on Mex 1 make sure to take the right fork marked Ensenada Centro just south of the Km 107 marker and the left fork at Km 109. You'll come to a stop light and see Pemex #2604 on the left. Zero your odometer here. You'll pass a Sanborn's coffee shop on the right and also a plaza with statues of three heads. At 1.2 miles (0.9 km) turn left onto Calle Agustin Sanginés, Pemex # 6036 is on the corner. Drive one block and turn left into Blvd. Las Dunas. The trailer park will be on your right after the turn.

⛺ HOTEL JOKER

Address:	Carretera Transpeninsular Km 12.5, Ex Ejido Chapultepec, Ensenada, B.C., México
Telephone:	(646) 176-7201
Fax:	(646) 177-4460
Website:	www.eljoker.com
Open:	All Year

GPS Location: N 31° 48' 12", W 116° 35' 43"

Just south of Ensenada, right on Mex 1, is a quirky little motel with a few RV slots. Once you enter the gates you'll probably find you like the place. The hotel specializes in special-event parties, there are play areas with castle-like crenellations, a piñata party plaza, a barbecue area and a general atmosphere of good clean family fun.

The Joker has only 2 spaces and they are small, RVs larger than 24 feet or so will have difficulty maneuvering and parking. The slots have 15-amp outlets, sewer, water, and patios with shade. There's also a large grass area that is perfect for tents. The restrooms are older but clean and in good repair and have hot water. The hotel also has a restaurant and a tiny swimming pool. At times when special events are planned the tent and RV sites may not be available.

The Joker is on the east side of Mex 1 just north of the Km 13 marker. Heading north watch for it after you pass the airport, about 1.4 miles (2.2 km) north of the Estero Beach road. Heading south it is 3.8 miles (6.1 km) south of the Gigante at the corner of Av. Reforma and Calle General Agustin Sanginés, watch for the hotel on your left. The RV park entrance is on the side street to the north, park outside and walk in to check space availability.

⛺ ESTERO BEACH HOTEL/RESORT

Reservations:	482 W. San Ysidro Blvd., PMP 1186, San Ysidro, CA 92173
Telephone:	(646) 176-6225
Fax:	(646) 176-6925)
Website:	www.hotelesterobeach.com
Email:	estero@telnor.net
Open:	All Year

GPS Location: N 31° 46' 41", W 116° 36' 15"

The Estero Beach Hotel has long been one of Mexico's finest RV parks, comparable in many ways (including cost) with the newer very expensive places on the road between Tijuana and Ensenada. This is really a large complex with a hotel as the centerpiece and many permanent RVs in a separate area from the RV park. Reservations are recommended because caravans often fill this place unexpectedly.

The modern RV park has 38 big back-in spaces with 30-amp outlets, sewer, and water. There is also a very large area for parking if you don't want utilities. There is grass under trees for tenters. The parked RVs look across an estuary (excellent birding) toward the hotel about a quarter-mile away. There's a paved walkway along the border of the estuary to the hotel. The restrooms are showing some age, hot water is sometimes not available. The hotel also has another area with full hookups for about 20 smaller units, they call it their trailer park. Check to see if there is room there for you if the RV park happens to be full. Rates are currently just under $30 with an additional fee of $5 for a towed vehicle. Holiday rates are higher. There is a 10% monthly discount.

The resort also has a restaurant, bar, museum, several upscale shops, boat launching ramp, tennis courts, and playground. RVers are not allowed to use the large main swimming pool but a special pool for the RV park is scheduled to be completed in October 2006. There's a public beach adjoining the resort on the far side of the grounds from the RV park.

To reach the Estero Beach Hotel take the Estero Beach road west from Mex 1 some 5.2 miles (8.4 km) south of the Gigante supermarket on the corner of Ave. Reforma (Mex 1) and Calle General Agustin Sanginés. Drive 1 mile (1.6 km) west and turn left at the sign for the Estero Beach Hotel. You'll soon come to a gate. There is a very long entrance drive and then a reception office where they'll sign you up and direct you to a campsite.

◼ EL FARO BEACH MOTEL AND TRAILER PARK

Address:	Apdo. 1008, Ensenada, CP 22785 B.C., México
Telephone:	(646) 177-4630
Open:	All Year

GPS Location: N 31° 46' 48", W 116° 37' 04"

The El Faro is a popular destination for beach-goers from Ensenada. Busses bring loads of them to the small public beach that is located between the El Faro and the Estero Beach Hotel. That means that on sunny days there are probably too many people wandering through the camping area for a really enjoyable experience. The mascot here is Leonardo, a huge male lion kept in a cage near the entrance. At one time it was a cute little cub, but, they say, "it just kept getting bigger!"

This is a simple place, RV parking is right next to the beach on a sandy lot surrounded by a low concrete curb. Tenters can pitch on the beach out front. There is room for about 3 RVs to back in for spaces with low-amp electricity. Much more space, enough for some 20 more RVs is available without hookups. Maximum RV length should be about 30 feet. Showers are old, in poor repair, and cold. You'll be happier if you have an RV and bring your own bathroom facilities along with you.

To reach the El Faro take the Estero Beach road west from Mex 1 about 5.2 miles (8.4 km) south of the Gigante supermarket on the corner of Ave. Reforma (Mex 1) and Calle Agustin Sanginés. Drive 1.9 mile (3.1 km) west, taking the left fork of the Y at 1.6 miles (2.6 km). The El Faro is at the end of the road.

BAJA BEACHES ARE POPULAR WITH LOCALS DURING THE HOLIDAYS

▣ MONA LISA RV PARK

Address:	Apdo. 607, Ensenada, B.C., México
Telephone:	(646) 177-5100
Website:	www.monalisabeach.com
Email:	lisated@telnor.net
Open:	All Year

GPS Location: N 31° 47'04", W 116° 37'02"

This is a interesting campground, a fun place to visit. The name apparently comes from the murals painted on every available wall. They depict scenes from Mexico's history and are themselves worth a special trip to the Mona Lisa.

The campground has 13 fairly large back-in spaces. All are paved and some have palapa-shaded tables. All also have 50-amp outlets, sewer, and water. The restrooms are old, dark, and poorly maintained. This is another place you'll appreciate having your own bathroom facilities. The Mona Lisa is near beaches but rock rip-rap fronts the actual RV park property, the current RV sites don't overlook the water. There's also a playground. The manager is in house #4. The RV rate in summer is $22, in winter it is $17.50. The monthly rate here is $300.

To reach the Mona Lisa take the Estero Beach road west from Mex 1 5.2 miles (8.4 km) south of the Gigante on the corner of Ave. Reforma (Mex 1) and Calle General Agustin Sanginés. Drive west and then north, taking the right fork of the Y at 1.6 miles (2.6 km). At 1.8 miles (2.9 km) turn left and you'll see the Mona Lisa ahead.

CORONA BEACH PARK

Address: PO Box 1149, Ensenada, México
Telephone: (646) 173-7326
Open: All Year

GPS Location: N 31° 47' 22", W 116° 36' 53"

This is a simple campground with parking in a large flat area with no view of the beach. There is parking for 28 RVs of any size with 15-amp outlets and water. There is also a dump station. The restrooms are clean and have cold water showers. A small grocery store sits next to the camping area but is not open in winter.

To reach the Corona Beach take the Estero Beach road west from Mex 1 some 5.2 miles (8.4 km) south of the Gigante on the corner of Ave. Reforma (Mex 1) and Calle General Agustin Sanginés. Drive west and then north, taking the right fork of the Y at 1.6 miles (2.6 km). At 1.9 miles (3.1 km) the road makes a quick right and then left to continue straight. You'll reach the campground at 2.1 miles (3.4 km).

CENTRO RECRETIVO MI REFUGIO

Address: Carretera a la Bufadora Km 8.5,
                         Ensenada, B.C.
Telephone: (646) 154-2756
Email: klaudiamt@yahoo.com
Open: All Year

GPS Location: N 31° 41' 54", W 116° 38' 06"

As you drive out toward La Bufadora you may notice a castle on the right, complete with crenellated towers. If you walk down the entrance road you'll find a nice little RV park right alongside. The castle is really a home and the whole establishment is obviously a labor of love, an unusual one. There's a Japanese restaurant above the park which may help you recognize it.

The campground has 15 full-hookup sites with 15-amp outlets, water, and sewer. These are small pull-in or back-in sites, some are suitable (with careful maneuvering) for RVs to about 30 feet. You'd be well advised to walk in and look before entering in anything over 30 feet because turning around could be difficult and the entrance is steep. The sites directly overlook the bay. The somewhat muddy beach with additional areas for tent camping is just below. There is a modern restroom building with hot showers, also a playground. The monthly rate is $250.

The campground is on the road to La Bufadora which leaves Mex 1 about 9.1 miles (14.7 km) south of the Gigante supermarket on the corner of Ave. Reforma (Mex 1) and Calle General Agustin Sanginés in Ensenada. You will see it on the right 5.5 miles (8.9 km) after taking the cutoff.

CAMPO MENESES

Address: Km 12 Carret. Maneadero a la Bufadora,
                         Punta Banda, CP 22791 Ensenada, BC, Mexico
Telephone: (646) 176-1363
Open: All Year

GPS Location: N 31° 42' 59", W 116° 39' 43"

This two-year old park is a work in progress. It's a long lot running from the road to the beach. There is room for perhaps 50 RVs to park along the central divider. Right now facilities include water, a dump station, and restrooms with toilets and warm showers. Cords can be run to obtain electricity. The plan is to put in full-hookup RV sites with cement patios.

Take the road toward La Bufadora from Mex 1 about 9.1 miles (14.7 km) south from the Gigante on the corner of Ave. Reforma (Mex 1) and Calle General Agustin Sanginés in Ensenada. You will see the Campo Meneses on the right 7.5 miles (11.9 km) from the cutoff.

🚐 LA JOLLA BEACH CAMP

Address:	Apdo. 102, Km 12.5 Carret. Maneadero a la Bufadora, Punta Banda, CP 22794 Ensenada, B.C., México
Telephone:	(646) 154-2005
Fax:	(646) 154-2004
Open:	All Year

GPS Location: N 31° 43' 00", W 116° 39' 54"

The La Jolla Beach Camp is a huge place. There are a lot of permanently-located trailers here but most of the transient trade is summer and holiday visitors using tents or RVs. Several big empty dirt lots, both on the waterfront and on the south side of the highway, have room for about 300 groups. During the winter these areas are practically empty. You can park on the waterfront and run a long cord for low-amp electricity from a few plugs near the restroom buildings. There is room for large RVs when the campground is not crowded. Water is available and there's a dump station. Restrooms are very basic, like what you'd expect next to a public beach, there are a few hot showers available. There is a small grocery store and basic English is spoken. There's also a launch ramp, it's only suitable for light boats since it's really just access to the sandy beach. The monthly rate here is $350.

Take the road toward La Bufadora from Mex 1 about 9.1 miles (14.7 km) south from the Gigante on the corner of Ave. Reforma (Mex 1) and Calle General Agustin Sanginés in Ensenada. You will see the La Jolla on the right 7.8 miles (12.6 km) from the cutoff.

🚐 VILLARINO RV PARK AND BEACH CAMPING

Address:	Km 13 Carr. la Bufadora, Punta Banda, B.C., México
Telephone:	(619) 819-8358 (US), (646) 154-2045
Fax:	(646) 154-2044
Email:	villarv@telnor.net
Open:	All Year

GPS Location: N 31° 43' 01", W 116° 40' 00"

This campground with lots of permanents also has a good-size transient area. It's close to Ensenada, on the beach, and a little off the beaten path.

Behind a glass-fronted terrace overlooking the beach is a large packed dirt area with some trees and about 25 larger hookup sites. Some sites have 15-amp outlets, sewer, and water and some have only electricity and water. There are a few pull-thrus. Most sites have picnic tables, some have fire rings. After careful maneuvering through the entrance and access road many of the sites in this campground will take big RVs. The restrooms are very clean and well maintained, they have hot showers. In front of the campground is a restaurant, a small store, a post office, and a public phone. There's also a small boat ramp. The monthly rate here is $400, much less if you pay your own electricity.

Take the road toward La Bufadora from Mex 1 about 9.1 miles (14.7 km) south from the Gigante on the corner of Ave. Reforma (Mex 1) and Calle General Agustin Sanginés in Ensenada. You will see the Villarino on the right 7.9 miles (12.6 km) from the cutoff.

CAMPO #5 – CORONEL ESTEBAN CANTU

Open: All Year

GPS Location: N 31° 43' 46", W 116° 43' 21"

This is the most popular of several ejido or Campo campgrounds along the road out to la Bufadora. It's difficult to miss since it's right alongside the road. The views here are spectacular, you're hundreds of feet up the mountain overlooking the ocean. There are no hookups but a restroom building does have a toilet and cold showers. Any size RV will fit just fine.

Take the road toward La Bufadora from Mex 1 about 9.1 miles (14.7 km) south from the Gigante on the corner of Ave. Reforma (Mex 1) and Calle General Agustin Sanginés in Ensenada. Some 11.9 miles (14.9 km) from the junction you'll see the campground on the right.

RANCHO LA BUFADORA

Open: All Year

GPS Location: N 31° 43' 33", W 116° 43' 00"

This is really just a parking area where RV parking is allowed for a fee. Tents are often pitched out front. It's located along the rocky shore just below the parking lots at La Bufadora blowhole. There's a small rocky beach. This is a popular scuba diving location and there is a dive shop. There are also restroom with flush toilets and dilapidated cold showers without shower heads.

To reach the parking area you must brave the crowded parking lots for the blowhole. Ignore the people waving you in to a parking space and watch for the sign for Rancho La Bufadora a bit down a side road to the left. This is the turn, follow the road down and around to the left and you'll find yourself in the camping lot.

Other Camping Possibilities

Out near La Bufadora there are at least two small camping operations in addition to Camp No. 5 and Rancho la Bufadora. These are very basic and inexpensive no-frills camping sites with names like Camp #7 and Campo #8. They offer no facilities except pit toilets and often very difficult access, but some have great views.

TECATE (TEH-**KAW**-TAY)
Population 80,000, Elevation 1,850 ft. (560 m)

Tecate is one of the most relaxed and pleasant border towns in Mexico. Besides being a great place to cross into Baja (there are decent roads south to Ensenada and east to Mexicali) the town is well worth a short visit.

Tecate is an agricultural center that is gradually turning industrial as the maquiladora industries arrive. The center of town is dominated by the park-like square which is just a couple of blocks from the laid-back border crossing. Probably the most famous tourist attraction here is the **Tecate brewery**.

Coming into Mexico here from the U.S. is pretty easy. If you need to pick up a tourist card we suggest that you park on the U.S. side and walk across to get the cards, it's easier to find a parking place on the U.S. side. After crossing in your vehicle just go down the hill four blocks to Av. Juarez (the street just before the park), jog one block left, and then turn right and head south, you're on the road to Ensenada.

Crossing back into the U.S. is pretty easy too. The line to cross the border northbound is on a road along the border fence east of the crossing. To get on it you must travel east of the city to a new entrance road. It's about .6 miles east of the crossing and accessible from Mex 2 (not the toll road). Turn north toward the border at the sign for Garita Tecate, the road name is Manuel Moreno. When you reach the fence you'll turn left. Get in the left lane, big RVs can make the necessary turn into the gate area much more easily from the left lane. If you wait too long you won't be able to get over. This setup is much better than in the past with less chance of running afoul of the local police. The crossing is open from 5 am to 11 pm.

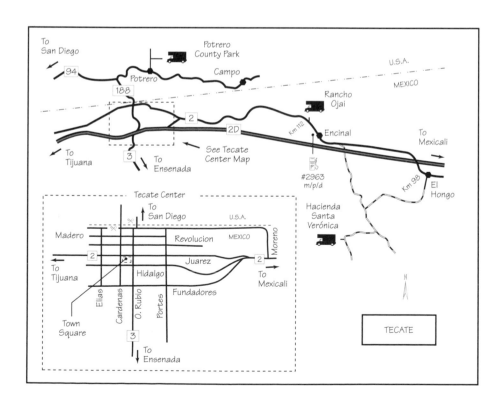

SOUTH TO ENSENADA

Tecate Campgrounds

POTRERO COUNTY PARK

Reservations: 5201 Ruffin Road, Suite P,
San Diego, CA 92123-1699
Telephone: (Reservations) (858) 565-3600,
(Info) (858) 694-3049
Website: www.co.san-diego.ca.us/parks
Open: All Year

GPS Location: N 32° 36'46", W 116° 35'41"

This is a good campground on the U.S. side of the border near Tecate. If you are headed south and want to get an early start in the morning consider spending the night here. It is only 5 miles (8 km) from Tecate, the small nearby town of Potrero offers a café. Another nearby town, Campo, has an interesting railroad museum.

There are 39 back-in sites with electrical and water hookups set under oak trees for shade and also 7 tent sites. Large RVs will find plenty of room in most RV sites. Picnic tables and fire pits are provided. Areas are also set aside for tents and there are hot water showers. There is a dump station. Reservations are accepted but probably not necessary during the winter season.

Follow Hwy. 94 from San Diego toward Tecate. Zero your odometer where Hwy. 188 to Tecate cuts off to the right but continue straight. Drive 2.3 miles (3.7 km) to the outskirts of Potrero and turn left. Then after another 0.3 miles (0.5 km) turn right on the entrance road to the campground.

RANCHO OJAI

Address: Km 112 Carretera Libre Mexicali-Tecate,
Tecate, B.C., Mexico
Telephone: (665) 655-3014
Fax: (665) 655-3015
Website: www.rancho-ojai.com
Email: reservations@campingbaja.com
Open: All Year

GPS Location: N 32° 33'33", W 116° 26'10"

Rancho Ojai is something a little different in Baja campgrounds. This is a former working ranch located in the rolling hills just east of Tecate off Mex 2. It's about two miles from the U.S. border as the crow flies. The facilities are new and nicely done. This is normally a summer destination, the area is known for its mild summer weather, but winters have an occasional frost.

This was formerly an award-winning KOA, for several years the only KOA in Mexico. KOA has pulled out of Mexico but this is still an outstanding park. There are 75 campsites, 41 have full hookups with 30 and 50-amp outlets, sewer, and water. These are large flat pull-thrus suitable for large RVs. There are tent camping sites but the price for these is a fairly high $11 per person. The tiled restrooms are new and clean with hot water showers. The ranch offers a ranch-style clubhouse, a barbecue area, swimming pool, spa, grocery shop, sports areas for volley ball and horseshoes, mini-golf, bicycle rentals and a children's playground. The campground is fenced and there is 24-hour security. There's a restaurant just outside the grounds, just a pleasant stroll through the pasture will take you there. The rate here is about $32 for a full hookup site.

The Rancho is located about 13 miles (21 km) east of Tecate on the north side of the free highway near the Km 112 marker. It is not accessible from the toll highway. There is a stone arch entrance near the highway and you can see the camping area across the valley.

HACIENDA SANTA VERÓNICA

Address:	Blvd. Agua Caliente No. 4558, Piso No. 1, Ofic. 105 Torres de Agua Caliente, CP 22420 Tijuana, B.C., Mexico
Telephone:	(665) 681-7428 (Tijuana), (665) 648-5234 (On site)
Open:	All Year

GPS Location: N 32° 27' 34", W 116° 21' 47"

Slightly farther east of Tecate than Rancho Ojai is Hacienda Santa Verónica. To get there you must negotiate a rough and partially paved back road but once you've reached the campground you're likely to want to spend some time. This is a 5,000 acre rancho. It is described in its own brochures as rustic, but other than the no-hookup campground it is really surprisingly polished. The rancho is very popular with off-road motorcycle riders and also offers quite a few amenities: rental rooms, a swimming pool, good tennis courts, a nice restaurant and bar, horseback riding, and occasionally even a bullfight. This is a popular summer destination, in the winter things are pretty quiet except on weekends.

The camping area is a grassy meadow with big oak trees for shade. Spaces are unmarked, you camp where you want to. Any size RV will find room. There are restrooms near the camping area and near the pool.

To find the hacienda head east on Mex 2 from the Rancho Ojai to the small town of El Hongo, a distance of 8.7 miles (14 km) from Rancho Ojai. Near the center of town there is a small road heading south through the village, it is marked with an easy-to-miss Hacienda Verónica sign. After 1.1 miles (1.8 km) the road curves right and leaves town. You'll reach a Y after 4.7 miles (7.6 km) take the right fork and you'll reach the gate in another 1.5 miles (2.4 km).

TECATE TO ENSENADA ON HIGHWAY 3
67 Miles (108 Km), 2 Hours

See the information in the Tecate section just above about crossing the border either way.

Highway 3 is a good two-lane paved road that runs 63 miles (102 km) south from Tecate to meet with the four-lane coastal road just before it enters Ensenada. The route is suitable for larger RVs if they take it easy, it does cross some higher elevations and have some long grades. Some 45 miles (73 km) south of Tecate the road passes through the **Guadalupe Valley**, Mexico's premier wine-growing region. Several wineries are located there. The Pedro Domecq winery, hard to miss on the west side of the highway, offers tastings and tours as does the nearby L.A. Cetto winery.

Tecate to Ensenada on Highway 3 Campground

🚐 RANCHO SORDO MUDO (DEAF RANCH)

Address:	PO Box 1376, Chula Vista, CA 91912 or Apdo. 1468, Ensenada, B.C., Mex.
Telephone:	(646) 155-2201
Website:	www.ranchosordomudo.org
Email:	ranchosordo@hotmail.com
Open:	All Year

GPS Location: N 32° 06' 41", W 116° 32' 48"

If you decide to follow the inland route on Mex 3 south from Tecate to Ensenada you might decide to spend the night at Rancho Sordo Mudo, about 24 miles (39 km) north of Ensenada. The ranch is actually a school for deaf children, the campground was originally constructed for the use of visitors helping at the school. The income from the RV park goes to a good cause and the surroundings are very pleasant. There is no fixed price, donations are accepted.

There are 7 back-in spaces in a grassy field, some with full hookups including 50-amp outlets. Twenty more pull-through spaces offer electricity and water only. There's a separate dump station and oranges grow on the trees between sites, you're welcome to help yourself to a few. This is a fine campground and it is well-signed on Mex 3.

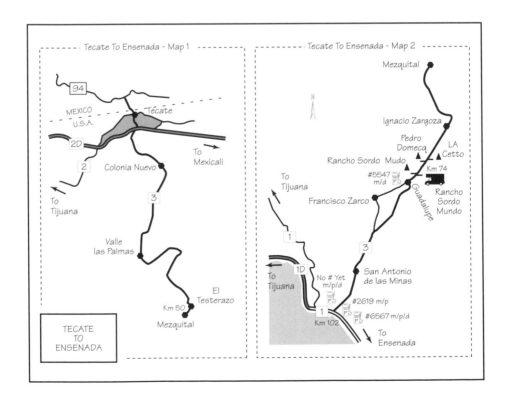

Driving south start watching as you pass the Domecq winery, it will be on your left right next to the highway just after the Km 74 marker. Heading north it is even easier to spot just north of the village of Guadalupe.

STOP FOR A TASTING AT ONE OF THE MANY WINERIES ON THE RUTA DEL VINO

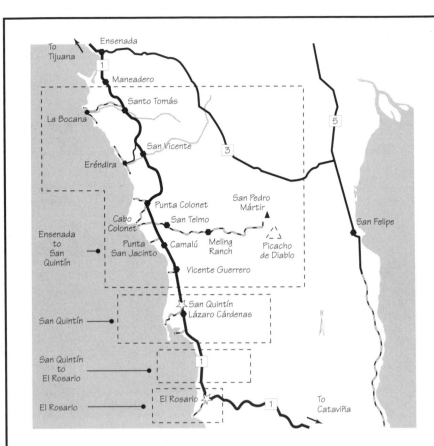

To
Tijuana

Ensenada

1

Maneadero

Santo Tomás

La Bocana

San Vicente

Eréndira

3

5

Punta Colonet

San Pedro
Mártir

San Felipe

Cabo
Colonet

San Telmo

Ensenada
to
San
Quintín

Punta
San Jacinto

Camalú

Meling
Ranch

Picacho
de Diablo

Vicente Guerrero

San Quintín

San Quintín
Lázaro Cárdenas

N

San Quintín
to
El Rosario

1

El Rosario

El Rosario

1

To
Cataviña

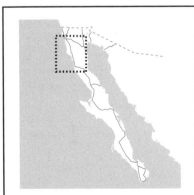

CHAPTER INDEX

Highlights .... Page 79
Roads and Fuel Availability .... Page 80
Sightseeing .... Page 81
Beaches and Water Sports .... Page 81
Fishing .... Page 81
Backroad Adventures .... Page 82
Ensenada to San Quintín .... Page 83
San Quintín .... Page 89
San Quintín to El Rosario .... Page 93
El Rosario .... Page 94

SOUTHERN NORTHWEST COAST

Chapter Five

Southern Northwest Coast

INTRODUCTION

South of Maneadero the character of the Baja changes considerably. There are far fewer people and less traffic. In the beginning the road climbs into coastal hill country, much of it is covered with greenery. One of the valleys you will cross is the Santo Tomás Valley, known for its vineyards. After some time the road flattens out and runs along a coastal plain. There is much irrigated farming in this fast-growing region with occasional roads toward the ocean which is out of sight to the west. Near San Quintín dirt roads lead west to Bahía San Quintín, a sheltered estuary offering a place to launch boats and also some history. Finally the road climbs to cross a barren mesa and then descends steeply into the town of El Rosario.

Enjoy the hustle and bustle of the fast-growing farming towns that often line the road. At the south end of this section you will be turning inland and driving through some of the Baja's most remote countryside.

Highlights

The **Santo Tomás Valley**, about 22 miles (35 km) south of Ensenada, is another of Mexico's wine regions. Many of the grapes from this area go to the Santo Tomás Winery, Mexico's largest, which is located in Ensenada. The ruins of the old **Misión Santo Tomás de Aquino** are located near the Balneario El Palomar.

Bahía San Quintín, about 110 miles (177 km) south of Ensenada, is a popular fishing destination. The bay provides a protected place to launch boats and the fishing outside the bay is excellent. Wide sandy beaches are easy to reach from the highway just to the south of Bahía San Quintín. In the 1890s an English company failed in an attempt to develop an agricultural town in the area, remains of a pier and cemetery can still be seen.

Inland from this stretch of road is the **Parque Nacional San Pedro Mártir** (San Pedro Mártir National Park). Access to this high pine country is via a long rough dirt road. See this chapter's *Backroad Adventures* for information about visiting this park.

One hundred and forty-six miles (235 km) south of Ensenada the road turns sharply left and heads inland. The small town here, **El Rosario**, is traditionally the spot to get gasoline and prepare for the isolated road to the south.

Roads and Fuel Availability

Much of the road in this section of the book is built to the narrow Baja Peninsula standard of about 19 feet wide. Additionally, there are seldom any shoulders. That means that all drivers much be cautious, particularly those driving large RVs. See the *Roads and Driving in Mexico* section in the *Details, Details, Details* chapter.

This section of Mex 1 is marked by kilometer markers that begin in Ensenada and end at Lázaro Cárdenas near Bahía San Quintín with Km 196. There the numbers start over and reach Km 59 in El Rosario.

Gasoline is not hard to find in this part of the Baja. There are several stations in Maneadero and also stations in most small towns along the route. The stations, the distances between them, and the type of fuel sold are as follows: **Santo Tomás**, 18 miles (29 km) gas; **San Vicente**, 24 miles (39 km), gas and diesel; **Punta Colonet**, 23 miles (37 km), gas and diesel; **Camalú**, 19 miles (31 km), gas and diesel; **Emiliano Zapata**, 6.2 miles (10.0 km), gas and diesel; **Vicente Guerrero**, 3.1 miles (5.0 km), gas and diesel; **Ejido Padre Kino**, 4.5 miles (7.3 km), gas and diesel: two stations in **San Quintín**, 5.2 miles (8.4 km), gas and diesel; two stations in **Lázaro Cárdenas**, 3 miles (5 km), gas and diesel; **Ejido El Papalote**, 2.8 miles (4.5 km), gas and diesel; **Rancho los Pinos**, 4 miles (6.5 km), gas and diesel; and **El Rosario**, 27 miles (44 km), gas and diesel.

A word of warning is in order about fuel. It is very important to fill up with gas or diesel in either San Quintín or El Rosario at the south end of this section. There will probably be no fuel available from filling stations until you reach Villa Jesús María, some 22 miles (35 km) north of Guerrero Negro. This is a gas gap of 195 miles (315 km). There are old Pemex filling stations at Cataviña and at the Bahía de L.A. Junction but they have been closed down and the pumps removed. Individuals with drums of gasoline in the back of their pickups often sell fuel at these stations, but we wouldn't want to count on these guys being around if we were in dire need. The La Pinta Hotel in Cataviña also has a pump for gasoline but it is usually not open. In an emergency stop and ask, they might have some fuel and be willing to open up. There is also now fuel in Bahía de Los Angeles, 39 miles (63 km) east of the Bahía de L.A. Junction.

Sightseeing

The **Parque Nacional Sierra San Pedro Mártir** is located high in the sierra east of the highway. It is an area of pine forest that is so free from human interference that there is actually an astronomical observatory at 9,300 feet in the park. On Saturdays you can drive to the observatory, tours are given from 11 am to 1 pm. **Picacho Diablo**, the highest mountain in Baja California at 10,150 feet, is accessible to climbers from the park. See *Backroad Adventures* in this chapter for more information about this road. See also the campground listings for **Parque Nacional Sierra San Pedro Mártir** and **Rancho Los Manzanos** in the Ensenada to San Quintín campground listings.

The ruins of several **Dominican missions** can be viewed as you travel down the peninsula in this section. Since all were constructed of adobe they have suffered from the occasional rain over the years and give the appearance of having melted. At Santo Tomás the ruins of **Misíon Santo Tomás de Aquino** are actually located on the grounds of a campground, the Balneario El Palomar. Ask for directions for finding them at the office. The ruins of **Misíon San Vicente Ferrer** are located in the town of San Vicente, about 43 miles (69 km) south of the La Bufadora cutoff in Maneadero. To find them take the dirt road west from about Km 88. Near Vicente Guerrero is the **Misíon Santo Domingo**. It is accessible by taking a road east at about Km 169 to the village of Santo Domingo. Finally, near El Rosario there are the ruins of **Misíon el Rosario**. The directions for finding the mission can be found in the *Backroad Adventures* section below.

One of the few **tourist information centers** on the Baja is located near Km 178 just south of the town of Vicente Guerrero. It might be worth a stop although we find the information offerings pretty slim.

The late 19th century wheat-farming scheme at San Quintín left a few remnants that you might want to track down. Near the Old Mill Trailer Park is the restored **grist mill** and southeast around the bay is the **old pier**. Just south of the latter is the **Old English Cemetery**.

Beaches and Water Sports

There are miles of long sandy beaches along this section of coast. The primary activities are surfing and surf fishing. Road access is actually not bad, see *Backroad Adventures* below for some ideas. Since many of the back roads lead to beaches in this area we've discussed the attractions in that section. Water temperatures along the coast are cool but that just makes the fishing better.

South of the mouth of the San Quintín estuary is a long beach called **Playa Santa María** at the north end and **Playa Pabellón** farther south. Both surfing and fishing are popular, access is from the Cielito Lindo, Gypsy's Beach Camp and El Pabellón RV parks, see the campground descriptions below for directions.

Fishing

From Punta Banda at the north end of the area covered by this chapter and south for about 200 miles upwelling water from the ocean depths brings nutrients that make fishing near the shore extremely good. The problem with this area is that it is unprotected and not really very safe for small boats. Launching sites for larger boats are scarce.

One way around this problem is to beach cast. Surf fishing is good along much of the coast. Another solution is to hire a panga and guide to take you out. You can do this at Puerto San Isidro, La Bocana near Puerto Santo Tomás, or at San Quintín at the Old Mill Trailer Park or the Cielito Lindo, also an RV park.

If you do decide to use your own boat the best launch site is San Quintín. However, from there you must find your way out through the weeds of the estuary, not easy to do for someone without local knowledge. There are also poor launch ramps at Puerto San Isidro and La Bocana that might be usable for small boats if the tide and weather are just right.

Backroad Adventures

See the ***Backroad Driving*** section of ***Chapter 2 - Details, Details, Details*** for essential information about driving off the main highway on the Baja and for a definition of road type classifications used below.

In the area covered by this chapter there are many small roads branching off the highway to the west and east. Most of those to the west are headed for the coast, one to the east is headed up into the Sierra San Pedro Mártir and the national park there. There are quite a number of people living between the highway and the coast, that means that there are a great number of roads of varying quality. Many of them are farm roads but they often reach the coast in places that offer good surf fishing and surfing. High clearance vehicles, especially with four-wheel drive are your best bet. The condition of these roads changes, we advise getting local information about road conditions before heading out.

Some places to try roads like this are as follows. In Santo Tomás near Km 51 a road leads to the coast at Punta San José and southwards all the way to Eréndira. The area is popular for surf fishing and surfing. There is also a web of roads west of Punta Colonet. They reach the long beach at San Antonio del Mar which is good for surf fishing and also Bahía Colonet, Punta Colonet, and Punta San Telmo. Surfing is popular south of the points, particularly south of Punta San Telmo which is widely known as "Quatro Casas". Consider these roads to be Type 3 roads unless you have local knowledge. More possibilities follow.

From Km 47 Near Santo Tomás - One and nine tenths miles (3.1 km) north of the El Palomar campground a gravel road goes along the Santo Tomás valley to **La Bocana** and then north along the coast to **Puerto Santo Tomás**. La Bocana is at the mouth of the Santo Tomás River and is 17.6 miles (28.7 km) from Mex 1. Puerto Santo Tomás is about three miles (5 km) to the north. This is usually a Type 2 road.

From Km 78 between Santo Tomás and San Vicente - A paved but sometimes rough road leads about 11 miles (18 km) to the coast at the ejido town of **Eréndira**. The road continues up the coast to **Puerto San Isidro**. You can also cross the river near the coast and drive south on dirt roads to Malibu Beach Sur RV Park, see the description below for this campground and instructions for reaching it. The paved road to Eréndira is usually a Type 1 road, beyond Eréndira the road is usually Type 2.

🚐 **From Km 141 North of San Quintín** - About 34 miles (55.5 km) north of San Quintín a road goes east to San Telmo, the **Meling Ranch**, and the **Parque Nacional Sierra San Pedro Mártir**. The first 14.5 miles (23.4 km) is paved, then as far as the Meling Ranch cutoff at about 31 miles (50 km) is usually a Type 2 road. The ranch is about a half-mile off the main road, it has an airstrip and offers overnight accommodations but not camping. Beyond the ranch to the park entrance gate at 53 miles (85 km) the road may not be as good and is sometimes a Type 3 road but is usually Type 2 letting small camping vehicles reach the park. The road continues to an astronomical observatory at 65 miles (106 km). You should be aware that the road may be closed due to snow in the winter. See also the campground listings for **Parque Nacional Sierra San Pedro Mártir** and **Rancho Los Manzanos** in the Ensenada to San Quintín campground listings.

🚐 **From the northern border of the town of Lázaro Cárdenas** - A road runs to **Bahía Falsa** on the coast where there is an oyster farm. The distance is 9 miles (14 km) along a graded gravel and sand road that is normally a Type 2 road. Bahía Falsa is the outer bay of the San Quintín estuary, the road takes you around the north end of Bahía San Quintín and past the volcanic cones that protect the bay. There are other less developed sand and dirt roads along the outer peninsula. The outer coast is a popular surfing destination.

🚐 **From the 90-degree turn in the town of El Rosario** - Heading south the highway takes a sharp left. If you go right here, then almost immediately left you will cross the river and within a mile reach the village of El Rosario de Abajo (Lower El Rosario). The ruins of **Misión el Rosario** are in this town on the right side of the road. Roads lead about 10 miles (16 km) out to the coast from here to Punta Baja and points south along the Bahía Rosario. The sandy beach along the bay is a popular surf-fishing location. This is usually a Type 3 road. The road is suitable for high-clearance vehicles only, the river crossing right at El Rosario is sometimes a problem, there is a makeshift bridge made from a large culvert that sometimes washes out. Fortunately you will reach this less than a mile from the highway so you won't waste much time if the crossing is not possible.

THE ROUTES, TOWNS, AND CAMPGROUNDS

ENSENADA TO SAN QUINTÍN
116 Miles (187 Km), 4 Hours

Mex 1 as it leaves Ensenada runs through some 7 miles (11 km) of suburbs until it reaches the town of Maneadero. At the north end of Maneadero is the road west out to La Bufadora, and you'll find several campgrounds there, they are described in the preceding chapter.

Leaving the south edge of Maneadero the road climbs into brush-covered hills. This is a scenic section of road but exercise caution because the road is narrow. Fifteen miles (24 km) after leaving Maneadero the road descends into the Santo Tomás Valley.

SOUTHERN NORTHWEST COAST

For a few miles the road runs along the valley floor which is used to grow grapes and olives. Then it once again climbs into the rolling hills. You'll pass through the small farming towns of San Vicente and Punta Colonet.

After Punta Colonet the road runs along a broad coastal plain which is covered with irrigated farmland. The ocean is occasionally visible in the distance to the right. It's really not far away and is accessible via the occasional rough dirt side road. Along this section are the villages of Camalú, Vicente Guerrero, San Quintín, and Lázaro Cárdenas. These last two towns almost seem to be one as they merge into one another along the highway, they and the bay that almost adjoins them to the west form the area that for the sake of convenience is often called San Quintín.

Ensenada to San Quintín Campgrounds

LAS CANADAS CAMPAMENTO

Address:	Km 31.5 de la Carretera Ensenada-San Quintin
Telephone:	(646) 153-1055 or (800) 027-3828
Website:	www.lascanadas.com
Email:	canadas@telnor.net
Open:	All Year

GPS Location: N 31° 39' 42", W 116° 31' 08"

This is a large new swimming resort or balneario which caters to the crowds from Ensenada and Tijuana to the north. There are swimming pools, water slides, pedal boats, a fishing lake and a store. It also is a campground. There are six full hookup sites suitable to any size RV. These have 20-amp power, water and sewer hookups as well as large patios, picnic tables, and barbeques and are located above and away from the crowded water park. There is also tent camping on grass in large areas nearer the water park. Restrooms for the tent camping area offer warm showers. The pools are closed in the middle of the winter but the camping stays open. There's a small grocery store at the entrance. Expect to pay more if you spend the day here to use the water park, the $12 per person rate above is for the evening only.

The campground is located directly off Mex 1 some 3 miles (5 km) south of Maneadero near Km 31.

CAMPING URUAPAN

Address:	Mex 1, Km 41
Open:	All Year

GPS Location: N 31° 37' 05", W 116° 27' 07"

This is a small rustic camping area and balneario run by the ejido in Uruapan. The camping area now has indoor-style electrical outlets nailed to the trees. The parking/camping area is shaded with big trees, with careful maneuvering large RVs can use some of the parking locations. There is a restroom building with poorly functioning flush toilets but a new one was under construction when we last visited. Most of the time the campground is unattended but someone comes by to collect. There is no security and we do not recommend camping here with just one RV. The campground is on the east side of Mex 1 near Km 41 some 8 miles (15 km) south of Maneadero.

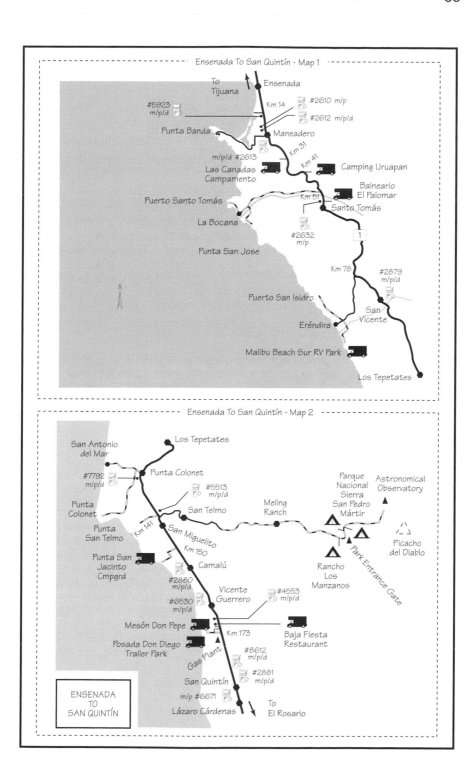

Ensenada To San Quintín - Map 1

To Tijuana
Ensenada
#5923 m/p/d
Km 14
#2610 m/p
#2612 m/p/d
Punta Banda
Maneadero
Km 31
m/p/d #2613
Km 41
Las Cañadas Campamento
Camping Uruapan
Balneario El Palomar
Puerto Santo Tomás
Km 51
Santo Tomás
La Bocana
#2632 m/p
1
Punta San Jose
Km 78
#2879 m/p/d
Puerto San Isidro
San Vicente
Eréndira
Malibu Beach Sur RV Park
Los Tepetates
N

Ensenada To San Quintín - Map 2

San Antonio del Mar
Los Tepetates
#7792 m/p/d
Punta Colonet
#5513 m/p/d
Parque Nacional Sierra San Pedro Mártir
Astronomical Observatory
Punta Colonet
San Telmo
Meling Ranch
Punta San Telmo
Km 141
San Miguelito
Park Entrance Gate
Picacho del Diablo
Km 150
Punta San Jacinto Cmpgrd
Camalú
Rancho Los Manzanos
#2880 m/p/d
Vicente Guerrero
#4553 m/p/d
#6530 m/p/d
Mesón Don Pepe
Km 173
Baja Fiesta Restaurant
Posada Don Diego Trailer Park
Gas Plant
#8612 m/p/d
San Quintín
#2881 m/p/d
ENSENADA TO SAN QUINTÍN
m/p #6671
Lázaro Cárdenas
To El Rosario

⛟ BALNEARIO EL PALOMAR

Address:	Moctezuma Entre 3 y 4, Ensenada, BC, México
Telephone:	(646) 153-8002 or (646) 153-8071
Open:	All Year

GPS Location: N 31° 33' 24", W 116° 24' 43"

Balnearios (swimming resorts) are very popular in Mexico, they often make a good place to camp. This is a good example although it is much less popular now that Las Canadas (see above) has opened.

The El Palomar has six pull-thrus large enough for RVs to about 30 feet and 20 or so very small back-in spaces. All have 15-amp outlets, sewer, water, patios and barbecues. Many also have picnic tables. Two restroom buildings are provided but are in poor condition, they sometimes have hot water for showers. There are two swimming pools near the camping area and a small lake and water slide about a half-mile away. Swimming areas are only open in summer. There's also a small zoo and large areas for picnicking. Across the street in the main building there is a store, a restaurant, and a small gas station. The store has a good collection of Mexican handicrafts. You should be aware that this is a very popular place with people from Ensenada on weekends during the summer and on holidays. It might be better to avoid the campground during those times since many of the sites are pretty much right in the center of things. At other times this place seems to be very, very quiet.

The El Palomar is at the north entrance to the town of Santo Tomás about 30 miles (49 km) south of Ensenada on Mex 1. The office is on the west side of the road and the campground on the east.

⛟ MALIBU BEACH SUR RV PARK

Telephone:	(646) 713-1816 or (646) 154-4028
Open:	All Year

GPS Location: N 31° 14' 15", W 116° 21' 26"

This is an isolated campground with decent facilities on a very nice beach. If you have a smaller RV that allows you to drive to it without problems you'll find it hard to beat. The owners live on site.

There are 14 pull-thru sites with full hookups. Outlets are 15 amps. Sites have cement patios and the 7 in front overlook the ocean. There is a 15-foot bluff here with stairs leading down to the beach. Sixteen more sites with no hookups or patios are located behind the serviced sites. The bathroom building has hot showers and there is also a washing machine and dryer. Fishing from the beach is excellent here, this coast is famous for it.

A portion of the access road to this campground is ungraded dirt road. We recommend that motorhomes over about 24 feet and trailers do not attempt to use this campground without local knowledge. The road condition undoubtedly changes from year to year and you may also have to do a little route-finding. To reach the campground leave Mex 1 just south of the Km 78 marker on the road toward Eréndira. Follow this paved road 10.2 miles (16.5 km), then take a left turn at a somewhat faded sign for Malibu Beach Sur RV Park. This is an unpaved track that will take you across the (hopefully) dry riverbed and up the bank on the other side through a group of houses. Continue following signs for the campground through a region of fields along the ocean. You'll reach the campground 3.2 miles (5.2 km) after leaving the pavement. If you reach a branch in the road that is not marked (there are several branches), just follow the one that seems to lead south along the coast. The countryside is open and you'll have a good view of the area.

⛺ PUNTA SAN JACINTO CAMPGROUND

Open: All Year

GPS Location: N 30° 51' 41", W 115° 10' 01"

This is a popular surfing location. There's a wrecked ship just off the beach, surfers call the location "Shipwreck".

The campground is a fenced compound with many permanently located trailers and small cottages owned by surfers. Visitors can park to the north of the permanent area near the beach. There are a few fire rings and not much else. It is possible to travel out here and park in any size RV although visitors are mostly surfers in smaller vehicles. Facilities are limited to pit toilets, cold showers may be available.

To reach the campground leave the highway near Km 150 and head west on a rough dirt road. At 1.2 miles (1.9 km) you'll enter a small village and see the Playa sign pointing left. Follow the sign and in another 0.2 mile (0.3 km) another sign will take you right. The road will take you out of town to the beach area and then bear right and in 3.1 mile (5 km) you'll arrive at the campground gate.

⛺ PARQUE NACIONAL SIERRA SAN PEDRO MÁRTIR

Open: All Year

GPS Location: N 31° 00' 01", W 115° 33' 25"

This park in the Sierra de San Pedro Mártir mountains is rumored to have become a state park but we've not seen any confirmation. The change from national to state status will probably have little effect on the camping there. See also the information about the park under *Sightseeing* and *Backroad Adventures* above.

This is a large and mostly undeveloped park. It's in a pine forest at the altitude of 8,000 to 9,000 feet so it's very cool in winter and often has snow. It's primarily a summer destination. There is a road through the park up to the observatory and also rough tracks requiring high clearance and sometimes four-wheel drive to other areas of the park, also lots of hiking. You can camp in several designated areas, the only facilities are fiberglass outhouses. RVers in small RVs can also park and stay in an area near the entrance gate.

The road to the park begins near Km 141 about 34 miles (55.5 km) north of San Quintín. The first 14.5 miles (23.4 km) is paved, then as far as the Meling Ranch cut-off at about 31 miles (50 km) is usually a Type 2 road. Beyond the ranch to the park entrance gate at 53 miles (85 km) the road may not be as good and is sometimes a Type 3 road but is usually Type 2 letting small camping vehicles reach the park. The road continues to an astronomical observatory at 65 miles (106 km). You should be aware that the road may be closed due to snow in the winter.

RANCHO LOS MANZANOS $ A 🚰 🏠

Open: Summer Only

GPS Location: N 30° 57' 46", W 115° 36' 09"

This small camping area is located 6 miles outside the Parque Nacional Sierra San Pedro Mártir gates along the access road. While really a tent campground it does have areas where small RVs could park. It is only open in summer and not always then. There are bathrooms with flush toilets and showers, they're in very poor condition.

The campground is located on the right 45.4 miles from Mex 1. See the listing for Parque Nacional Sierra San Pedro Mártir for more information about access to the campground.

BAJA FIESTA RESTAURANT   FREE 🚿HOT 🍴 👤ENGLISH

Address: Av. Benito Suarez Sur, Vicente Guerrero, BC, México   🚌BIG RIGS
Telephone: (616) 166-4011
Open: All Year

GPS Location: N 30° 44' 08", W 115° 59' 20"

This is a very popular new Mexican restaurant located in Vicente Guerrero just north of the Méson Don Pepe (below). It has a large lot behind the restaurant, RVers are welcome to spend the night (no hookups) if they have dinner. There are bathrooms and showers (20 pesos for showers) and the owners live behind the restaurant so someone is on-site all night. The restaurant is at the south end of Vicente Guerrero on the west side of the highway, just north of Km 173.

MESÓN DON PEPE $$ A ♿ 🚰

Address: Calle del Turismo No. 102, CP 22920 Vicente   🚐 🚿HOT 🍴
                     Guerrero, B.C, México
Telephone: (616) 166-2216
Fax: (616) 166-2268
Open: All Year

GPS Location: N 30° 42' 59", W 115° 59' 21"

This campground and the one following are in the town of Vicente Guerrero, about 8 miles (13 km) north of San Quintín. Both of these parks have been popular for a long time with travelers heading south or north, they are a comfortable day's drive from the border. Both are located on the same entrance road, they're within a half-mile of each other. The Don Pepe is the one on the highway and the first one the visitor reaches, it is also the smaller of the two.

Just below the restaurant is a grassy area with electrical outlets and water that is set aside for tenters, there's also parking on dirt for RVs. Access and site size limit RV size to about 30 feet. There is room for about 8 traveling RVs. The campground has a dump station and old but useable restrooms with hot water showers. The restaurant at the Don Pepe is well known and considered to be good.

The entrance to the trailer park is on the west side of Mex 1 just south of Col. Vicente Guerrero where the road climbs a small hill at the Km 173 marker. Near the top of the hill, just north of the gas plant, turn into the road that leads westward. Almost immediately turn into the parking lot for the small restaurant and office. After checking in you'll see a road curving around the back of the trailer park to lead you back down the camping area.

▥ POSADA DON DIEGO TRAILER PARK

Address:	Carr. Transpeninsular Km 174,
	CP 22920 Vicente Guerrero, B.C., México
Telephone:	(616) 166-2181
Fax:	(616) 166-2248
Website:	www.posadadondiego.com
Email:	posadadondiego@yahoo.com
Open:	All Year

GPS Location: N 30° 42' 44", W 115° 59' 52"

This second Col. Vicente Guerrero trailer park is very popular with caravans, it is roomy and has lots of spaces, in fact it is the only large campground with full hook-ups in this area.

The campground has 100 spaces, about a third of these are usually occupied by permanents. Most of the available slots are large enough for big RVs with slide-outs, they have 15-amp outlets, water, and patios. A few are pull-thrus, most are back-ins. About half have sewer, there is also a dump station available. The restrooms are older but in good repair and clean, they have hot water showers. The campground also has a restaurant/bar, a store, a meeting room and a playground. Wi-Fi is available at some of the sites near the restaurant, there is a charge. The monthly rate here is $275.

To reach the Posada Don Diego follow the road going west from just north of the gas plant at Km 173. This is just south of Col. Vicente Guerrero. The same road runs right past the restaurant at the Don Pepe, described above. The campground is about 0.5 miles (0.8 km) down this sometimes rough but passable gravel road.

SAN QUINTÍN (SAHN KEEN-TEEN)
Population 40,000 in the area

San Quintín is an interesting place, both geological and historically. The area is a large salt water lagoon system which fronts a fertile plain. Long sandy beaches stretch north and south. The lagoon and plain probably would have eroded away long ago except that there are eight small volcanoes (seven onshore and one an island offshore) that shelter the area from the sea. For the last few decades the plain has been heavily farmed, unfortunately there is not enough fresh water in the aquifer and salt water has started to displace the fresh water. Farming is gradually retreating to the east side of Mex 1.

Farming is also responsible for the interesting history of the area. During the late 19th century the region was the focus of a settlement scheme by an American company and then later an English company under a grant from Mexican President Porfirio Díaz. The plan was to grow wheat but it turned out that there wasn't enough rainfall. Today there are several ruined structures to remind visitors of the colony, they include the Molino Viejo (old mill), the Muelle Viejo (old pier), and the English cemetery.

Outdoorsmen love the area. Goose and duck hunting is good in the winter, fishing offshore is excellent. The protected waters are a good place to launch a trailer boat if you've pulled one south, but the shallow waters of the bay are difficult to navigate and the offshore waters can be dangerous.

The large influx of workers into this area from throughout Mexico to work on the farms, particularly single males, has meant that the area has a crime problem. Camping outside campgrounds is definitely not recommended throughout this region or in the neighboring areas to the north and south.

San Quintín Campgrounds

CIELITO LINDO MOTEL AND RV PARK

Address:	Apdo. 7, San Quintín, B.C., México
Telephone:	(616) 165-9246 or (616) 159-6158
Email:	cielitolindo@bajasi.com, josem@telnor.net
Open:	All Year

GPS Location: N 30° 24' 32", W 115° 55' 27"

The Cielito Lindo Motel has been around for a long time. It is well-known for its restaurant and fishing charters. The long and sandy Playa Santa María is a short walk from the campground. On our last visit we found it in much better condition than usual.

The hotel camping area has 8 back-in slots, they have generator produced electric-

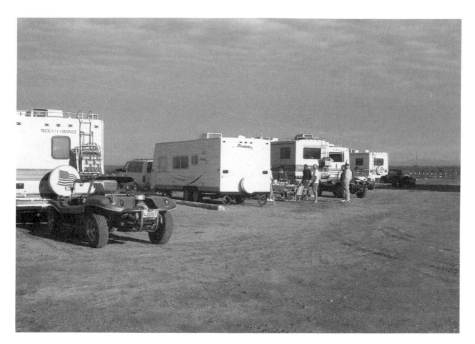

CAMPING AT GYPSY'S BEACH CAMP

ity with 15-amp outlets, water and sewer. These are long sites suitable for big RVs and there's lots of maneuvering room. There is a row of pine trees to provide shade and some shelter from the frequent wind in this area. The bar also serves as a restaurant, some people come here just because of the food. There is live music three nights a week. There is also an area set aside for tent campers not needing hookups. Restrooms with hot showers are located in a building on the north side of the central courtyard area and have been recently refurbished, they were spotless when we visited.

The Cielito Lindo is located near the San Quintín La Pinta Motel. The paved road with lots of potholes leads west from Mex 1 near the Km 11 marker. It is signed for both the La Pinta and the Cielito Lindo. Follow the road west for 2.8 miles (4.5 km) past the La Pinta entrance (where the road turns to gravel) to the Cielito Lindo entrance, .8 miles beyond the La Pinta entrance.

GYPSY'S BEACH CAMP

Address:	APDO 7, San Quintin, Baja California, México
Telephone:	(619) 593-2252
Website:	www.bajasi.com
Email:	gypsys@bajasi.com
Open:	All Year

GPS Location: N 30° 24' 26", W 115° 55' 53"

This is an old camping area that has been resurrected. It's located at the beach near the Cielito Lindo.

The campground has lots of room for RVs to park on packed dirt. Some sites are separated by cement curbs but much of the area is not formally laid out as sites. An old abandoned restroom building has been turned into a covered area for tent campers and there's another restroom building with flush toilets and hot showers. There's also a restaurant, Laura's Zopilote Mojado (Wet Buzzard).

To reach the campground drive to the Cielito Lindo as outlined above. Continue on past the Cielito Lindo, you'll see the Gypsy Beach Camp in the distance about a quarter-mile away.

OLD MILL TRAILER PARK

Address:	PO Box 2448, Chula Vista, CA 91912
Telephone:	044 (616) 105-0788
Open:	All Year

GPS Location: N 30° 29' 05", W 115° 58' 36"

The Old Mill Trailer Park is primarily a fishing destination. It is located some 3 miles (5 km) off Mex 1 on a washboard but otherwise fine dirt road. The long rough entrance road makes it unpopular for overnight stays but even big RVs do come in here.

The campground has 20 spaces. They all have paved parking pads, patios, electricity with 15-amp outlets, sewer, and water. Fifteen are in the front row with a good view of the estuary and its birds. These are poor for big RVs because the pads aren't long enough. Behind are several sites more suitable for long RVs. There is also an area set aside for dry or tent campers. The bathrooms have hot water showers. Check in at the bait shop across the driveway from the restaurant or, if it is closed, at the bar. Fishing is good in open water outside the bay. There's a boat launch if you've brought your own (big) boat or you can hire a boat and guide.

The access road to the Old Mill leads west from Mex 1 south of Col. Lázaro Cárdenas. It is well- signed at the 1 Km marker. The wide dirt road leads west for 3.3 miles (5.3 km), then you'll see a sign pointing left to the restaurant and RV park. Don't follow signs for Old Pier, that is a different place.

EL PABELLÓN RV PARK

Open:	All Year

GPS Location: N 30° 22' 27", W 115° 52' 09"

Miles of sand dunes and ocean. That's El Pabellón RV Park. There really isn't much else. This is a large graded area set in sand dunes close to the ocean. The restrooms are very good, they're exceptionally clean and have flush toilets and hot showers. There's also a long line of interesting table-like structures with sinks and barbecues but everyone just ignores them and parks where they want. Caravans often stop here and circle wagon-train style. Tenters pitch in the dunes in front of the campground or behind rows of trees that provide some shelter if the wind is blowing. There is water in the faucets at this campground but it is salty so don't fill up with it. This campground is suitable for any size RV. There is usually an attendant at the entrance gate.

The turn for El Pabellón is between Km 16 and 17 south of San Quintín. Turn south at the sign and follow the 1.2 mile dirt and gravel road to the campground.

EL PABELLÓN PALAPAS ALVINOS

Open: All Year

GPS Location: N 30° 22' 16", W 115° 51' 49"

This new campground appears to be an extension of El Pabellón. They are virtually identical with Palapas Alvinos adjoining El Pabellón to the east. They are now separated by a chain-link fence so you cannot drive between them.

Like El Pabellón this campground is a large parking area adjoining the beach and suitable for any RV. Water hookups run in a line with the water trucked in so that it is not brackish. Restrooms are good with hot showers and there is a dump station here. Unlike El Pabellón there is generally someone on-site 24 hours.

You'll find a large sign marking the entrance near Km 16.5, 0.2 miles (0.3 km) east of the El Pabellón entrance. The road will take you toward the ocean along power lines and then turn right toward the campground, the distance is 1 mile (1.6 km) and the road is generally solid and fine for even big RVs.

SAN QUINTÍN TO EL ROSARIO
37 Miles (60 Km), 1.25 Hours

After leaving San Quintín the road continues southward along the coastal plain. It

SAN QUINTÍN
TO
EL ROSARIO

SOUTHERN NORTHWEST COAST

soon crosses a long bridge over the Río Santa María, which is usually dry. After a few more miles the ocean is within sight to the west, occasionally a small track leads to the bluff above the ocean. About 40 miles (65 km) south of Lázaro Cárdenas the road turns inland into the San Quintín Canyon and begins to climb to the top of El Rosario Mesa. Soon after reaching the top of the mesa the road descends steeply into the town of El Rosario.

EL ROSARIO (EL ROE-**SAHR**-EEYOH)
Population 4,000

For many years El Rosario was as far south as you could drive unless you were an off-roader. Today's road turns inland here and heads for the center of the peninsula, it won't return to the west coast until it cuts back to Guerrero Negro, and even there it won't stay for long. **Espinosa's Place**, a local restaurant, has been famous for years for its seafood burritos (lobster and crab meat). The town of El Rosario is actually in two places, El Rosario de Arriba is on the main highway, El Rosario de Abajo is 1.5 miles (2.4 km) away down and across the arroyo (river bed). Each has the ruins of an old mission, the first is in El Rosario de Arriba, it was abandoned when the mission moved to El Rosario de Abajo. Little remains of the first except the foundations, there are still standing walls at the second, which was abandoned in 1832. See *Backroad Adventures* in this chapter for directions to the mission.

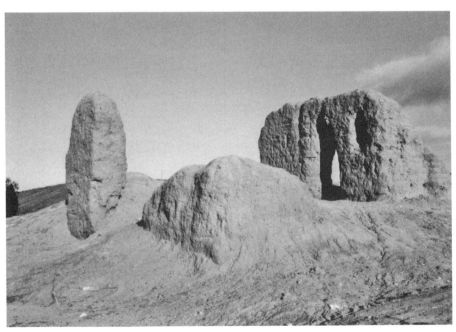

RUINS OF MISIÓN EL ROSARIO

El Rosario Campground

🚐 **MOTEL SINAHI RV PARK**

Address:	Carret. Transp. Km 56 #1056, El Rosario, B.C., México
Telephone:	(616) 165-8818
Open:	All Year

GPS Location: N 30° 04' 01", W 115° 42' 55"

The Motel Sinahi in el Rosario has 33 RV or tent camping sites on a plateau behind the motel and in the yard below. There are 25 sites for RVs or tent campers up a ramp above the motel, but they are so close together that there will probably be room for fewer campers most of the time. All sites have electricity (15 amp), water and sewer drains are available to most of them. There are also eight sites below in a large lot adjacent to the motel. There is a very nice toilet cubicle and two nice little shower rooms with hot water. There is plenty of room for big RVs to maneuver and sites are flat. The motel also has a little restaurant. Very limited English is spoken.

The Motel Sinahi is near the eastern outskirts of El Rosario on the north side of the highway. It is 0.9 miles (1.5 km) east of the 90-degree turn in the middle of town.

To
San Quintín

El Rosario

El Mármol

El Rosario
to
Cataviña

Cataviña

Cataviña

Side Trip
to
Bahía de
los Angeles

N

1

Cataviña
to
Guerrero
Negro

Bahía de los Angeles

Bahía Las Animas

Guerrero
Negro

Rosarito

Villa
Jesús
Maria

Bahía San Rafael

San Francisquito

Punta
Eugenia

Guerrero Negro

El Arco

Guerrero
Negro
to
San Ignacio

Bahia
Tortugas

Vizcaíno

1

Bahía la Asunción

San
Ignacio

San
Ignacio

To
Loreto

CHAPTER INDEX

Highlights .... Page 97
Roads and Fuel Availability .... Page 98
Sightseeing .... Page 98
Beaches and Water Sports .... Page 99
Fishing .... Page 100
Backroad Adventures .... Page 101
El Rosario to Cataviña .... Page 102
Cataviña .... Page 104
Cataviña to Guerrero Negro ...... Page 106
Guerrero Negro .... Page 108
Side Trip to Bahía de los
    Angeles .... Page 112
Guerrero Negro to San Ignacio .... Page 117
San Ignacio .... Page 119

CENTRAL BAJA

Chapter Six

Central Baja

INTRODUCTION

This central section of the Baja Peninsula is much different than that to the north. The area has far fewer people, and the landscape is definitely desert. In fact, the area from El Rosario to the cutoff to Bahía de los Angeles has some of the most scenic and interesting desert country in the world.

Highlights

The desert country around **Cataviña** is filled with huge granite boulders. Between them grow a variety of desert cactus, this is great country for short hikes and photography. In this area you'll see a unique type of cactus, the **cirio** or boojum tree. These large cactus look like upside-down green carrots. The Baja is the only place in the world that you are likely to see them.

The **Ojo de Liebre** lagoon near Guerrero Negro is one of only three places on the Baja where you can get right up close to **California gray whales**. They give birth to their young in the lagoon, you can see them from January to March each year. A second location for this is **Laguna San Ignacio**, accessible from San Ignacio and also described in this chapter.

Bahía de los Angeles is beautiful, you'll want to see it. The bright blue bay and string of islands offshore are a real spectacle as you approach on the highway. The town itself can be a bit of a letdown, but there are some very popular primitive but accessible camping sites near town and excellent summer fishing locations some distance to the south.

Roads and Fuel Availability

The main road, Mex 1, from El Rosario to Guerrero Negro and on to San Ignacio is in good condition. The countryside is made up of rolling hills so the road rises and falls and snakes around looking for the best route. This may be the area where you really begin to notice the 9.5-foot-wide lanes. Just keep your speed down and watch for traffic. When you meet someone, slow to a safe speed and get as near the right edge of the pavement as you safely can.

Kilometer markers in this section are in three segments. The first two count up as you go south: El Rosario to a point near the Bahía de los Angeles Junction (60 to 280) and Bahía L.A. Junction to the Baja/Baja Sur Border (0 to 128). From the border to San Ignacio (and for the rest of the trip south) the kilometer markers run from south to north. They begin at the border with Km 221 and reach Km 74 at San Ignacio.

The road out to Bahía de los Angeles is paved and until lately has been in very poor condition with lots of potholes. The entire 42 mile (68 km) length has been repaved and is in excellent condition.

This section of the peninsula is home to the famous "Baja Gas Gap". It is the one place on the Baja highway where even cautious travelers might run in to trouble. From the gas station at El Rosario to the gas station at Villa Jesús María just north of Guerrero Negro is a distance of 195 miles (315 km). If either the gas station at El Rosario or the one at Villa Jesús Maria was temporarily out of fuel the gap would be even larger. Even so, few vehicles are permanently lost in the "gas gap", just be sure to fuel up before entering it.

Fuel locations, types available, and distances between stations is as follows: **El Rosario**, gas and diesel; **Villa Jesús María**, gas and diesel, 195 miles (315 km); **Guerrero Negro**, several stations, gas and diesel, 19 miles (31 km); **Vizcaíno**, gas and diesel, 44 miles (71 km); and **San Ignacio**, gas and diesel, 43 miles (69 km). There are also two stations in **Bahía de Los Angeles**, both gas and diesel are available.

Sightseeing

El Mármol is an abandoned onyx mine located in the desert about nine miles north of the highway. From the early 1900's to about 1950 this was the world's major source of onyx, if you have some this is probably where it came from. Today the place is abandoned but there is a well-known onyx-walled school-house and blocks of onyx scattered around. See the *Backroad Adventures* section below for driving instructions.

Near **Cataviña** there is an area of extremely photogenic cactus set among rounded granite boulders. The highway goes right through the middle of this area so you can't miss it.

From late December to about the middle of April the **California gray whales** come to the Baja. They congregate in shallow bays along the west coast where their young are born. It is possible to take a ride in a panga out to see them up close. There are three places where this is done: Guerrero Negro, Laguna San Ignacio, and Bahía

RUPESTRIAN ART

Magdalena. This is discussed in much more detail in the sections about Guerrero Negro and San Ignacio later in this chapter.

Misión San Fernando Velicatá, Misión Santa Maria, and **Misión San Borja** are located in the area covered by this chapter. See the *Backroad Adventures* section below for detailed information about visiting the sites.

The **28th Parallel** forms the border between the states of Baja California and Baja California Sur. The spot is marked by a huge metal statue of an eagle, also by a huge Mexican flag at the military base located at the base of the statue. The road runs right by both so you'll have a good look.

San Ignacio appears to be a classic desert oasis, and it really is. The town has thousands of date palms, as well as an attractive square bordered by the Misión San Ignacio. There is also a museum describing the cave paintings found in the surrounding Sierra de San Francisco, they're known as **rupestrian art**. Guides are available in Guerrero Negro, San Ignacio, Mulegé, Loreto and also near some of the sites and are required. You must also register to visit many of the sites at the museum in San Ignacio.

Beaches and Water Sports

Surfing in this area, of course, is limited to the Pacific Coast. Since the main highway runs far from the coast, road access to surfing generally requires long drives on pretty poor roads. Exceptions are the places accessible from El Rosario in the north and also where the road nears the coast north of Rosarito.

One of the popular surfing spots near Rosarito is Punta Santa Rosalillita, also known as "The Wall". See *Backroad Adventures* below for more about this location. This is also a popular sailboarding location, it is sometimes called "Sandy Point".

A few miles south is Punta Rosarito, also a surfing destination. To the south of the point is the long Altamara beach. See *Backroad Adventures* below for driving instructions.

Still farther south, near Villa Jesús María a roads lead out to Laguna Manuela. This is a popular fishing destination, but there is a long beach called Playa Pacheco to the north of the lagoon. Between the beach and the lagoon is Morro Santo Domingo, a high headland ringed with small coves. There's also a small beach near the fish camp at the end of the road at the lagoon, it is often used by the folks from Guerrero Negro for picnics. Watch for soft sand, access to the long Playa Pacheco is very sandy and requires 4WD or a walk. See *Backroad Adventures* below for more about this road.

Kayaking is popular on the Gulf of California coast. Winds tend to be from the north so long-distance kayakers usually travel from north to south. Bahía de los Angeles makes a good place to explore with beaches for camping that don't require long passages.

Fishing

Since much of this route is inland fishing possibilities are limited to Bahía de los Angeles and areas that you can reach using back roads.

The **Bahía de los Angeles** area is probably the most popular destination on the Baja for fishermen with large and small trailer boats. There are good boat launches, a reasonable number of fish, and the weather is much warmer than on the west side of the peninsula at this latitude.

Unfortunately, boating conditions can be dangerous here. A combination of often very strong winds (generally either from the north or the west) and very active tidal currents can make boating a challenge.

The best fishing is in the summer and fall and the most popular fishing is for yellowtail. Expect daytime temperatures to 100 degrees Fahrenheit in the middle of the summer.

Unfortunately the fishing is not as good as it once was due to commercial overfishing. Your best fishing opportunities are north and south of the bay. Access to the north by vehicle is nonexistent much past Playa La Gringa, but to the south there are several fishing destinations for those with the RVs to travel rough roads. Destinations include Bahía las Animas (30 miles south), Playa San Rafael (45 miles south of L.A. Bay with good shore fishing), and Bahía San Francisquito (85 miles south of L.A. Bay). See the *Backroad Adventures* of this section for more information about access to these locations.

At the southern end of the section covered by this chapter is Laguna Manuela. You reach it on a marked road heading westward from Villa Jesús Maria. You can launch small boats across the beach here and fish the lagoon for bass, halibut, sierra, and corvina. See *Backroad Adventures* for road information.

Backroad Adventures

See the *Backroad Driving* section of *Chapter 2 - Details, Details, Details* for essential information about driving off the main highway on the Baja and for a definition of road type classifications used below.

From Km 121 Between El Rosario and Cataviña - The ruin of **Misión San Fernando Velicatá** is a short distance off the highway on this road east of El Rosario. This is usually a Type 2 road, the distance is about 3 miles (5 km).

From Km 149 Between El Rosario and Cataviña - The virtually abandoned onyx mining area called **El Mármol** makes an interesting day trip. The access road is about 19 miles (31 km) west of Cataviña. This is a graded road that is about 10 miles long, it is usually a Type 1 road. Take a look at the old school house built entirely of onyx. The mine was very active in the early part of the century, the quarried onyx slabs were shipped by water from Puerto Santa Catarina about 50 miles west on the Pacific coast. You might also want to make the 3-mile hike (6 miles round trip) from the mine to El Volcán where you can see a small seep forming new onyx.

From Km 229 Between Cataviña and L.A. Bay Junction - This road runs to the coast and then north all the way to Puertecitos (81 miles (131 km)) and then San Felipe. It is a long rough Type 2 road that is planned for an eventual upgrade so that there will be paved access from the north along the east side of the Baja Peninsula.

From Km 38 Between L.A. Bay Junction and Guerrero Negro - A good road leads west to the small community of Santa Rosalillita, Bahía Santa Rosalillita, and Punta Santa Rosalillita. It leaves Mex 1 near Km 38, some 8 miles (13 km) north of Rosarito. The road leads 9.5 miles (15 km) to the village. At about 8 miles (13 km) a side track leads north toward the community of San José de las Palomas giving access to many more beaches. The road to Santa Rosalillita is usually Type 1, the others in the area vary, some are Type 2 or even 3, watch for soft sand.

From Km 52 Between L.A. Bay Junction and Guerrero Negro - Another mission, **Misión San Borja** is also accessible if you have four-wheel drive or a lightly loaded pickup with good ground clearance. From Rosarito, located about 97 miles (158 km) south of Cataviña on Mex 1 drive east, roads leave the highway both north and south of the bridge over the arroyo. At about 15 miles (24 km) the road reaches Rancho San Ignacio, the mission is beyond at about 22 miles (36 km). Misión San Francisco de Borja was built in 1759 and has been restored by the government. This is usually a Type 3 road.

From Km 68 Between L.A. Bay Junction and Guerrero Negro - A short 2.8 mile (4.5 km) road leads to **El Tomatal** which is popular for surfing, board sailing, and surf fishing. There is also room for boondocking. This road is usually Type 1, but watch for soft sand.

From Km 96 Between L.A. Bay Junction and Guerrero Negro - From the town of Villa Jesús María a road heads 7 miles westward to the Laguna Manuela. This area is popular for fishing, primitive camping, and the beach. Drive about a mile west on a paved road, then turn south on a graded dirt road, you'll reach the lagoon in another 6 miles (10 km). This is usually a Type 1 road.

From Bahía de los Angeles - A road leads south from Bahía de los Angeles for many miles. Along the way it passes beaches on the southern curve of Bahía de los Angeles, an abandoned silver-smelting operation at Los Flores, a side road to Bahía las Animas, Bahía San Rafael, and eventually reaches Punta and Bahía San Francisquito. The road is a badly washboarded Type 1 for about 10 miles (16 km), then becomes a bad Type 2 road.

From Km 189 Between Guerrero Negro and San Ignacio - From 16 miles east of Guerrero Negro a road that was paved at one time goes north to the almost-abandoned mining town of **El Arco**. The road is very poor, many drivers actually find the sand alongside to be faster and smoother. The distance is 26 miles (42 kilometers). The road continues beyond El Arco for 23 miles (37 km) to **Misión Santa Gertrudis**, which is being restored. The road to El Arco is usually a marginal Type 1, the one to the mission usually a Type 3 road.

From Km 144 Between Guerrero Negro and San Ignacio - There's a junction here at Ejido Vizcaíno for a road that runs southwest to the coast at **Bahía Tortugas**, only the first twenty miles or so are paved, the remainder is a Type 1 road often with soft sand in places. The distance to the coast is about 107 miles (173 km), this is a long, rough, lonely road across Baja's dryest desert, but fuel trucks do travel to Bahía Tortugas, which is a popular refueling station for power boats traveling between California and Cabo. Type 2 and 3 side roads allow you to travel on to Punta Eugenia or off to the southwest to Bahía Asunción and other coastal locations.

From Km 118 Between Guerrero Negro and San Ignacio - This is a 22-mile (35 km) drive into the Sierra San Francisco to the village of **San Francisco**. This is a cave-art location, **Cueva Ratón** is located near the village, you must have a guide from the village to get in the locked gate. Guides can take you to other caves too, some trips require several days. Before visiting you must register in San Ignacio. This is usually a Type 2 road.

From San Ignacio - This 40-mile (65 km) road leads southeast from the village to **Laguna San Ignacio**. This is one of the best California gray whale observation sites on the peninsula. Most people opt to leave their RVs in San Ignacio and ride down with a van tour. You can drive it yourself although route-finding can be difficult due to there being many alternate tracks in some areas. Panga operators at the lagoon give whale-watching tours. This is usually a Type 2 road, watch out for soft sand.

THE ROUTES, TOWNS, AND CAMPGROUNDS

EL ROSARIO TO CATAVIÑA
73 Miles (118 Km), 2.25 Hours

From El Rosario the highway heads northeast for about four miles (6 km) along the north side of the El Rosario River. It then crosses and follows a climbing canyon into rolling hills that can be surprisingly green during the winter. This is the beginning of the longest mountainous section of Mex 1 as the highway passes along the western edge of the Peninsular Range for some 180 miles (290 km) but never crosses to the Gulf of California side.

From this point until well past Cataviña the scenery is fascinating, you are in what is known as the Sonoran Desert Vegetation Region. You'll soon see your first cirios (boojum trees) and as you drive along there will be more and more of them. Other cactus include huge cardóns, barrel cactus, chollas, and agaves. Many of these cactus are found only in this area.

Near Km 121 a short road runs south to the ruins of Misión San Fernando Velicatá. See *Backroad Adventures* for more information about this road.

Near Km 149 is the cutoff to the north to El Mármol. See the *Backroad Adventures* section above for a description of this road and destination.

As you near Cataviña, near Km 160, you enter a region of large granite boulders. These are known as the Cataviña boulder fields. Around and among them grow all types of cactus, and together they are extremely photogenic. You'll be tempted to pull off and camp on one of the short roads leading into the boulders, but you'll be much safer at one of the inexpensive campgrounds just a few miles ahead.

El Rosario to Cataviña Campground

SONORA RV CAMPING (LONCHERIA SONORA)

Telephone: (556) 151-9446
Open: All Year

GPS Location: N 29° 54'51", W 114° 56'20"

Next to a small restaurant along the highway is one of Baja's newest campgrounds. Actually, this is a large lot surrounded by tires half buried in the ground. Out front next to the highway with the door swinging open as if in invitation is an outhouse. This is a great place to stay if you are in an RV and want to visit El Marmol in a smaller tow vehicle. It's also a convenient place to overnight if you can't quite make Cataviña.

The campground is located near Km 149. This is a few hundred yards from where the road out to El Marmol leaves the highway. It's 55 miles (89 km) from El Rosario and 18 miles (29 km) from Cataviña.

CATAVIÑA (CAT-AH-**VEE**-NYA)

You can't really call Cataviña a town. There is little more here than a Hotel La Pinta, an abandoned Pemex, an old government-built campground, and a few shacks and restaurants. The area, however, is one of the most interesting on the Baja. The Cataviña boulder fields are striking. The road threads its way for several miles through a jumble of huge granite boulders sprinkled liberally with attractive cacti and desert plants. It is a photographer's paradise. Gas is sometimes still available at the La Pinta Motel, they have a Pemex gas pump with limited and irregular supplies.

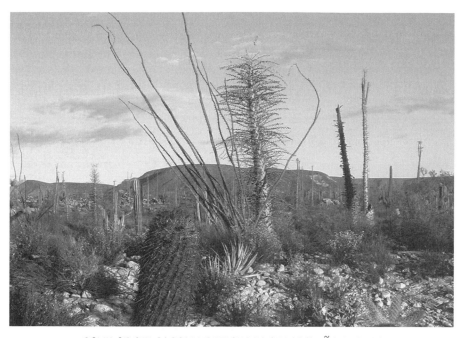

SOME OF THE CACTUS VARIETIES IN THE CATAVIÑA DESERT

Cataviña Campgrounds

PARQUE NATURAL DESIERTO CENTRAL TRAILER PARK
Open: All Year

GPS Location: N 29° 43' 52", W 114° 43' 20"

This is one of the fenced compounds that were built by the government soon after the road south was finished. None of the hookups other than sewer work any more, but last time we visited it had been cleaned up and looked pretty good. The landscaping has boulders and cactus, just like the surrounding area. Sites are large, most are pull-thrus. There are bathrooms with toilets that are flushed with a bucket of water but no showers. Many people use this campground, perhaps because they don't know about Rancho Santa Inez (see below). It's a noisy place at night because it's right next to the highway.

The campground is located in Cataviña off Mex 1 just west of the La Pinta Motel and the abandoned Pemex, it's on the south side of the road.

RANCHO SANTA INEZ
Open: All Year

GPS Location: N 29° 43' 48", W 114° 41' 53"

Many folks drive right by the entrance road to this camping spot, and that's a mistake. We think it is the best place to stay in this area.

The camping area is a large flat dirt lot with only a few trees for shade. There's room for lots of RVs of any size, that's why many of the caravans stay here. Other facilities include a water faucet and a small building with a flush toilet. Best of all is the small restaurant. An advantage here is that the campground is quiet because it is off the main highway.

To reach the campground turn north on the well-marked road near Km 181, less than a mile east of the La Pinta Motel. Follow the paved side road for about 0.8 miles (1.3 km), the camping area is on the left.

CATAVIÑA TO GUERRERO NEGRO
145 Miles (234 Km), 4.25 Hours

The two-lane highway continues snaking its way southeastwards from Cataviña. It passes signs for a few small ranchos, along the road is the occasional small restaurant, often with a truck or two parked out front. Eighteen miles (29 km) from Cataviña on the right side of the road you'll see a very large pile of rocks. The small mountain is called **Cerro Pedregoso** (rocky hill). It has long been a landmark for travelers along the highway.

About 15 miles (24 km) beyond Cerro Pedregoso the highway descends and runs along **Laguna Chapala**. This is a large dry lake bed, before the current highway was completed a very rough road followed pretty much the same route in this region. Here it ran over the dry lake bed, it was very dusty and often heavily rutted.

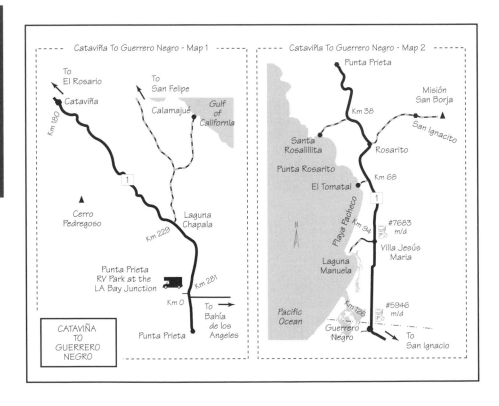

CENTRAL BAJA

Just north of the lake bed, near Km 229 you may see a road headed northeast. It is signed for San Felipe and Calamajué, they're both on the Gulf of California. At one time, before Mex 1 was constructed, this was sometimes a preferred alternate to the road you've followed coming south, but no more. See *Backroad Adventures* for more information about this road.

Thirty miles beyond the dirt road to San Felipe is the cutoff to Bahía de los Angeles, often called the **L.A. Bay Junction**. The road to Bahía de los Angeles and the attractions there are discussed in a separate section later in this chapter. In the past there was a gas station at this junction, the buildings remain but the pumps are gone. Sometimes you will find an entrepreneur here in a pickup with gas drums in the back, a welcome sight if you are low on gas.

South of the L.A. Bay Junction the road begins to gradually approach the west coast. There are roads out to the coast at Km 38 to **Santa Rosalillita**, Km 68 for **El Tomatal**, and Km 96 for **Laguna Manuela**. See *Backroad Adventures* above for more about all of these roads.

In Rosarito, 33 miles (53 km) south of the L.A. Bay Junction there is a back road northeastwards to the **Misión San Borja**. See *Backroad Adventures* for more about this trip.

Fifty-six miles (90 km) from L.A. Bay Junction you will reach the small town of Villa Jesús Maria which has a Pemex gas station with both gas and diesel. This is also the cutoff for the road out to Laguna Manuela.

Twenty-two miles (35 km) beyond Villa Jesús Maria is the border between Baja California and Baja California Sur. The **border** is marked by a huge metal **statue of an eagle**, as you approach the border you can see it for miles, it looks like a giant tuning fork from this direction. At the border there is a military base with a huge flag, a motel, a restaurant with RV parking behind, and an RV park. A checkpoint at the border will check to make sure you have tourist cards and fumigate the wheels of your RV. They charge a small fee for doing this. They'll also take citrus fruits (except small limes), apples, potatoes, avocados and perhaps other fruits and vegetables to combat the spread of farm diseases so plan to have used them all up by the time you reach this crossing. Just a short distance beyond the checkpoint is the side road in to the town of Guerrero Negro.

Baja California Sur observes Mountain time while Baja California observes Pacific time so you will have to change your clocks at the border.

Cataviña to Guerrero Negro Campground

PUNTA PRIETA RV PARK AT THE L.A. BAY JUNCTION

Open: All Year

GPS Location: N 29° 02' 51", W 114° 09' 13"

This is another of the old government campgrounds. It is often closed, but occasionally the gates are open and someone is operating the place. It has the standard nice desert plant landscaping, as well as the standard non-functional hookups. There's lots of room for big RVs. Toilets are flushed using a bucket of water if there's enough on hand and there are no showers.

The campground is very near the cutoff to Bahía de los Angeles, just to the north on Mex 1. While we wouldn't depend on it being open on the way south we might stop here going north if we had noticed that it was open on our southward journey.

GUERRERO NEGRO (GEH-**RER**-row **NEH**-GROW)
Population 8,000

The 28th parallel is the dividing line between the states of Baja and Baja South. You'll know when you pass over the line because it is marked by a very large statue of a stylized eagle, most people think it looks like a tuning fork and it is visible for miles. Two miles (3 km) south of the eagle the road to Guerrero Negro goes west.

Guerrero Negro is one of the newest towns on the Baja, and it's a company town. Founded in 1955 the town owes its existence to the Exportadora de Sal (ESSA) salt works. Large flats near the town are flooded with seawater which quickly evaporates leaving salt. This is gathered up using heavy equipment and shipped on barges to Isla Cedros offshore where there is enough water to allow cargo ships to dock.

More recently the town has gained fame for the California gray whales that congregate each winter in the nearby Ojo de Liebre or Scammon's Lagoon. There is now a lively tourist industry catering to the many people who come to visit the whales.

The town itself is small and the places of interest, restaurants and stores, are almost all arranged along the main street. Guerrero Negro has small supermarkets and also three Pemexes if you count the new one just north of the border crossing.

Guerrero Negro Campgrounds

LA ESPINITA MOTEL AND RESTAURANT
Open: All Year

GPS Location: N 28° 00' 23", W 114° 00' 44"

This is a restaurant and small tienda along the road just north of the border between Baja Norte and Baja Sur. Over the years they've added more and more RVer amenities. Now there are 8 RV sites with 15-amp electricity, water, and sewer. There's also a dump station. The restrooms have hot showers ($2) and you can dry camp for $5. There are also motel rooms for about 200 pesos per night.

La Espinita is 0.2 mile (0.3 km) north of the giant eagle that marks the border.

BENITO JUÁREZ TRAILER PARK

Address:	Asunción Morian Canales, Apdo. 188,
	Guerrero Negro, B.C.S., México
Telephone:	(615) 157-0025
Open:	All Year

GPS Location: N 27° 59' 56", W 114° 00' 49"

The Benito Juárez is another of the government-built trailer parks. This one is run by the Ejido Benito Juárez. It is the only one left on the Baja that offers electrical hook-

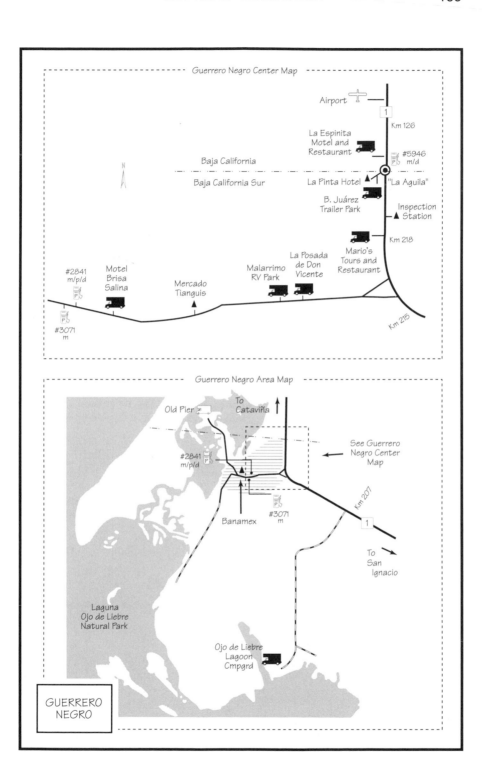

Guerrero Negro Center Map

Airport

1

Km 126

La Espinita
Motel and
Restaurant

#5946
m/d

Baja California

Baja California Sur   La Pinta Hotel   "La Aguila"

B. Juárez
Trailer Park

Inspection
Station

Km 218

#2841
m/p/d

Motel
Brisa
Salina

Mercado
Tianguis

Malarrimo
RV Park

La Posada
de Don
Vicente

Mario's
Tours and
Restaurant

#3071
m

Km 215

Guerrero Negro Area Map

Old Pier

To
Cataviña

See Guerrero
Negro Center
Map

#2841
m/p/d

Banamex

#3071
m

Km 207

1

To
San
Ignacio

Laguna
Ojo de Liebre
Natural Park

Ojo de Liebre
Lagoon
Cmpgrd

GUERRERO
NEGRO

CENTRAL BAJA

ups. Watch the voltage, it sometimes varies dramatically and can cause damage to your equipment. Also, note that this campground is accessed from north of the border so if you plan to be traveling back and forth to town you'll have to pass through the border inspection point each time.

This is a large campground. The spaces are pull-thrus with electricity, sewer, and water. Cactus are planted throughout for landscaping, there's a pretty complete collection of the different types you've been seeing along the road on the way south, including boojums. The restrooms are old but work, there are usually hot showers. A small store with limited supplies is now open at the campground too. Site are large and easy to access, many caravans stay here for that reason. The campground is fully fenced and has a manager who speaks some English.

This is an easy campground to find. Just watch for the eagle monument at the border between North and South Baja. The campground is just to the west, south of the La Pinta hotel. The campground is located almost exactly on the border.

⚎ MARIO'S TOURS AND RESTAURANT

Address:	Carretera Transpeninsular Km 217.3, CP 23940 Guerrero Negro, B.C.S.
Telephone:	(615) 157-1940
Fax:	(615) 157-0120
Website:	www.mariostours.com
Email:	mariostours@hotmail.com
Open:	All Year

GPS Location: N 27° 59' 00", W 114° 00' 48"

Mario's is a large palapa-style restaurant located along Mex 1 between the border station and town. That means, of course, that access to town is easy, you don't have to pass through the border station.

The restaurant has a large number of large pull-thru camping sites in the rear, they're about 70 feet long. Forty eight have electricity (30-amp outlets) and sewer hookups. Mario expects to get city water within a few months and will add water hookups. He's also planning to add another 25 sites. There's a new restroom building with hot showers. Mario's also offers good whale-watching tours. The tenter rate here is $5.

The restaurant is located on the west side of Mex 1 near the Km 218 marker some 0.6 mile (1 km) south of the border between Baja California and Baja California Sur.

⚎ LA POSADA DE DON VICENTE,

Address:	Blvd. Emiliano Zapata S/N, CP 23940 Guerrero Negro, B.C.S., México
Telephone:	(615) 157-0288
Open:	All Year

GPS Location: N 27° 58' 04", W 114° 01' 30"

This place is a motel enclosing a courtyard with RV parking inside and a restaurant out front. It has 10 back-in RV slots with 15-amp electrical outlets and water hookups, there's also a place to dump. Guerrero Negro electricity is marginal, watch voltage while hooked up to avoid damage to your RV. There are bathrooms with flush toilets and reportedly (by the owner) hot showers. There is limited maneuvering room so RVs over about 30 feet may find things a little tight. This is a seldom-used campground, last time we visited no one was staying here while Malarrimo's just

CENTRAL BAJA

down the street was pretty active.

To find the campground just drive in to Guerrero Negro from the east. It's 0.7 mile (1.1 km) from the turnoff. It is on the right about a block before you reach Malarrimo's.

MALARRIMO RV PARK

Address:	Blvd. Emiliano Zapata S/N, Col. Fundo Legal,
	CP 23940 Guerrero Negro, B.C.S., México
Reservations:	PO Box 284, Chula Vista, CA 91912
Telephone:	(615) 157-0100
Fax:	(615) 157-0250
Website:	www.malarrimo.com
Email:	malarrimo@telnor.net
Open:	All Year

GPS Location: N 27° 58' 04", W 114° 01' 48"

The Malarrimo is generally considered the best place to stay in Guerrero Negro. Not only are the campground facilities pretty good, the restaurant is the best in this section of Baja.

There are about 65 RV spaces with 15-amp electrical outlets, sewer, and water in all. They are in three different areas including the normally used sites directly behind the motel. There are also sites in a walled area farther back and others across the street but these areas are usually not used except when caravans arrive or there are an unusually large number of visitors. Large RVs can crowd into a few sites up front, the back sites are larger. It is possible to park RVs to 40 feet with careful maneuvering. Guerrero Negro electricity is marginal, watch voltage while hooked up to avoid damage to your RV. Restrooms are modern and clean and have hot water showers. This is a well-run place and English is spoken. They run tours to see the gray whales and cave art, and even have a gift shop. There's also a convenience store along the street out front. Many people make a special point to overnight in Guerrero Negro so they can eat at the restaurant. There's a slightly reduced rate here of $14 for vans and pickup campers, tenters pay $12.

To find the campground drive in to Guerrero Negro from the east. Almost immediately after entering town, 1 mile (1.6 km) from the turn off Mex 1, you will see the Malarrimo on the right.

MOTEL BRISA SALINA

Address:	Blvd. Emiliano Zapata S/N, CP 23940
	Guerrero Negro, B.C.S., México
Telephone:	(615) 157-1795
Open:	All Year

GPS Location: N 27° 58' 04", W 114° 02' 32"

This is a small motel that has just installed RV hookups in an enclosed courtyard out back. There are electricity (15-amp outlets but 30-amp breakers), water, and sewer hookups for 22 RVs. The place would be very crowded with that number of RVs, they probably couldn't all fit, but with half that number it would be fine. If this place were full it would be hard to enter with a big RV but if empty any size RV will fit. Restrooms have hot showers and there is a restaurant too.

The motel is on the right in central Guerrero Negro, 1.6 mile (2.6 km) from Mex 1.

CENTRAL BAJA

🚐 OJO DE LIEBRE LAGOON CAMPGROUND

Open: Dec 20 – April 15 (Varies)

GPS Location: N 27° 44' 56", W 114° 00' 42"

One of the top attractions of the Baja Peninsula is a whale-watching trip. One way to do this is to drive across the salt flats to the edge of Laguna Ojo de Liebre (Scammon's Lagoon). It costs a little less to take a tour here than from in town, and camping along the edge of the lagoon is excellent. This place is only accessible during the whale-watching season, approximately the last third of December to the middle of April.

When you arrive at the lagoon there is an entrance kiosk where a $3 fee is collected. There is a large parking lot where visitors on whale-watching trips can park. A large new building houses the tour ticket sales as well as a souvenir store, and restaurant. Camping stretches for a long distance beyond the parking lot along a dirt road with pullouts along the beach of the lagoon for camping. Some site are fine for big RVs, watch for soft spots and be aware of tides. Pit toilets are provided for campers.

To reach the lagoon turn westward from Mex 1 at about Km 207. This is 5 miles south of the turnoff for the town of Guerrero Negro. The turn is marked with a large sign for Laguna Ojo de Liebre. The road is graded dirt, it is fine for even the largest RVs. At 4 miles (6 km) you will reach an entrance gate where your name will be recorded as you enter the salt flats working area. You'll probably see heavy equipment collecting the salt from the flats. At 13.8 miles (22.3 km) there is a Y, go right as indicated by the sign. Finally, at 14.9 miles (24 km) you will reach the entrance gate at the lagoon.

SIDE TRIP TO BAHÍA DE LOS ANGELES
42 Miles (68 Km), 1.75 Hours

From a junction on Mex 1 a paved road runs 42 miles (68 km) down to the coast at Bahía de los Angeles. Recently the road has been repaved so this is a very worthwhile trip.

BAHÍA DE LOS ANGELES (BAH-**HEE**-AH DAY LOES AHN-**HAIL**-ACE)
Population 500

The Bahía de los Angeles (Bay of the Angels) is one of the most scenic spots in Baja California with blue waters and barren desert shoreline backed by rocky mountains. The huge bay is protected by a chain of small islands, and also by Isla Angel de la Guarda, which is 45 miles (75 km) long. Even with this protection boating is often dangerous because of strong winds from the north and evening "gravity" winds that whistle downhill from the west. Fishing, boating, diving, and kayaking are good in the bay, among the islands, and offshore and there are several launch ramps in town. Exercise caution, these are considered dangerous waters due to the frequent strong winds.

There is a turtle rescue and research facility in Bahía de los Angeles near the Brisa Marina RV Park where you can see some of these endangered animals. For more in-

Drive to Bahía de los Angeles

To Cataviña

1

42 Miles
68 Kms

Km 0

Km 42

Gulf of California

Punta
la Gringa

Km 64

Bahía de
los Angeles

Punta
Prieta

1

N

To
Misíon
San Borja

To
Guerrero
Negro

Bahía de los Angeles Area

N

Gulf
of
California

Playa
La Gringa

Military

To
Hwy 1

No # yet
m/p/d

#8026
m/p/d

See Bahía
de Los
Angeles Center
Map

Camp
Gecko

El Porvenir

Bahía de los Angeles Center

Daggett's
Beach Camping

To
Hwy 1

Airport

Camp
Archelon

No # yet
m/p/d

Brisa Marina
RV Park

Km 64

#8026
m/p/d

Ⓐ

Ⓑ

Ⓒ

Villa Vitta
Hotel
Resort

Ⓔ   Ⓓ

Guillermo's
Hotel and
RV Park

Casa Diaz

Ⓐ   Market
Ⓑ   Market
Ⓒ   Villa Vitta
      Hotel
Ⓓ   Plaza
Ⓔ   Museum

CENTRAL BAJA

SIDE TRIP TO BAHÍA DE LOS ANGELES

formation visit Camp Archelon and talk to the owner, he runs the turtle facility. The village itself doesn't offer much except a couple of motels, several RV parks and a few small stores. Electricity in town is currently produced by a generator that only runs part time.

Big things are happening in Bahía LA. First the road is now newly paved all the way from the Transpeninsular. It's beautiful, complete with large pull-off areas related to the new "marine staircase" project that proposes to bring yachts across the peninsula on trucks so that thousands of boats from the States will come to the Mar de Cortez. Second, there are now not one, but two Pemexes in town, both have both gas and diesel. And finally, power lines are being installed from Guerrero Negro, the town should soon have full-time electricity.

It is still important, however, when coming to Bahía de los Angeles, to remember that all supplies are trucked in at great expense and services are limited. Arrive with those water tanks full.

Bahía de los Angeles Campgrounds

This area offers many places to camp. You may find, as we do, that the campgrounds in town with hookups are much less attractive than the more informal places outside town to the north and south.

GUILLERMO'S HOTEL AND RV PARK

Address:	Expendio #11, Boulevard Bahía de Los Angeles, CP 22950 Bahía de Los Angeles, B.C., México
Telephone:	(200) 124-9104
Website:	www.guillermos.net
Email:	guillermospanga@hotmail.com
Open:	All Year

GPS Location: N 28° 56' 52", W 113° 33' 33"

This campground has about 40 camping spaces, some have working full hookups with 15-amp outlets. On a recent visit we found that many of the electrical outlets had been repaired and that there was a new toilet and shower building. Water is not always available, it is trucked in. Sites have patios. Permanents here block any view of the water. There are also a few parking spots south of the restaurant along the water, they have no hookups. Large RVs will fit in most sites. There is a restaurant, bar, store and also a launch ramp. Bear in mind that electricity in Bahía de los Angeles is not available 24 hours a day. If it is important to you ask when the campground will have electricity before checking in.

To find Guillermo's drive into town, pass the Villa Vitta, and you'll soon see the campground on the left.

VILLA VITTA HOTEL RESORT

Reservations:	416 W. San Ysidro Blvd, S. 564, San Ysidro, CA 92173 (Res. in U.S.)
Telephone:	(664) 686-1152 (Res. in Tijuana.)
Website:	www.villavitta.com
Email:	Adrian@villavitta.com
Open:	All Year

GPS Location: N 28° 57' 04", W 113° 33' 30"

The Villa Vitta RV Park is located across the street from the hotel of the same name. This is probably the best campground for large RVs in town. The campground is a flat dirt lot with no landscaping, however, it is right next to the beach with no permanently located RVs out front. There are 36 large sites, 19 are pull-thrus and the others are back-ins along the beach. There are patios and electrical outlets. Electricity is only provided for a few hours each evening, normally from sundown to 9:30 p.m. If it is important to you ask when the campground will have electricity before checking in. There is no water but there is a dump station. A toilet building is available, ask for a key. There are no showers. This motel/campground has a good launch ramp, available for an extra fee.

You'll find that the Villa Vitta is hard to miss, you'll see the hotel on the right and the RV park on the left soon after entering town.

CASA DIAZ

Address: PO Box 579, CP 86007 Ensenada, México
Telephone: (200) 124-9112
Reservations: (619) 278-9676 (San Diego)
Open: All Year

GPS Location: N 28° 56' 42", W 113° 33' 27"

This campground is part of one of the oldest establishments in Bahia Los Angeles. This compound at the end of the highway at the south end of town has a motel, a restaurant, a small store, and a launch ramp.

There are six sites, they have 15-amp electricity, water, and sewer. Small structures provide shade. This camping area gets little maintenance and is in poor shape, the toilet building is unusable. There is another toilet and shower at the motel that you can use. If it is important to you ask when the campground will have electricity before checking in.

To find the Casa Diaz just follow the main highway south through town, when you come to the T at the end turn left and drive around the wall, you're there.

CAMP GECKO

Website: www.campgecko.com
Email: gecko@starband.net
Open: All Year

GPS Location: N 28° 54' 02", W 113° 31' 46"

This waterside campground has a quiet location on a nice beach some distance south of town. Unfortunately you must drive almost four miles of washboard gravel road to reach it.

Camp Gecko has a number of rental cabins above the beach, there are also several places where you can put a tent under a palapa or park an RV. There is also parking for large RVs away from the beach. There are no hookups but the camp does have flush toilets and hot water showers. There is also a small boat ramp.

As you head south through Bahía de los Angeles village you will come to a rock wall and the entrance to Diaz RV park. Go to the right around it and follow a washboard gravel road south. At 4.0 miles (6.5 km) take the sandy road left toward the beach and Camp Gecko.

⛟ BRISA MARINA RV PARK

$ ⛺ 🚐 🚌 BIG RIGS

Open: All Year

GPS Location: N 28° 58'06", W 113° 32'51"

This is one of the old government RV parks. It is located next to the bay, and along the front of the campground is a sea turtle research project. Sea turtles are kept in tanks, visitors are allowed. In fact, they might put you to work.

The campground is little more than a place to park and boondock. Only the sewer hookups are useable and there are no bathroom facilities. Still, there are generally a few people staying here since it is a quiet place in a decent location with a low price. It's easy to find a place to park a big RV here.

The road to the campgrounds north of Bahía de Los Angeles leaves the highway near the point where the highway enters town and is usually marked for the airport. It is a paved road. After 0.8 miles (1.3 km) follow the road as it curves right (the airport is straight) and follow it straight (and off the pavement) to the campground in 0.8 mile (1.3 km).

⛟ CAMP ARCHELON

$$ ⛺ 🚿 HOT ～

Email: resendizshidalgo@yahoo.com
Open: All Year

GPS Location: N 28° 58'17", W 113° 32'49"

This camp is located just north of the Brisa Marina along the beach. It is run by the same folks who are in charge of the sea turtle research project, this is the place to come for information about the project.

This camping area is really more appropriate to tent-campers than RVers. There are several palapas near the beach as well as rental cabins. Several areas are suitable for RV parking with no hookups. RV size should be limited to about 25 feet. Clean and well maintained toilets are provided as are limited hot water showers.

To reach Camp Archelon follow the directions above to Brisa Marina. Turn left when you reach Brisa Marina and drive north parallel to the beach for just a tenth of a mile to Camp Archelon.

⛟ DAGGETT'S BEACH CAMPING

$$ ⛺ 🚐 🚿 HOT 🍴 ～ 🚌 BIG RIGS

Telephone: (200) 124-9101
Website: www.campdaggetts.com
Email: rubendaggett@hotmail.com
Open: All Year

GPS Location: N 28° 58'32", W 113° 32'49"

This is one or our favorite places to stay in Bahía de los Angeles for tent camping or an RV. There are 20 beachside palapas with room to park an RV alongside and an additional 10 palapas just for tent campers. There are no hookups but there is a dump station, flush toilets, and hot showers. There's a restaurant, kayak rentals, and fishing and snorkeling charters.

To drive to the campground follow the north beaches road from Bahía L.A. After 0.8 mile (1.3 km) the road jogs right, than in 0.5 miles (0.8 km) it jogs left to continue north. Three-tenths mile (0.5 km) after this last turn you'll see the sign for Daggett's Beach to the right. Follow the road to the beach and campground.

Playa La Gringa

Open: All Year

GPS Location: N 29° 02' 26", W 113° 32' 41"

This beach seems to be known by beach campers throughout the Baja, it is a real favorite. There is absolutely nothing in the way of facilities, just a long sandy beach backed by mostly solid side roads branching from the main gravel road and providing access to camping sites above the beach.

To reach the campground just drive north from town along the north beaches road as described in the descriptions above. Playa La Gringa is 7 miles (11.3 km) north of town, the road is paved for only the first 2 miles (3.2 km). The road is passable in any RV, but sections of bad washboard often make it slow going. While big RVs can drive out here they cannot park right next to the water because the surface is soft, there are places they can park away from the beach. This is a remote location, solo camping is not recommended.

GUERRERO NEGRO TO SAN IGNACIO
89 Miles (144 Km), 2.25 Hours

Now that you have crossed the border you will note that the kilometer markers are counting down instead of up as they have been doing in the state of Baja California. All sections of kilometer markers on Mex 1 in Baja California Sur go from south to north. The markers for this section of road begin in Santa Rosalía, the town where the highway reaches the coast of the Gulf of California.

About 5 miles from the Guerrero Negro junction you will see a sign and a road headed toward the coast. This is the access road for whale watching at Laguna Ojo de Liebre, or Scammon's Lagoon. The distance is about 17 miles to the lagoon on a road that is usually passable for any RV but often washboarded. The road to the lagoon is only open during the whale-watching season from December through some time in April.

The highway from Guerrero Negro to the mountains runs across the Vizcaíno Desert. Much of the way you are crossing stabilized sand dunes that have blown eastward from the Laguna Ojo de Liebre area. The most noticeable vegetation is datilillo, a member of the yucca family, and small mesquite trees.

Sixteen miles (26 km) south of the Guerrero Negro junction is the road northeast to an old mining town, El Arco. See *Backroad Adventures* in this chapter for more information about this trip.

Forty-four miles (71) km) from the Guerrero Negro cutoff you will reach the small community of **Vizcaíno**. There's a junction there for a road that runs southwest to the coast at Punta Eugenia and Bahía Tortugas. See the *Backroad Adventures* section above for more information.

The road begins a gradual climb into Sierra San Francisco that form the spine of the peninsula at about 70 miles (113 km) from the Guerrero Negro junction. The pass through the mountains used by the highway is fairly mild with no major grades on the western slopes. As you near the mountains you will begin to see the large cardón cactus.

Fifty-nine miles from the Guerrero Negro cutoff there is a road to the left that leads to the most accessible of the pinturas rupestres or cave painting locations in this section of the Baja. Cueva Ratón is near the small village of **San Francisco de la Sierra**. See the *Backroad Adventures* section above for more information about this road. You must register and obtain information at the cave painting museum in San Ignacio before visiting the cave.

Finally, 86 miles (139 km) from the Guerrero Negro junction you will enter the outskirts of San Ignacio. The road to the right to San Lino is first, then you'll see the side road leading to the village of San Ignacio.

Guerrero Negro to San Ignacio Campground

🚐 **MOTEL KADEKAMAN**

Address:	Blvd. Lazaro Cardenas S/N, Vizcaino, B.C.S., México
Telephone:	(615) 156-4112
Email:	kadekaman@yahoo.com
Open:	All Year

GPS Location: N 27° 38' 46", W 113° 23' 06"

If you find yourself on the road east of Guerrero Negro when night falls you have no problem, the Motel Kadekaman makes a convenient place to pull off and spend the night with electricity and water hookups.

This motel has a nice restaurant out front and about six spaces for RVs to park in the back. There are electricity (15 amp) and water hookups but no sewer. Efforts have been going into modernizing this motel and plans are to put in quite a few full hookup sites sometime in the not too distant future. A bathroom in the motel building is clean and modern and has a toilet and hot shower.

The campground is located near the Km 143 marker on Mex 1 in the town of Vizcaíno. It is 0.4 miles (0.6 km) southeast of the Pemex station.

SAN IGNACIO (SAHN EEG-NAH-SEE-OH)
Population 4,000, Elevation 510 ft (155 m)

San Ignacio is a date-palm oasis built around lagoons formed by damming a river which emerges from the earth nearby. The town is located just south of Mex 1. The road into town is paved and big RVs should have no problems since they can drive around the main square to turn around. The main square is also the location of the **mission church of San Ignacio**, one of the easiest to find and most impressive mission churches on the Baja. This one is built of lava rock and has walls that are four feet thick.

From San Ignacio it is possible to take a guided tour to see rock paintings in the surrounding hills. You should visit the rock art museum located just south of the church, next door is where you register to visit rock-art sites. It is also possible to follow the thirty mile long unpaved road to **Laguna San Ignacio** to see gray whales from January through March. Tours to do this are available in San Ignacio.

San Ignacio Campgrounds

RICE AND BEANS OASIS

Address:	Carretera Transpeninsular, CP 23930
	San Ignacio, B.C.S, México
Telephone:	(615) 154-0283
Open:	All Year

GPS Location: N 27° 17' 55", W 112° 54' 16"

This is San Ignacio's nicest RV park and definitely the best choice for big RVs. The campground also boasts a restaurant, arguably the best place to eat in San Ignacio. Both the RV park and associated restaurant are owned and operated by the same family that has the popular Rice and Beans Restaurant in San Felipe.

There are 29 spaces all with full hookups with 15-amp outlets but 30-amp breakers. They are located on two terraces overlooking San Ignacio's date palm forest. Tents are allowed but there is no separate area for them. There is no shade and unfortunately the highway runs just above the campground so it can be noisy. Restrooms are separate rooms with flush toilets and hot showers. The restaurant is at the entrance, we found the food to be excellent. They have a computer set up in the restaurant for customer use, also Wi-Fi which you can sometimes pick up in the sites that are closest to the restaurant, there is a fee. This is a Passport America campground, cardholders can stay overnight for $15 rather than the normal $30.

The campground is not located on the main road into San Ignacio like the other five mentioned here. Instead it is in the village of San Lino. The paved road to the campground leaves Mex 1 some 0.3 miles (0.5 km) west of the main road in to San Ignacio. The right turn when coming from the north is difficult, if it looks too sharp for you just continue on a short distance to the Pemex to make a U-turn. The campground is 0.4 miles (0.6 km) from the highway on the right.

RV PARK EL PADRINO

Telephone:	(615) 154-0089
Open:	All Year

GPS Location: N 27° 17' 08", W 112° 54' 05"

The El Padrino is the closest RV park to town, you can easily stroll in to the central square or over to the nearby La Pinta Motel for dinner.

There are 6 back-in spaces with low-amp electricity (some outlets hanging loose) and water and the campground has a dump station. There are also large areas for camping without hookups. These dry sites have shade, parking is on dirt. This is a good campground for tents and big RVs also often use it, there's plenty of room to maneuver. The restrooms have flush toilets but are in poor condition, when we visited recently the hot water heater was working so the showers were hot. A centrally located restaurant also serves as an office and has a computer for internet access. The campground offers gray whale watching tours to San Ignacio Lagoon which is about two hours away in their van. The price for tents or no-hookup RVs is 80 pesos.

Take the San Ignacio cutoff near the Pemex. The campground is just past the La Pinta, 1.3 miles (2.1 km) from the cutoff.

🚐 TRAILER PARK MARTIN QUEZADA RUÍZ

Open: All Year

GPS Location: N 27° 17'19", W 112° 53'59"

This is a grass-covered clearing in the trees with a pit toilet. Tent camping is very pleasant. Smaller RVs fit just fine but there are no hookups. You may find dates drying on platforms near the front of the property.

To find Martin's zero your odometer at the exit from Mex 1 and head toward town. The campground entrance is on the left at 1.1 miles (1.8 km). If no one is around don't worry, someone will be around to collect. The owner is not on-site overnight.

🚐 CAMPING PETATES

Open: All Year

GPS Location: N 27° 17'50", W 112° 53'52"

This is a newly established camping area in the date palms next to the San Ignacio lagoon. There is room for perhaps 15 RVs here. Bigger RVs will have to exercise caution to avoid the palms. There are no hookups, facilities include only pit toilets. The managers are not on-site overnight.

From the San Ignacio cutoff near the Pemex head toward town. In .5 miles (.8 km), just past the lagoon crossing, you'll see the entrance on the right.

🚐 RESTAURANT MIKASA

Open: All Year

GPS Location: N 27° 17'55", W 112° 53'50"

This is a small restaurant on the shore of the San Ignacio lagoon. The parking lot has room for perhaps 4 RVs of any size. There are no hookups but the restaurant offers hot showers. The owners are not on-site overnight.

From the San Ignacio cutoff near the Pemex head toward town. In .4 mile (.6 km), just before the road crosses the lagoon, the restaurant is on the left.

🚐 LAKESIDE RV PARK

Open: All Year

GPS Location: N 27° 17'58", W 112° 53'39"

This campground is easy to spot as you drive the side road in to San Ignacio. It's a very simple place with parking for any size RV on dirt under date palms next to the lagoon. The only facilities are dilapidated pit toilets. The campground is often unattended, someone will surely come by to collect when they see you parked there. The manager is not on-site overnight.

To reach the campground take the San Ignacio cutoff near the Pemex. In just 0.2 mile (0.3 km) from the turn you'll see a sign indicating the entrance to the Lakeside on the left. A painted car door also identifies the campground as Camping Don Chow's.

To
Guerrero Negro

1

San Ignacio

N

Mulegé

Bahía Concepción

Bahía
Concepción
to
Loreto

Loreto
to
Puerto
Escondido

Puerto Escondido

San Ignacio
to
Santa Rosalía

Santa Rosalía

Santa Rosalía

Santa Rosalía
to
Mulegé

Mulegé
to
Bahía Concepción

1

1

Loreto

Loreto

Puerto Escondido

To
Ciudad Constitución

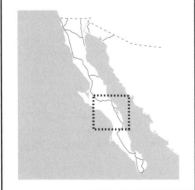

CHAPTER INDEX

Highlights	Page 123
Roads and Fuel Availability	Page 123
Sightseeing	Page 124
Golf	Page 124
Beaches and Water Sports	Page 124
Fishing	Page 125
Backroad Adventures	Page 125
San Ignacio to Santa Rosalía	Page 126
Santa Rosalía	Page 127
Santa Rosalía to Mulegé	Page 129
Mulegé	Page 132
Mulegé to Bahía Concepción	Page 136
Bahía Concepción	Page 136
Bahía Concepción to Loreto	Page 142
Loreto	Page 143
Loreto to Puerto Escondido	Page 146
Puerto Escondido	Page 148

CENTRAL GULF COAST

Chapter Seven

Central Gulf of California Coast

INTRODUCTION

The section covered in this chapter is one of the most popular areas of the whole Baja Peninsula. Here Mex 1, the Transpeninsular, reaches the warm Gulf of California for the first time. There are tourist resorts, quiet tropical towns, and sandy beaches suitable for RV parking. What more could you want?

Highlights

The sandy beaches lining **Bahía Concepción** are the primary destination for many RVers headed down the Baja. Here you can camp right next to the water, there are enough nearby services so that you can stay for an extended period, and there is plenty to keep you busy with sightseeing trips to the north and south and water sports right at your doorstep.

Loreto, a town toward the southern end of this section, is just about the only fly-in destination with scheduled air service north of La Paz and Cabo. It has hotels, restaurants, a golf course, and resort-type services like guided fishing, diving, and sightseeing trips.

Roads and Fuel Availability

The Transpeninsular is two lanes wide for the length of this section, just as it is along most of the peninsula. It is narrow but relatively uncrowded, so continue to exercise caution and keep the speed down.

Kilometer markers along here decrease as you drive south. The segment from San Ignacio to Santa Rosalía counts down from 74 to zero. In Santa Rosalía a new segment of kilometer posts begins with 197, it counts down to zero at Loreto. At the Loreto cutoff the kilometer posts start again at 119, these reach zero at the 90 degree corner in Ciudad Insurgentes on the west side of the Sierra Gigante where the road turns south toward La Paz and the Cape.

Fuel is readily available in this section. Here are the locations, with types, and distances between stations: **San Ignacio**, gas and diesel; **Santa Rosalía**, two stations with gas and diesel, 45 miles (83 km)(watch these guys!); **just south of Mulegé**, gas and diesel, 41 miles (66 km); and **Loreto**, gas and diesel, 80 miles (129 km). From Loreto to the next station at **Cuidad Insurgentes** is a distance of 74 miles (119 km).

Sightseeing

At the northern end of this section is the coastal town of **Santa Rosalía**. It has an unusual history for a Baja town and some unusual sights, including a church designed by the same man who designed the Eiffel tower, a French-style bakery, and wood buildings dating from the 19th century. See the Santa Rosalía section for more information.

Mulegé is a date-palm oasis located on an estuary along the Gulf of California. It's a friendly little town that is very accustomed to visitors from north of the border. It also has some interesting sights including an old mission and a jail that only locked the doors at night when it was in operation.

You can visit some missions in this section. One is the **Misión Santa Rosalía de Mulegé** mentioned above. The other is the well-preserved Jesuit **Misión San Javier** in the hills behind Loreto, the road is described in *Backroad Adventures* below. Easiest of all to visit is the **Misión Nuestra Señora de Loreto** right in central Loreto, it also has a museum with exhibits about the Jesuit missions in the region.

There are several **rock-art sites** in the mountains behind the coast. Most popular is probably the one near Rancho La Trinidad. You can find a guide in Mulegé. The drive is described below in the *Backroad Adventures* section.

Golf

Just a few miles south of Loreto is a resort - Nopoló. This is a FONATUR complex. FONATUR is the Mexican governmental agency that has planned and constructed places you are probably more familiar with: Cancun, Cabo San Lucas, Ixtapa, and Bahías de Huatulco. The resort has a golf course, the only one between Ensenada and Cabo San Lucas. It is an 18-hole course and tee-time reservations are easy to get. There is also a driving range and a tennis center.

Beaches and Water Sports

Punta Chivato is a campground offering excellent water sports opportunities. The beach is fine for swimming with nice sand. Snorkeling is good along rocky reefs just offshore, winds are good for board-sailing, and the fishing is good too. There is a nearby boat ramp and a sheltered area for small boats right at the campground.

The white sand beaches on the west side of **Bahía Concepción** are one of the area's biggest attractions. The waters of the bay are protected and excellent for swimming and water sports. Kayakers especially love the area. Most beaches near the highway are available for camping, they are listed under *Bahía Concepción Campgrounds* below.

Kayakers also like to make 1 to 2 week trips from Mulegé to Loreto or even from Puerto Escondido south to La Paz.

Fishing

It is not too hard to find launching ramps in this section. There are ramps in Santa Rosalía, San Lucas Cove, Punta Chivato, Mulegé, Bahía Concepción, Loreto, and Puerto Escondido. Some are better than others, in fact some are just beaches with hard sand, but you should be able to find a place to launch most any trailer boat along here somewhere.

In this section the two most popular fisheries are probably for yellowtail during December through January and for Dorado in July and August. The winter yellowtail season coincides with great weather for camping.

Pangas can be chartered in many places along this coast so don't think that you can't fish if you don't have a boat.

San Lucas Cove, located between Santa Rosalía and Mulegé, has two campgrounds and is very popular with fishermen. It offers protected waters for your boat at the campgrounds and easy access to 10-fathom water in Craig Channel behind Isla San Marcos.

Backroad Adventures

See the *Backroad Driving* section of *Chapter 2 - Details, Details, Details* for essential information about driving off the main highway on the Baja and for a definition of road types used below.

🚙 **From Km 169 Between Santa Rosalía and Mulegé** - This is a usually Type 2 road that leads 9 miles (14 km) to the village of **San José de Magdalena**. This town is known as the garlic capital of the Baja. You can buy long braids of garlic here from March to December. The road continues beyond town but deteriorates to a Type 3.

🚙 **From Km 136 at Mulegé** - This road leading westward from near the Mulegé cutoff leads quite a distance into the mountains, but the most popular destination is **Rancho La Trinidad** and nearby cave art in La Trinidad canyon. You can find a guide in Mulegé. The road to the rancho is usually a Type 2 but beyond it deteriorates to Type 3 requiring 4WD. Eventually the road circles around to San José de Magdalena, reaching it 50 miles (81 km) after passing Rancho La Trinidad. From **San José de Magdalena**, of course, you can return to Mex 1 at Km 169 as described above.

🚙 **From Km 77 Between Bahía Concepción and Loreto** - This road takes you around the south end of Bahía Concepción, up the east side of the bay, and then across the tip of the peninsula on the far side to an old mine site on the coast. The distance is about 35 miles (56 km) out to the mine. This is usually a Type 3 road. There's a Y at about 5 miles (8 km) that takes you across the peninsula to **San Sebastián** on the coast, the distance from the Y is 9 miles (15 km), this is usually a Type 3 road. San Sebastian can more easily be reached as described below.

From Km 62 Between Bahía Concepción and Loreto - From this point a graded road leads 10 miles (16 km) to the village of **San Nicolas**, then 6 miles (10 km) along the coast northward to **San Sebastian**. This is usually a Type 2 road.

From Km 118 Between Loreto and Puerto Escondido - The **Misión San Javier** is a popular excursion for tourists in Loreto. The distance from the junction to the church is 22 miles (35 km) on a graded Type 2 road with some steep sections. At about 18 miles (29 km) you will pass a cutoff for the long road to San Miguel de Comondú and San Jose de Comondú. That is usually a Type 3 road, you can reach these two towns more easily from the far side of the mountains on better roads.

THE ROUTES, TOWNS, AND CAMPGROUNDS

SAN IGNACIO TO SANTA ROSALÍA
45 Miles (73 Km), 1.25 Hours

The road in this section is passing through the Sierra San Francisco. Grades are not difficult, other than the descent to the coast, but the road is sinuous in places so you'll want to keep the speed down.

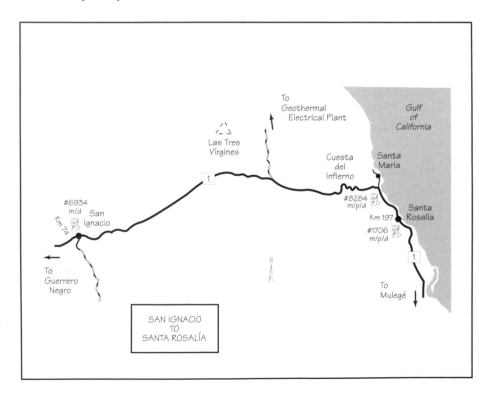

About 20 miles eastward from San Ignacio you may notice that the road is crossing lava flows. They are from **Las Tres Vírgines** (The Three Virgins), a volcanic mountain with three separate cones on the north side of the highway. In a short distance you'll pass the road left to an experimental geothermal electrical plant. The volcano is thought to have last shown significant activity about 1847 in the form of quite a bit of vapor. At about this point the road begins a long descent toward the Gulf of California.

Thirty-five miles from San Ignacio the descent becomes much steeper. This grade is called the **Cuesta del Infierno** (loosely translated as Grade to Hell), it is about 2.5 miles (3.1 km) long and the steepest grade on Mex 1. Be sure to gear down and keep the speed low as you descend, there are several curves. Soon the grade becomes less steep and after another 4 miles (6.5 km) or so you'll reach the coast and turn south to enter Santa Rosalía.

Santa Rosalía (SAHN-TAH ROH-SAH-LEE-AH)
Population 15,000

Don't pass through Santa Rosalía without stopping. This old mining town is unlike any other town on the Baja. Located at the point where Mex 1 finally reaches the Gulf of California, Santa Rosalía was founded in the 1880s by a French company to extract the large amounts of copper ore located here. The mining operation lasted until the 1950s. Now the town is a fishing and ferry port, it serves as a hub for the

THE INTERIOR OF EIFFEL'S CHURCH IN SANTA ROSALIA

surrounding area. The ferries run from here to Guaymas on Mexico's west coast. For information see *Ferries* in *Chapter 2 - Details, Details, Details.*

Much of the town is constructed of wood imported from the Pacific Northwest, the building designs are French colonial. **Santa Rosalía's church** is unique, it was designed by A.G. Eiffel who is better known for his tower in Paris. It was prefabricated in France and shipped by boat around Cape Horn. The town also has a well-known **French-style bakery**.

It is best not to drive a large RV in to town, although the town is built on a grid plan the roads are fairly constricted. It is better to park along the road north of town and then walk in. Be careful where you park, the police here are notorious for giving tickets.

Santa Rosalía Campground

🚐 **LAS PALMAS RV PARK**

Address:	Apdo. 123, Santa Rosalía, B.C.S., México
Telephone:	(615) 152-2070
Email:	jramiro-contreras@hotmail.com
Open:	All Year

GPS Location: N 27° 18' 53", W 112° 14' 35"

The Las Palmas is the most convenient place to stay if you want to be close to Santa

Rosalía. It's a well-done full-hookup facility, but suffers from being away from the water. However, during the summer there is a balneario with two swimming pools right next door.

There are 30 large grassy spaces separated by concrete curbs arranged around the edge of the campground. It's a good place for tent camping. Access and parking for big RVs is fine. All sites have electricity with 15-amp outlets (40-amp breakers), sewer, and water. The restrooms are showing neglect, they have hot water showers. There is a coin-operated laundry onsite. When we visited the owner did not stay at the facility so there was no security, he dropped by in the evening to collect.

The Las Palmas is just off Mex 1 about 2 miles (3.2 km) south of Santa Rosalía on the east side of the highway.

SANTA ROSALÍA TO MULEGÉ
37 Miles (60 Km), 1 Hour

As you make the short climb south out of Santa Rosalía watch for the Las Palmas RV park to the left. It's a good place to base yourself if you find Santa Rosalía to be an interesting town.

Nine miles (15 km) south of Santa Rosalía, is San Lucas. Caleta San Lucas, a large cove just a half mile east of town, is the location of two RV parks popular with fishermen. They are RV Park San Lucas Cove and much smaller RV Camacho, both

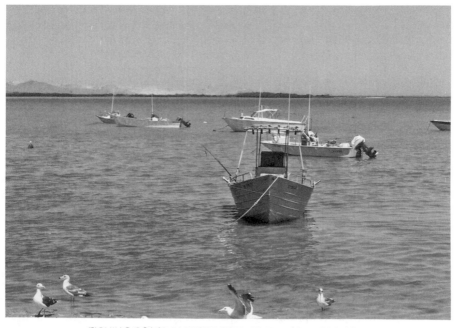

FISHING BOATS IN FRONT OF RV PARK SAN LUCAS COVE

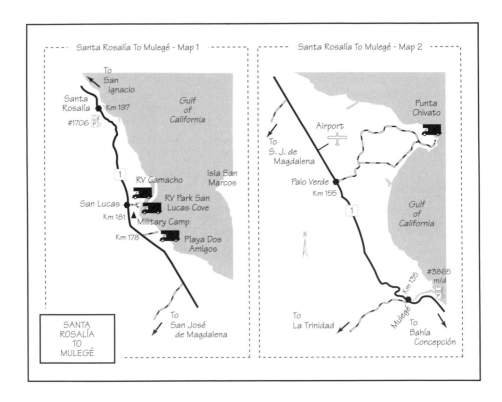

discussed below. The island offshore is Isla San Marcos, there is a large gypsum mine on the island. Just a bit farther south you'll see the sign for another RV park, Playa Dos Amigos.

Twenty-five miles (41 km) south of Santa Rosalía, near Km 155, is a road leading to the coast and a campground known as Punta Chivato. The road is 11 miles (18 km) long, unpaved and dusty, but usually suitable for any RV. The waterfront camping area is very popular with folks who know about it, it is covered below.

You'll arrive at Mulegé 37 miles (60 km) from Santa Rosalía, near Km 136. Do not take the left in to town, the roads are narrow and not at all suitable for RVs. Instead select an RV park from the ones described below and explore town in a tow car or on foot.

Santa Rosalía to Mulegé Campgrounds

RV CAMACHO
Telephone: (615) 155-4063
Open: All Year

GPS Location: N 27° 13' 14", W 112° 12' 47"

This is a small campground just north of the much larger RV park called San Lucas Cove. There are 10 waterfront sites with palapas. A large area behind the waterfront sites provides lots of room for additional parking, big RVs are fine. There are hot water showers and flush toilets as well as a dump station. The campground is fenced and there is a small office at the entrance gate which is usually manned. The monthly rate here is $165.

To reach the campground watch for the sign at Km 181 south of Santa Rosalía. The 0.6 mile (1 km) dirt road east to the campground is fine for any size RV.

🚐 RV PARK SAN LUCAS COVE

Address:	Apdo. 50, Santa Rosalía, B.C.S., México
Open:	All Year

GPS Location: N 27° 13' 07", W 112° 12' 51"

This is a waterfront campground that may remind you of those farther south on Bahía Concepción. It is not quite as scenic as those but has a similar ambiance. The fishing in this area is excellent and most of the campers in this park are here for the fishing.

There are about 20 parking sites along the beach and at least 40 more on a large hard-packed sandy area behind. There is lots of room for big RVs. The campground has flush toilets and usually hot water showers as well as a dump station, so it is possible to make an extended visit. Municipal water is now connected to the campground so the water is not salty. Folks either pull their boats up on the beach or anchor them out front. The monthly rate is $140.

Access is now via the same road as RV Camacho above. It is near Km 181 south of Santa Rosalía. At about 0.5 mile (0.8 km) take the right fork into the campground. The road in to the campground is packed sand and is about 0.6 miles (1 km) long. Big RVs will have no problems negotiating it.

🚐 PLAYA DOS AMIGOS

Telephone:	(615) 152-1020 (Santa Rosalia) or
	044 (615) 155-4097 (at park)
Open:	All Year

GPS Location: N 27° 12' 09", W 112° 12' 30"

This camping area is located on the south shore of the Bahía el Islote de San Lucas, RV Camacho and RV Park San Lucas Cove are on the north shore of the same bay. The beach out front of this campground is shallow and very gradually sloping so it's not good for larger boats but fine for kayaks.

The campground is a large field just back from the beach. The restroom building has flush toilets and hot showers. The access road has been improved considerably and is now suitable for any size RV. There's a small restaurant at the campground run by the manager who lives onsite.

The access road is well marked with billboards, it heads east to the campground just north of the Km 178 marker. It's about 0.6 mile (1 km) long. Near the beach bear left, the large lot to the right is privately owned.

🚐 PUNTA CHIVATO

Open:	All Year

GPS Location: N 27° 04' 27", W 111° 56' 52"

Punta Chivato has long been a popular beachside camping spot with few amenities, a good trade-off for having the ocean just outside your front door. This area is associated with a nearby hotel which was a fly-in fishing destination for years. Many homes have been built along the coast, mostly to the east of the hotel between it and the camping area.

Camping is in a large parking area behind a sandy beach. A small spit provides enough protection for small fishing skiffs. Sand drifts into the camping area so most areas are only suitable for smaller RVs, preferably with four-wheel drive. The long access road and limited parking room mean that this is not really a suitable camp-ground for most big RVs although we often see some pretty big ones here. Tent campers love this beach. A building behind the beach has cold showers and there are pit toilets. Water is available at the camping area and there is a dump station back near the hotel and airport.

Access to the resort and camping area is via a long dirt road. The access road leaves Mex 1 just north of Km 155 between Santa Rosalía and Mulegé in the village of Palo Verde. The distance from Mex 1 to the camping area is 11.2 miles (18.1 km). After 2.1 miles (3.4 km) there is a fork in the road, take the right fork for the new road. The road nears the shoreline at 5.7 miles (9.2 km) and turns left to parallel the shoreline some quarter-mile back from the beach. At about 8.5 miles (13.7 km) from the high-way the road turns inland and rounds the end of a runway, then returns toward the beach reaching the resort at 10.5 miles (16.9 km). The dump station is on the right at this point. Turn left here following signs for Playa Camping and proceed another 0.7 mile (1.1 km) eastward to the camping area. En route you will pass through a row of houses which overlooks the beach and campground.

MULEGÉ (MOO-LAH-HAY)
Population 6,000

Situated near the mouth of the palm and mangrove-lined Río Santa Rosalía, Mulegé is a welcome tropical paradise after the long drive across desert country to the north. In many ways Mulegé may remind you of San Ignacio, both have a definite desert oasis ambiance. Mulegé is a popular RVer destination, many permanents make their seasonal home here, there are four decent RV parks, and the beaches and coves of the Bahía Concepción begin only 12 miles (19.6 km) to the south.

Fishing, diving, and kayaking are all popular here. Yellowtail are often thick during the winter and summer anglers go offshore for deep water fish. The nearby Santa Inés Islands are popular diving destinations, dive shops in Mulegé offer trips to the islands and other sites. Kayakers love Bahía Concepción and the coastline north and south.

Sights in Mulegé itself are limited. The **Misión Santa Rosalía** is located about 2 miles (3.3 km) upstream from the bridge on the right bank (facing downstream). It is usually locked except during services but the excursion offers excellent views of the town and river. Mulegé is also known for its **prison**. Now closed the prison building houses a museum and you can take a look at the cells. You can drive out to the mouth of the river (if you have a smaller RV) on the north shore, there you'll find a rock formation and lighthouse known as El Sombrerito, you can't miss it.

Mulegé is accustomed to visitors and takes them in stride, there's a large Norteamericano population. There are quite a few good restaurants and some small grocery shops. Street-side phones are available. A few miles south of town is a Pemex, it has lots of room for big RVs and is an easy place to fill up.

Mulegé Campgrounds

⛺ HACIENDA DE LA HABANA

Address: PO Box 123, Mulegé, BCS, México
Telephone: 044 (615) 161-4316
Open: All Year

GPS Location: N 26° 52' 22", W 112° 01' 08"

This new campground is owned and operated by Ray Lima, the owner of Ray's Place, the well-known restaurant at Playa Santispac. Hacienda de la Habana is located back in the wide valley behind Mulegé. It's a pleasant well-watered area, very unusual for the Baja.

The hacienda has 24 large full-hookup pull-thru sites with parking on grass. Electrical outlets are the 20-amp style but have 30-amp breakers. There are flush toilets, showers, a swimming pool, and a beautiful lounge area overlooking the pool. Under construction at the same location is Ray's second restaurant, this one is to have Cuban cuisine. The monthly rate here is $350.

Reaching the campground requires driving on dirt roads, they are scheduled for im-

Ⓐ   Former Prision and Museum
Ⓑ   Cemetery
Ⓒ   El Sombrerito
Ⓓ   Misión Santa Rosalía

MULEGÉ

HACIENDA DE LA HABANA'S LOUNGE AREA OVERLOOKING THE POOL

provement but even before that is done they can be still be driven by any RV. From Mulege drive west on Icehouse Road. This is the road that goes inland just north of Km 135, about .5 mile (.8 km) north of the bridge over the Río Mulegé. Icehouse Road is also Calle Manuel M De Leon but neither name is signed at the intersection, there may be a sign for the campground. Drive inland for .6 mile (1 km). At the end of the pavement turn left, this turn is just past the Icehouse. In just .1 mile (.2 km) turn right. From here it's 1.8 miles (2.9 km) to the campground. Just stick to the main road. It makes a quick left and then a right, then in a bit another left turn and then a right turn. The campground is on the left.

HOTEL CUESTA REAL

Address:	Km 132 (PO Box 74), CP 23900 Mulegé, B.C.S., México
Telephone:	(615) 153-0321
Website:	http://cuestareal.tripod.com
Email:	htl_cuesta-rl@hotmail.com
Open:	All Year

GPS Location: N 26° 53' 50", W 111° 57' 55"

This little motel and campground are excellent for smaller RVs. It's a great alternative for a stay in Mulegé.

There are 10 back-in sites here suitable for RVs to about 35 feet, 4 are available for short-term use. These are full hookup sites with 15, 30 and 50-amp outlets. Restrooms have hot showers and there's a restaurant, a small store, a laundry room, and internet access. There's also a swimming pool. Since this is a small park we recommend that you park near the entrance and walk down to see if there is room for you. The monthly rate is $325.

The entrance road is 1.1 miles (1.8 km) southeast of the Mulegé bridge off Mex 1.

VILLA MARIA ISABEL RECREATIONAL PARK

Address:	Apdo. 5, CP 23900 Mulegé, B.C.S., México
Telephone and Fax:	(615) 153-0246
Email:	mulegevillamariarvpark@yahoo.com
Open:	All Year

GPS Location: N 26° 53' 49", W 111° 57' 51"

This is an excellent place to stay if you are looking for an RV park with full hookups in Mulegé. Like the other Mulegé campgrounds it sits near the south shore of the Mulegé River. The park has a great swimming pool and a laundry room.

The campground has about 40 sites, some have water and electric only but there are about 18 pull-thru spaces with 30-amp outlets, sewer, and water. Parking is on dirt and the sites will accommodate larger RVs although they're narrow and if the park is full it is difficult to find room to extend an awning. There is also an area for tent campers with a shared palapa. The restrooms have hot water showers. The swimming pool is a big attraction, especially during hot summer weather. There is a boat ramp and a dry long-term storage area. Caravans like this park so if one is scheduled you won't get in. The monthly rate here is $475.

The campground is 1.3 miles (2.1 km) south of the Mulegé bridge off Mex 1.

HOTEL SERENIDAD

Address:	Apdo. 9, CP 23900 Mulegé, B.C.S., México
Telephone:	(615) 153-0530
Fax:	(615) 153-0311
Website:	www.serenidad.com
Email:	hotelserenidad@prodigy.net.mx
Open:	All Year

GPS Location: N 26° 53' 50", W 111° 57' 32"

The Serenidad is a hotel located on the south bank of the Mulegé River near the mouth. It has its own airstrip and was a popular fly-in fishing destination even before the Transpeninsular Highway was built.

The hotel has 8 RV spaces along a wall at the back of the property. Sites are not suitable for big RVs, a 30-footer could fit. The location is hot and unappealing considering the nearby alternatives, but there are full hookups with 15-amp outlets. Restrooms are available with hot showers. The hotel has nice facilities, there is a swimming pool and restaurant. A pig roast, Mexican buffet, and folklorico performance draws people from around the area on Saturday night.

The entrance to the Serenidad is the farthest south along Mex 1 of all the Mulegé campgrounds. If you zero your odometer at the bridge you'll see the entrance road at 2.2 miles (3.5 km). There's a half-mile gravel entrance road leading along the side of the airstrip to the hotel.

MULEGÉ TO BAHÍA CONCEPCIÓN
12 Miles (19 Km), .25 Hour

This is only a short drive to the northernmost of the beaches, of course it's a lot farther to the southernmost beaches on the bay. An important stop along the road is the Pemex station 3 miles (5 km) south of the Mulegé bridge. It has excellent access for big RVs.

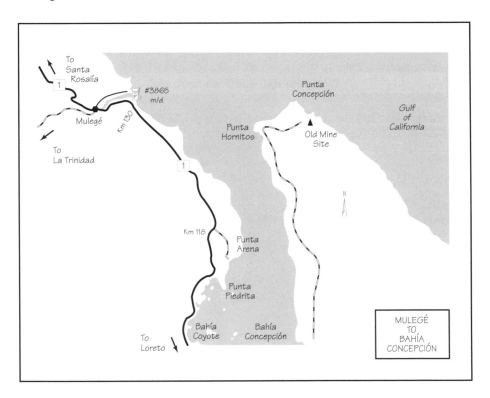

BAHÍA CONCEPCIÓN (BAH-HEE-AH KOHN-SEP-SEE-OHN)

For many people, especially RVers, Bahía Concepción is the ultimate Baja destination. This huge shallow bay offers many beaches where you can park your camping vehicle just feet from the water and spend the winter months soaking in the sunshine. Mex 1 parallels the western shore of the bay for about 20 miles (33 km), you'll see many very attractive spots and undoubtedly decide to stop. The many beaches offer different levels of services. Full hookups are seldom available, but many have toilets, showers, water, and restaurants. Information about the most popular beaches is offered below. While many of these places seem to have no formal organization do not be surprised if someone comes by in the evening to collect a small fee. This usually covers keeping the area picked up, trash removal and pit toilets. Ask one of your fellow campers about arrangements if you have questions. You'll seldom be alone on these beaches. The closest place to get supplies is Mulegé.

It is important to be concerned about sanitation, particularly about disposal of both black and gray water at all of the beaches along here. A lot of RVers winter here and some people feel that in recent years there's been a noticeable increase in the growth of vegetation offshore at some beaches. If the trend continues it's possible that camping along these beaches might be restricted, something no one wants to happen. You should assure yourself that waste is being properly handled before using any of the dump stations on these beaches.

Bahía Concepción Campgrounds

LOS NARANJOS BEACH

Address:	Armando y Delia Naranjos, Mulegé, B.C.S., México (Reservations)
Telephone:	(615) 153-0121
Open:	All Year

GPS Location: N 26° 47'02", W 111° 51'49"

Two camping areas occupy Punta Arena. The one to the north is Los Naranjos.

This campground occupies the actual point. To the north along open beach there is a large open parking area. Since the wind during the winter often blows from the north this is the least desirable area. Along the more protected beach to the south are permanent structures, however there is some space to camp behind them. There is a small restaurant, as well as primitive restrooms with flush toilets and hot showers. It takes some time to get the showers going, you need to make a request ahead of time. There's also a dump station and water is available.

The entrance to Playa Los Naranjos is 0.2 miles (0.3 km) north of the Km 118 marker. It is marked with a sign to Punta Arena. The road in to the beach can be rough but should be negotiable by any RV at very slow speeds. It is 2.1 miles (3.4 km) long, at 0.4 miles (0.7 km) there is a Y where you go left for Playa los Naranjos and right for Playa Punta Arena.

PUNTA ARENA

Open:	All Year

GPS Location: N 26° 46'44", W 111° 52'23"

There are actually two different camping area on this large beach: Playa los Naranjos to the north and Playa Punta Arena to the south. The entry road branches not far from the highway and you make your decision there. Punta Arena is the fork to the right.

The beach at Punta Arena is long and not nearly as crowded as the many beaches to the south on Bahía Concepción. It is quite easy to find a place along the water most of the time. There are pit toilets. Small palapas are available. In the scrub behind the beach the residents have set up a small sand golf course.

The entrance to Punta Arena is 0.2 miles (0.3 km) north of the Km 118 marker. The road in to the beach is rough but should be negotiable by any RV at very slow speeds. It is two miles (3 km) long, at 0.4 miles (0.7 km) there is a Y where you go left for Playa los Naranjos and right for Playa Punta Arena.

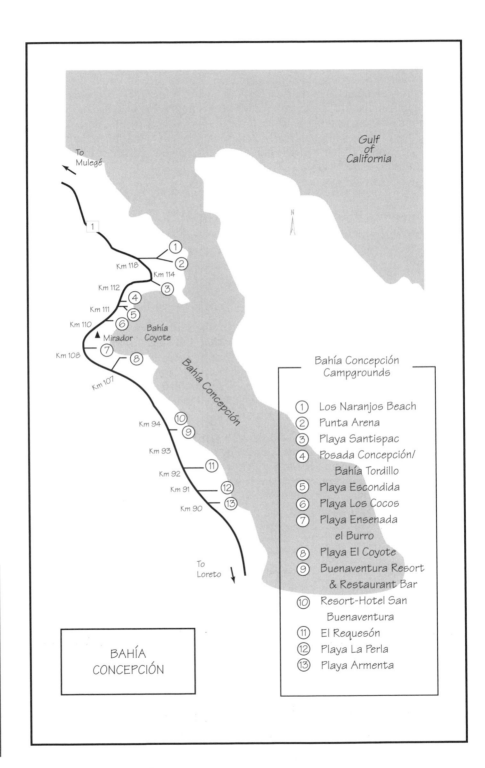

Gulf
of
California

To
Mulegé

Km 118
Km 114
Km 112
Km 111
Km 110
Mirador
Bahía
Coyote
Km 108
Km 107

Bahía Concepción

Km 94
Km 93
Km 92
Km 91
Km 90

To
Loreto

Bahía Concepción
Campgrounds

① Los Naranjos Beach
② Punta Arena
③ Playa Santispac
④ Posada Concepción/
   Bahía Tordillo
⑤ Playa Escondida
⑥ Playa Los Cocos
⑦ Playa Ensenada
   el Burro
⑧ Playa El Coyote
⑨ Buenaventura Resort
   & Restaurant Bar
⑩ Resort-Hotel San
   Buenaventura
⑪ El Requesón
⑫ Playa La Perla
⑬ Playa Armenta

BAHÍA
CONCEPCIÓN

PLAYA SANTISPAC

Open: All Year

GPS Location: N 26° 45'57", W 111° 53'15"

The most northerly beach on sheltered Bahía Coyote is very popular, partly because the entrance road is so short and easy. The fee here is slightly higher than most other beaches in the area.

The long beach offers beachside parking for many, but you will find that the beach sites are often very crowded together and full. There are flush toilets, a dump station, hot (20 pesos) and cold showers, and two restaurants. One of them, Ray's, is very good. There is also a small muddy hot spring located a short walk to the west just below the highway and at the back of a grove of mangroves. There are rumors that this property is sold and a hotel will be built here soon, but at the time we went to press it remains open for camping.

The entrance to Playa Santispac is just south of the Km 114 marker. The beach is visible from the road, it's hard to miss since it's the first of Bahiá Concepcion's great beach campgrounds that you'll see from the road as you head south. While short and in good shape the entrance road is a little steep and at the bottom of a hill if you're coming from the north, exercise care when leaving the highway. There is a manned entrance station where the fee is collected. It's the only one on any beach along here, that will give you some idea of the popularity of this beach.

LARGE RVS CAMPING ON THE SAND AT PLAYA SANTISPAC

CENTRAL GULF COAST

▦ Posada Concepción/Bahía Tordillo

$$	⚗	🚰	🚐	🚿 HOT	⚓	🚌 BIG RIGS

Address: Apdo. 14, Mulegé, B.C.S., México
Open: All Year

GPS Location: N 26° 45' 11", W 111° 53' 56"

Posada Concepción is really more subdivision than beachfront camping area, most of the people here live in houses or permanently installed trailers. There are a few spaces for travelers, they are nowhere near the water but they do have hookups.

There are six slots here with full hookups, electricity is from 15-amp outlets. The spaces are fine for large RVs. Restrooms have flush toilets and hot showers. This beach is well-protected, at low tide the water is very shallow and there are a few hot-water seeps in shallow water. There is also a tennis court.

The entrance to Posada Concepción is 0.2 mile(0.3 km) south of the Km 112 marker.

▦ Playa Escondida

$$	⛺	🚿	⚓

Open: All Year

GPS Location: N 26° 44' 42", W 111° 53' 45"

This small isolated beach is picture-perfect. There is a row of palapas along the water. Outhouses and cold water showers are on the hillside behind.

The road in to this beach is very rough, we recommend it only for high clearance cars and vans and pickup campers. The entrance road is just south of Posada Concepción, 0.4 mile (0.6 km) south of the Km 112 marker. The same road is shared by the Eco Mundo kayaking operation. At first glance you'll think the road leads to the south side of the same bay occupied by Posada Concepción, but instead it leads 0.5 miles (0.8 km) up over a low saddle to an unexpected beach, hence the name which means hidden beach.

▦ Playa Los Cocos

$$	⛺	🚐	⚓

Open: All Year

GPS Location: N 26° 44' 33", W 111° 54' 04"

Playa los Cocos is another beautiful beach with minimal facilities. There are palapas, pit toilets, and a dump station. Mangroves are at the rear.

The entrance is midway between Km 110 and 111 markers. There is no sign and the entrance road is about 0.3 miles (0.5 km) long. It's in poor condition, recommended only for RVs to 30 feet. The campground can easily be seen from the highway because it runs very close by.

▦ Playa Ensenada el Burro

$$	⛺	🚐	🍴	🛒	⚓	🚌 BIG RIGS

Open: All Year

GPS Location: N 26° 43' 46", W 111° 54' 27"

This beach offers the standard pit toilets but also has a restaurant as well as a dump site. There's even a small store across the highway. Parking is along the water but there are so many palapas with long-term residents that beach sites have become hard to come by. Caravans often stay here.

The entrance to Playa el Burro is midway between Km 108 and Km 109. You can easily see the beach from the highway.

⚟ PLAYA EL COYOTE

Open: All Year

GPS Location: N 26° 42' 50", W 111° 54' 13"

Another good beach with few facilities. A tree or two provide shade on this beach and it is not quite as crowded as the spots farther north, perhaps because the road is slightly more difficult. It has pit toilets and a questionable dump station. There is a hot spring along the rocks to the east. Many books about the Baja have a picture on the cover of RVs parked on this beach, palm trees right next to the water, often with RVs parked beneath, make an enticing shot from above.

The entrance road to El Coyote is just north of the Km 107 marker. After leaving the highway and driving down to the water turn right and proceed 0.5 miles (0.8 km) along the water below the cliff to the camping area. Big RVs occasionally go in here but if you have one it would be best to scout this in a tow car or on foot before trying it. The entrance road is a long stretch right along the water with no wide places for vehicles to pass, possible soft spots, and frequent erosion by the ocean.

⚟ BUENAVENTURA RESORT & RESTAURANT BAR

Telephone: (615) 161-1077
Email: bajabuenaventura@hotmail.com

GPS Location: N 26° 38' 35", W 111° 50' 39"

This restaurant and bar has no-hookup parking for RVs and camping for tents along the water. In addition to the restaurant there are flush toilets and hot water showers. This campground is on the same cove as the similarly named Resort Hotel San Buenaventura (a motel). This one is to the south.

The entrance is near Km 94 on Mex 1. The main road is almost at beach level here. There's quite a bit of room out front making this a good turn-around spot if you have missed a turn-off to the north or south.

⚟ RESORT-HOTEL SAN BUENAVENTURA

Address: PO Box 20, Mulegé, B.C.S., México
Telephone: (615) 155-5616
Website: www.hotelsanbuenaventura.com
Open: All Year

GPS Location: N 26° 38' 35", W 111° 50' 44"

This is a small motel near the beach. There is a flat area back from the beach where about 10 RVs of any size can park. A restroom in the office has flush toilets and hot showers.

The entrance is at Km 94 and is shared with the campground described above. This one is on the left.

⚟ EL REQUESÓN

Open: All Year

GPS Location: N 26° 38' 13", W 111° 49' 53"

CENTRAL GULF COAST

This is the most picturesque of the Bahía Concepción beaches. The beach is a short sand spit which connects a small island to the mainland at low tide. Small, shallow bays border both sides of the spit. There are pit toilets but no other amenities. You can hike along the water to the south beyond Playa La Perla. Someone will come by to collect a fee each evening.

The entrance to El Requesón is just north of the Km 92 marker. The entrance road is rough but should present no problems for most RVs, it is about 0.2 miles (0.3 km) long. Bushes alongside sometimes can cause scratching problems however. Large RVs, the Green Tortoise tourist bus, and even caravans drive in here and there's lots of maneuvering room for big RVs once they're in. You will find that it is easier to enter the road if you are approaching from the north so northbound travelers may drive on less than a mile and turn around in front of Playa Buenaventura.

PLAYA LA PERLA

Open: All Year

GPS Location: N 26° 38' 06", W 111° 49' 30"

This beachside camping area offers pit toilets and many palapas. It is a small sandy cove with a lot of additional camping locations to the north and south of the cove. The cove itself is probably better for tent campers while RVs may prefer the adjoining areas.

The entrance road is just south of the Km 91 marker. If you enter this way the road is about 0.4 mile (0.6 km) long and bushes along the side can scratch the side of your RV. You can also use the entrance road to El Requesón, turn right as you reach the beach, and trundle slowly along the shoreline south to Playa La Perla. We find this entrance to be easier with larger RVs, there is less chance of scratching the side of your RV. Rigs over 35 feet probably will find access to this beach inadequate. Scout either route first on foot or in a tow vehicle if you have a big RV.

PLAYA ARMENTA

Open: All Year

GPS Location: N 26° 37' 31", W 111° 48' 37"

The most southerly of the Bahía Concepción campgrounds has an exposed location but a decent beach in a north-facing cove. There are palapas and pit toilets.

The entrance road is a little south of where the Km 91 marker should be. There is no longer a sign for the km marker or the beach. The entrance road is 0.5 miles long (0.9 km) and somewhat difficult for big RVs although we've seen 35-foot motorhomes in here.

BAHÍA CONCEPCIÓN TO LORETO
71 Miles (115 Km), 2 Hours (from the northern end of the bay)

From Bahía Concepción to Loreto the kilometer markers continue to count down with zero at Loreto. After winding alongside Bahía Concepción for about 26 miles (42 km) the road climbs over a low saddle and then runs along a wide inland valley all the way south to Loreto. In some areas where water is available you'll see scattered ranchos in the valley. Off to the right are the Sierra de la Giganta. Prepare yourself, you'll soon be crossing them.

LORETO (LOH-**RAY**-TOE)
Population 7,200

Loreto is considered the oldest continuously occupied town on the Baja having been founded in 1697. This is theoretically true, however the town was virtually abandoned from the time of a major hurricane in 1829 until resettlement in the 1850s. The **Museo de los Misiones** has exhibits explaining the history of the area and also of the missions throughout the Baja. It is located next to the **Misión Nuestra Señora de Loreto**.

Today the town is part of a FONATUR development scheme like those in Cancún, Huatulco, Ixtapa, and Los Cabos (Cabo San Lucas and San José del Cabo). Most of the infrastructure was put in Nopoló, about 5 miles (8.2 km) south of Loreto. There you'll find an uncrowded but very nice golf course, a tennis center, the Loreto Inn, and a convention center. Even Bahía Escondido is part of the scheme, it is now supposed to be called Puerto Loreto. See the Puerto Escondido section below for more information.

CENTRAL GULF COAST

TOURS OR FISHING CHARTERS ARE AVAILABLE FROM LORETO'S BOAT HARBOR

Fishing and boating are popular activities in Loreto. You can arrange a trip in a panga or larger fishing cruiser. Just offshore from Loreto is Isla Carmen, the island has beaches and sheltered anchorages. Many experienced kayakers visit the island or you can arrange a panga for the trip.

Loreto Campgrounds

🚐 LORETO SHORES VILLAS AND RV PARK

Address:	Colonia Zaragoza (Apdo. 219), CP 23880
	Loreto, B.C.S., México
Telephone:	(613) 135-1513
Fax:	(613) 135-0711
Email:	loretoshores@yahoo.com
Open:	All Year

GPS Location: N 25° 59' 56", W 111° 20' 19"

This is the largest RV park in Loreto and a good place to stop for the night if you're traveling. It has plenty of room for big RVs on entry roads and inside the park. The spaces look a lot like those in the government parks, perhaps this was one of them. If so it has an unusually good waterfront location. Unfortunately the waterfront is now blocked by permanent structures.

There are about 35 pull-thru spaces remaining here, all with 15-amp outlets, sewer, water and patios. The restrooms are clean and have hot water showers. There's also a laundry. This is the best big RV campground in Loreto, almost all of the caravans stop here or at the Tripui to the south in Bahía Escondido. The monthly full-hookup rate here is $360.

Zero your odometer as you turn from Mex 1 at the main entrance to town on Paseo Pedro de Ugarte which is just north of Km 119. This will take you toward the ocean through a traffic circle and then a stop light. Take the turn to the right at 1.4 miles (2.3 km) onto Francisco Madero at another light. You'll cross a dry arroyo and continue straight. When you are 0.8 miles (1.3 km) from the turn make a left turn onto Ildefonso Green, the RV park is directly ahead.

RIVERA DEL MAR RV PARK AND CAMPING

Address:	Francisco I. Madero Norte No. 100, CP 23880
	Loreto, B.C.S., México
Telephone:	(613) 135-0718
Website:	www.riveradelmar.com
Email:	info@riveradelmar.com
Open:	All Year

GPS Location: N 26° 01' 02", W 111° 20' 45"

This is the new campground in Loreto, it's a great place to stay. The campground sits behind the house of the very friendly and accommodating owners so it is well-supervised and security is excellent. Space is limited (see below) but we'd check this place first before staying anywhere else in town. By staying here you're within walking distance of the beach and the center of town.

The park has 25 back-in RV spaces with full hook-ups (15-amp outlets) and also a nice tent-camping area with shade. These sites vary in length but the longest is really only about 35 feet. That's the rub here, there's just not enough room. The spaces are narrow without room for wide slide-outs or awnings. As a practical matter large RVs have been staying here, the owners let them take up two spaces (or sometimes 3) so that they have room for slides, awnings, and tow cars. The restrooms are brand new and very clean and well-maintained, they are individual rooms with showers, toilets, and sinks. There's also a laundry area with washer and dryer and a barbeque area. Wi-Fi is available for a fee, it can be received in the RV parking area.

The campground is in a residential area about a kilometer north of the business district. Access is a little convoluted but not difficult in any size RV. There are many routes, we think the following is the easiest. Enter Loreto at the main entrance to town on Paseo Pedro de Ugarte which is just north of Km 119. After 0.8 mile (0.5 km) you'll see Pemex #1698 on the right, continue for another 0.7 mile (1.1 km) to the end of the road where it meets the ocean. Turn left and drive to the end of the waterfront street, a distance of 0.5 miles (0.8 km). Now drive inland one block to a T. Turn right and then left at the second street. You'll again come to a T, turn right and the RV park is immediately on your left.

⊟ MOTEL & RV PARK EL MORO

Address:	Rosendo Robles No. 8, Col. Centro, CP 23880
	Loreto, B.C.S., México
Telephone and Fax:	(613) 135-0542
Open:	All Year
Website:	www.loreto.com/elmoro/

GPS Location: N 26° 00' 42", W 111° 20' 27"

The El Moro doesn't have a lot of extras in the way of facilities, just hookups and restrooms. There is also a motel on the property. This is the closest campground to central Loreto, it's within a block or two of almost everything.

There are 10 spaces, all are back-in slots with 30-amp outlets, sewer, and water. These are suitable for RVs to about 35 feet, they're wide enough for slide-outs or awnings, not both. Normally six or seven are available for travelers. The restrooms are simple but clean and have hot water showers. Wi-Fi is available for a fee. The monthly rate here is 2,640 pesos per month.

Zero your odometer as you turn from Mex 1 at the main entrance to town on Paseo Pedro de Ugarte which is just north of Km 119. Drive straight into and through town until you reach the waterfront malecón at 1.6 miles (2.6 km). Turn left and take the second left turn on Rosendo Robles at odometer 1.7 miles (2.7 km). The RV park is on the left at odometer 1.8 miles (2.9 km).

LORETO TO PUERTO ESCONDIDO
16 Miles (26 Km), .5 Hour

Just south of the entrance road to Loreto is a road leading westward into the mountains to the **Misión San Francisco Javier**. This is the only mission on the Baja still standing that has not been rebuilt. The distance to the mission is 22 miles (35 km).

See the *Backroad Adventures* section of this chapter for more information.

Five miles (8 km) south of the Loreto junction a road leads east to the **Nopoló resort area**. There's a hotel, a golf course, and tennis courts open to the public for reasonable fees.

South of the Nopoló junction you'll see the golf course along the road, as well as two bridges used to cross water hazards.

Near Km 97 you'll see a road to the left which leads to the camping beach called Juncalito. See the listing below for more information.

You'll reach the junction for the short stub road eastward to Puerto Escondido 15 miles (24 km) south of the Loreto junction.

Loreto to Puerto Escondido Campground

🚐 **JUNCALITO BEACH**

Open: All Year

GPS Location: N 25° 49' 10", W 111° 18' 59"

This little beach has nothing in the way of amenities except pit toilets. However, it is a nice beach, close to the road, and excellent for self-contained campers. The road in is pretty good, better than a lot of the roads up at Bahía Concepción, and is only 0.7 mile (1.1 km) long. The beach is ok for any size RV, carefully driven.

The road to the beach is just south of the Km 98 marker, that's 1.7 miles (2.7 km) north of the road out to Puerto Escondido.

PUERTO ESCONDIDO (PWER-toe ess-kohn-DEE-doe)
Population 100

Long popular as a camping and yachting destination, Puerto Escondido is now a part of the FONATUR plan to turn the Loreto area into a world-class resort. You'll be amazed at the paved but deteriorating boulevards, quay, and abandoned half-built hotel sitting next to this beautiful hurricane hole. Yachts are thick in the bay. There's a boat ramp here so fishermen like to use Puerto Escondido as a base for accessing the offshore waters and long stretch of coast to the south toward La Paz which has little road access. Kayakers put in here for the trips down the coast to La Paz.

Puerto Escondido Campgrounds

TRIPUI HOTEL - RV PARK

Address:	Apdo. 100, CP 23880 Loreto, B.C.S., México
Telephone:	(613) 133-0814
Fax:	(613) 133-0828
Website:	www.tripui.com
Email:	tripuivacation@hotmail.com
Open:	All Year

GPS Location: N 25° 48' 22", W 111° 19' 10"

The Tripui had a big fire not long ago. Many of the palapas housing permanently-located RVs were destroyed. The traveler section of the park was not affected and even the burnt sections are now repaired.

The traveler park here is a somewhat barren gravel parking lot. Some small palm trees have been planted to help make the place more attractive. Still, full hookup campgrounds with lots of amenities are scarce in this area so the Tripui is well-used. Many caravans stop here, it's good if you have a big RV and want full hookups. Another reason the Tripui is popular is the boat-launch ramp a short distance away at the port.

There are 31 back-in spaces in a fenced gravel lot with 20, 30 and 50-amp outlets, sewer, and water. Cement curbs separate the sites. The sites are short but no problem for big RVs since you can project far into the central area without really getting in anyone's way. The restrooms are fine, they have hot showers and flush toilets and are in good repair. This resort also has a lot of permanent RVs in a separate area, there's a small store, a gift shop, and a laundry as well as a nice pool area and a restaurant. The monthly rate here is $428.40. This park gives discounts for Passport America, Good Sam, Discover Baja Travel Club, and Club Vagabundos del Mar.

Take the Puerto Escondido cutoff from Mex 1 near Km 94 about 16 miles (26 km) south of Loreto. Drive 0.6 miles (1 km) on the paved road and you'll see the campground on the right. You'll first pass the traveler camping area and then see the sign for the office. Big RVs may want to pull into the camping area if there appear to be empty spaces and then walk over to sign in.

PUERTO
ESCONDIDO

 Ligui Beach

Open: All Year

GPS Location: N 25° 11'49", W 112° 07'13"

This is another beach south of Loreto that is popular with RVers. Drive in and look around, you may like it. There is a maze of roads behind the beach here leading out to camping locations, some spots are private and others have quite a few campers. Watch for brush that may scratch the side of your RV, also for soft spots and dead-end roads. It might be better to explore on foot. There are some pit toilets, the only amenities other than the beach. There's also a mini-super out on Mex 1.

The access road to Ligui Beach is just south of Km 84. The gravel road to the beach is fine for any RV, it's a distance of 0.9 miles (1.5 km). Near the highway there are some residences and you may see a sign indicating that this is private property, campers and fishermen ignore it. Once you approach the beach watch out for those soft spots, brush, and dead-ends.

Central Gulf Coast

To
Bahía Concepción

San
Juanico

La
Purisima

San
José
Comondú

San
Miguel
Comondú

Puerto Escondido

Side Trip
to
San Juanico

Side Trip
to
Lopez Mateos

Agua
Verde

Puerto Escondido
to
Ciudad Constitución

Lopez
Mateos

Ciudad Insurgentes

Ciudad Constitución

Ciudad Constitución

San Carlos

San Evaristo

Ciudad Constitución
to
La Paz

La Paz

Side Trip to
La Ventana

Side Trip
to
Puerto
San Carlos

El Cien

San
Juan
de la
Costa

La
Paz

La Ventana

Punta Conejo

To
Los Cabos

N

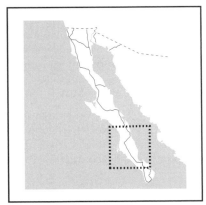

CHAPTER INDEX

Highlights .... Page 151
Roads and Fuel Availability .... Page 151
Sightseeing .... Page 152
Beaches and Water Sports .... Page 152
Fishing .... Page 153
Backroad Adventures .... Page 153
Puerto Escondido to Ciudad
    Constitución .... Page 154
Ciudad Constitución .... Page 155
Side Trip to San Juanico .... Page 157
Side Trip to Lopez Mateos .... Page 159
Side Trip to Puerto San Carlos .... Page 160
Ciudad Constitución to La Paz .... Page 162
La Paz .... Page 163
Side Trip to La Ventana .... Page 169

SOUTH TO LA PAZ

Chapter Eight

South to La Paz

INTRODUCTION

This chapter of the book covers the peninsula from the point where the highway turns inland south of Loreto to the point where it again reaches the Gulf at Baja Sur's largest town, La Paz. Between the two is a huge farming area centered around Ciudad Constitución. Many folks just hurry through this section bound for points farther south, but if you want to slow down there are several side trips offering fishing, whale watching, and sightseeing possibilities .

Highlights

La Paz is the largest city in Baja Sur and the one that feels the most like a mainland Mexican city. It is the best place to buy supplies south of Ensenada, many people spend the winter at one of the town's RV parks. La Paz celebrates Carnival, its a fun time to be here.

Roads and Fuel Availability

South of Loreto the road climbs to cross the Sierra la Giganta. On the far side you'll find a long and very gradual descent to the town of Ciudad Insurgentes. After a 90-degree left turn you'll drive for almost 50 miles (81 km) on an arrow-straight road through irrigated farming country. After that the road crosses dry rolling hills for another 90 miles (145 km) until it again reaches the east coast on the Gulf of California at the town of La Paz.

CARNAVAL IN LA PAZ IS A HIGHLIGHT OF ANY TRIP TO BAJA

Kilometer markers on this section of the Baja count down from Loreto to Ciudad Insurgentes, a distance of 119 kilometers. Then they again count down until you reach La Paz, a distance of 239 kilometers.

Fuel is readily available in this section. Here are the locations, with types and distances between stations: **Loreto**, gas and diesel; **Ciudad Insurgentes**, gas and diesel, 72 miles (116 km); **Ciudad Constitución**, gas and diesel, 14 miles (23 km); **El Centenario**, gas and diesel, 120 miles (194 km); **La Paz**, gas and diesel, 7 miles (11 km).

Sightseeing

During the months of January to March it is possible to visit the **gray whales** in Bahía Magdalena. Pangas go out to visit the whales from two different towns: San Carlos and Puerto Lopez Mateos. Both of them have places to boondock and are described below.

You can visit the remote and scenic villages of **San José Comondú** and **San Miguel Comondú**, see *Backroad Adventures* below.

Beaches and Water Sports

Access to beaches in this section, except in the La Paz vicinity, requires taking side roads since the Transpeninsular does not run along the coast.

Bahía Magdalena is one of the three places on the Baja were gray whales can easily be seen in their nursery lagoons. The others, of course, are near Guerrero Negro and San Ignacio. Access to the bay is easiest at Puerto Adolfo Lopez Mateos and at Puerto San Carlos, paved roads lead to both of them. The northern part of the bay is also an excellent kayaking and fishing location during months when access is not restricted due to the presence of the whales.

South of Bahía Magdalena are miles of Pacific Ocean beaches. Side roads lead from the highway, see *Backroad Adventures* below.

Ensenada de Aripes at La Paz doesn't have great beaches inside the protecting Peninsula el Mogote, but there are several good ones off the paved road that runs a few miles north to the ferry terminal at Pichilingue and beyond. They include Playas **Palmira**, **El Coromuel**, **Caimancito**, **El Tesoro**, **Pichilingue**, **Balandra** and **Tecolote**. Some are suitable for camping.

Southeast of La Paz Highway BCS 286 leads to **Bahía La Ventana**. There's a long sandy beach bordering the bay, this is a very popular windsurfing location. There are also campgrounds. See *La Ventana Side Trip* from La Paz below.

Fishing

The waters of the northern half of **Magdalena Bay**, north of Puerto San Carlos, are good small-boat fishing waters when the whales are not present. Small car-top aluminum boats and kayaks work well. These are mangrove waters and offer bass, pargo, and corvina. Launch sites for larger boats are not available, you will be launching over the sand. Waters outside Bahía Magdalena are difficult to reach and hazardous because of strong surf and sand bars at the bay entrances.

La Paz has a lot more to offer. At one time this was a top destination for big game fish and it continues to be pretty good although not as good as farther south. Charter cruisers and pangas are readily available in La Paz, the best season for billfish is May through October.

Small aluminum boat fishermen around La Paz will find few fish, there is just too much fishing activity near town. Try heading north on the **coastal road toward San Evaristo** or southeast to **Ensenada Los Muertos**, both are described in the *Backroad Adventures* section of this chapter.

Backroad Adventures

See the ***Backroad Driving*** section of ***Chapter 2 - Details, Details, Details*** for essential information about driving off the main highway on the Baja and for a definition of road types used below.

➤ **From Km 63 Between Loreto and Ciudad Constitución** - For a last visit to the Gulf of California before heading east you might try the road to **Agua Verde**. This small and isolated village sits on the shore of a bay and is a popular yachting destination. There are spots for primitive camping and the location is good for kayaking and sailboarding. The distance is 25 miles (40 km) on what has lately become a Type 3 road as the result of storm damage. Be prepared for a narrow road along cliffs as it descends to the coast.

➤ **From Km 0 at the Ciudad Insurgentes Junction** - At the 90-degree turn of

Mex 1 in Ciudad Insurgentes turn right and head north. Follow the paved road for 78 miles (126 km) to the oasis villages of **La Purísima** and **San Isidro**. Continue through these towns and take the right fork beyond on a Type 2 road that runs another 17.5 miles (28 km) to **San José Comondú** and neighboring **San Miguel Comondú**. These towns are small villages in verdant valleys, they are well worth the sightseeing trip. After passing through San Miguel Comondú you can follow another road 20 miles (33 km) back to the paved road north of Ciudad Insurgentes.

From Km 0 at the Ciudad Insurgentes Junction - At the 90-degree turn of Mex 1 in Ciudad Insurgentes turn right and head north. Follow the paved road for 68 miles (110 km) and then take the unpaved road left for 29 miles (47 km) to the coastal village of **San Juanico**. This unpaved road is usually a Type 2 road. A camping area with no hookups is next to the excellent beach. See the description of this trip and campground under *Side Trip to San Juanico* section below.

From Km 80 Between Ciudad Constitución and La Paz - A 10-mile (16 km) Type 2 road leads to the windswept coast at **El Conejo**. Punta Conejo is popular with surfers, it can also be good for experienced board-sailors and for surf fishing.

From Km 17 Between Ciudad Constitución and La Paz - This road leads up the coast from near La Paz. For the first 24 miles (39 km) to the mining town of **San Juan de la Costa** the road is paved. Just before reaching San Juan a fork leads right and a Type 2 road begins which leads another 34 miles (55 km) north to where the road becomes a rugged Type 3 road and continues another 16 miles (26 km) to **San Evaristo**. This is a very scenic road, there are a few places along it that are suitable for boondocking and the fishing offshore can be good.

From the Road to La Ventana - Follow the route described below from La Paz for the side trip to La Ventana. At mile 23 (km 37) do not take the left turn, continue instead straight on through San Juan de los Planes and then follow the highway as it takes a 90-degree left turn. The paved road leads on now almost all the way to **Ensenada los Muertos** at mile 30 (km 48), site of a real estate development. This bay has been renamed from Bay of the Dead to the more salable Bay of Dreams or Bahía de Sueños. From Ensenada Los Muertos pangas can take you fishing in winter and early spring out to Isla Cerralvo, about 8 miles out. There's a nice restaurant at the end of the road. Boondocking on the beach here is no longer possible.

THE ROUTES, TOWNS, AND CAMPGROUNDS

PUERTO ESCONDIDO TO CIUDAD CONSTITUCIÓN
72 Miles (116 Km), 2 Hours

Five miles south of the junction for Puerto Escondido the highway begins to climb up into the Sierra Giganta.

At about Km 63 the road to Bahía Agua Verde goes left. See *Backroad Adventures* in this chapter for more information about this road.

Once the climb is over the road enters Arroyo Huatamote which leads out onto the gently sloping Magdalena Plain. The road is relatively straight and easy to drive as it gradually descends into irrigated farming country. You'll pass the closed gas station at Ley Federal de Aguas Número Uno and come to the Ciudad Insurgentes intersection where the highway turns 90 degrees left to head for Ciudad Constitución. If you turn right here you have access to Puerto Lopez Mateos, La Purísima, San José Comondú, San Miguel Comondú, and San Juanico. See the *Backroad Adventures* section of this chapter for more information about these destinations.

About 15 miles (24 km) after making the turn you'll enter Ciudad Constitución and see a Pemex station on the right side of the highway.

CIUDAD CONSTITUCIÓN (SEE-OOH-**DAHD** KOHN-STIH-TOO-**SEE**-OHN)
Population 45,000

This burgeoning farm town isn't found in most tourist guides. It has little to offer tourists but RV travelers will find services they can use. It has RV parks, supermarkets and automobile dealerships. A new addition is a modern Ley supermarket. It's the first large supermarket you'll see south of Ensenada. Ciudad Constitución's location makes it a handy stop if you're headed north from beyond La Paz (only 130 easy miles (212 km) southeast) or need a base for whale watching in Bahía Magdalena to the west.

Ciudad Constitución Campgrounds

MANFRED'S RV TRAILER PARK

Address:	Km 213, Colonia Vargas, Cd. Constitución, B.C.S., México
Telephone:	(613) 132-1103
Website:	www.manfredsrvpark.com
Email:	npso@hotmail.com
Open:	All Year

GPS Location: N 25° 02' 54", W 111° 40' 49"

The new owners of Manfred's seem to be doing a great job. When we last visited the place looked great, and Manfred's 1,600 shrubs and trees were doing well too.

There are tents spaces as well as 30 large pull-thrus with 15-amp outlets, sewer, and water. Two spotless restroom buildings have hot showers. There is a spa and small swimming pool. There is internet access using the owner's computer or you can plug into their network.

The campground is very near the northwestern border of Ciudad Constitución and right on Mex 1 at about Km 212.

PALAPA 206 RV PARK

Address:	PO Box 186, Km 206, Ciudad Constitución, B.C.S.
Telephone:	(613) 132-3463
Email:	palapa206@prodigy.net.mx
Open:	All Year

GPS Location: N 24° 59' 59", W 111° 39' 33"

This new campground just outside Ciudad Constitución to the south is becoming a very popular stop for big RVs and caravans.

The campground has 24 pull-thru sites, suitable for any size RV. There's lots of maneuvering room. Twenty-three are full-hookup sites, 1 is water and electric only. Power is 20 amps. Restrooms have hot showers and English is spoken although with a British accent. The owner is very helpful and knows the area well.

The campground is on the west side of the highway near Km 206, that's about 1.4 miles (2.3 km) south of Ciudad Constitución.

CAMPESTRE LA PILA BALNEARIO AND TRAILER PARK

Address:	Apdo. 261, Ciudad Constitución, B.C.S., México
Telephone:	(613) 132-0582
Open:	All Year

GPS Location: N 25° 01' 04", W 111° 40' 39"

The La Pila is a balneario trailer park like El Palomar south of Ensenada. Winter travelers will probably not appreciate the pool quite as much as those passing this way during the really hot months.

There are 18 back-in spaces with 15-amp outlets and water. Sites are separated by relatively unkempt grassy areas and the camping area is a very large lot surrounded by palm trees. The nicely landscaped pool area next to the camping area has the bathrooms and there are hot water showers. There is a dump station.

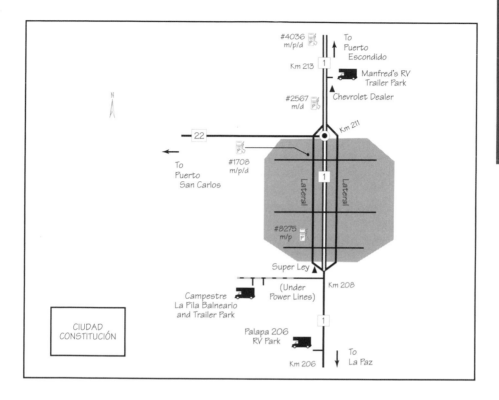

The turn-off from Mex 1 to the campground is near the south end of Ciudad Constitución at the point where the lateral streets begin. Turn west and follow the high tension electrical lines for .7 miles (1.1 km) and turn left into the campground at the sign. The campground is around to the left near the pools, the office in the red building on the right. There is plenty of room to maneuver.

SIDE TRIP TO SAN JUANICO
111 Miles (179 Km), 3 Hours

From Ciudad Constitución you can drive north on first paved roads and then a rocky, dusty desert road to the remote surfing and fishing village of San Juanico, known to surfers as Scorpion Bay. Only do this in a very small RV (a van or pickup camper) or a high clearance tow vehicle. First, drive north on Mex 1 for 14 miles (22.6 kilometers) to the intersection where Mex 1 goes 90 degrees right toward Loreto. Instead of turning go straight. You'll immediately pass through the town of Ciudad Insurgents and continue north on a paved road. This paved road goes all the way to La Purisima, a distance of about 71 miles (114 km). Instead of going all the way you only want to drive to the cutoff for San Juanico at Km 107 which is about 68 miles (110 km) from the junction with Mex 1 according to our odometer. Turn left following the signs for San Juanico, you'll find yourself on a Type 2 road. See the **Backroad Driving** section of **Chapter 2 - Details, Details, Details** for essential information about driving off the main highway on the Baja and for a definition of road types. From here the going is slow since the road is very rough, there are lateral roads alongside the main one that have been created by drivers trying to avoid the bumps on the main road. In 29.5 miles (47.6 km) you'll arrive in San Juanico. This dirt/gravel portion of the drive can easily take an hour and a half.

SAN JUANICO
Population 500

San Juanico is an isolated little fishing village that is growing as Norteamericanos buy land and build houses. It's particularly popular with the surfing set. There's not much here in the way of tourist facilities other than a couple of restaurants and a camping area. Of course there is the beach and the surf.

SCORPION BAY

Telephone:	(613) 138-2850
Website:	www.scorpionbay.net
Email:	ruben@scorpionbay.net
Open:	All Year

GPS Location: N 26° 14' 38", W 112° 28' 36"

The camping area here is simple but very convenient for surfers, you can park on the bluff and watch the action right out front.

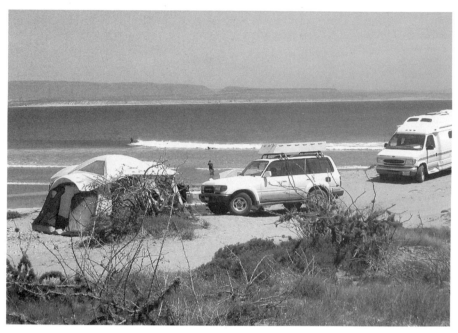

CAMPING ABOVE THE BEACH AT SCORPION BAY

Campers park pretty much where they like along several hundred yards of bluff area above a nice sandy beach and rocky headland. It can be tough to find a level spot. There are no hookups but there is a nice palapa restaurant/cantina as well as a modern recently built toilet and shower building, cold showers only.

To reach the campground after reaching town from the south just stay on the road above the bluff. The campground sits at the point northwest of town, you'll soon come to the entrance road which is well signed.

SIDE TRIP TO LOPEZ MATEOS
36.6 Miles (59 Km), 1 Hour

From Ciudad Constitución drive north on Mex 1 for 14 miles (22.6 kilometers) to the intersection where Mex 1 goes 90 degrees right toward Loreto. Drive straight on through Ciudad Insurgents for another 1.6 miles (2.6 km) to the cutoff where the paved road to Lopez Mateos goes left. Turn here and you'll arrive in Lopez Mateos in another 21 miles (34 km).

LOPEZ MATEOS
Population 2,000

This small but easy to reach fishing village has become one of the best places on the Baja to see gray whales. The whale-watching area is fairly restricted so there's a good concentration of whales and they're easy to find. The village has a nice embarcadero area where the pangas dock with lots of parking, a new restroom building, and several restaurants. To find it just follow the embarcadero signs through town. It's a little convoluted but this is a small town, the map will help.

Camping in Lopez Mateos

There are no formal campgrounds in this town but campers boondock in two different places. The first is the level parking areas at the panga docks along the water. The GPS Location is N 25° 11' 32", W 112° 07' 28". There is no security in this area, solo camping is not recommended.

The second area is at the fish processing plant. This is also the airport and there is a chain-link fenced area that the plant guards often let RVers use for overnight parking. You'll have to sweet talk them, a good test of your diplomatic skills – and your Spanish. The GPS location here is N 25° 11' 50", W 112° 07' 13".

SIDE TRIP TO PUERTO SAN CARLOS
34 Miles (55 Km), .75 Hour

The road out to San Carlos heads west from the middle of Ciudad Constitución. This is a fine two-lane paved highway running across the very flat coastal plain. You'll know you're getting close when you spot the big electrical generation plant.

PUERTO SAN CARLOS (PWER-TOW SAHN KAR-LOHS)
Population 5,000

This little town serves as one of the only two deep-water ports on the west coast of the Baja, the other is Ensenada far to the north. Puerto San Carlos' port is primarily used for exporting the farm products of the plain to the east, and also for offloading fuel for the big electrical plant that is located there, one of three on the Baja. Puerto San Carlos also provides access to Bahía Magdalena, one of the three gray-whale watching locations on the Baja. The cannery is the largest building in town, the smell of fish processing tends to be noticeable almost everywhere.

Bahía Magdalena's protected waters are a good place to use your small boat, the fishing is excellent. It's also good kayaking and windsurfing water. There is a concrete launch ramp in town. Gray whales are present from January to March and during this season boating is limited to certain areas and boating permits are required. Panga operators offer whale-watching tours.

Puerto San Carlos has only small stores but does have several restaurants. During whale-watching season there are actually quite a few tourists in town.

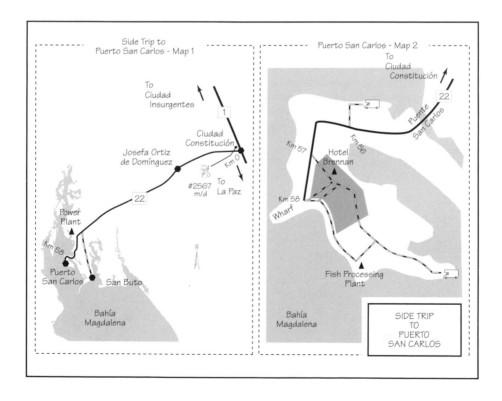

Camping in Puerto San Carlos

Two boondocking locations are commonly used by visitors to this town. These should only be used by two or more RVs, solo camping is not recommended. The best is near the beach used by the whale tour pangas. It has signs recommending it as an RV camping area. To get there follow the main road as it comes in to town and then continue on along the waterfront until you see the fish processing plant ahead. You have to turn inland here to get past the plant so turn left, go a block inland, and then right again. From here it's about 1.1 mile (1.8 km) to the parking area on the water. During the whale-watching season there are commonly several RVs parked here. The GPS location is N 24° 46' 45", W 112° 05' 46".

Another spot occasionally used is near the entrance to town. Near Km 56 as you come in to town turn right and follow the road to a small park area overlooking the estuary and power plant across the water. This is not as good for camping and is not recommended, it's reported to be a common teenage hangout area in the evenings. The GPS location is N 24° 48' 19", W 112° 06' 43".

CIUDAD CONSTITUCIÓN TO LA PAZ
130 Miles (210 Km), 3.75 Hours

The road south from Ciudad Constitución is flat and pretty much straight for 50 miles

(82 km). You'll soon pass through the roadside town of El Cien, so named because it is 100 kilometers from La Paz.

Fourteen miles (23 km) south of El Cien the road goes west for **Punta Conejo** which offers access to the coast. See this chapter's *Backroad Adventures* for more information about this road.

From El Cien the road crosses a region of hills and the highway is slower going, just exercise a little patience and soon you'll be in La Paz. As you finally begin to descend toward the coast you'll see La Paz ahead. Just before you reach the outlying town of El Centenario the road to **San Evaristo** goes left, this road is described in this chapter's *Backroad Adventures*.

LA PAZ (LAW **PAHS**)
Population 170,000

A favorite city on the Baja Peninsula, La Paz has lots of stores for supplies and a number of good campgrounds. Good, not fancy! This is not really a tourist town although it does have tourist amenities like hotels, good restaurants, beaches, and tour operators.

La Paz has been continuously occupied by Europeans only since 1811. Earlier settlement attempts, including one by Cortez in person, were not successful. The local Indians were not cooperative.

THE WHALE'S TALE-DOVE STATUE MARKS THE ENTRANCE TO LA PAZ

The city feels more like a larger mainland city than any other on the Baja. The waterfront **malecón** is good for strolling and you'll enjoy exploring the older part of town a few blocks back from the water. La Paz's best **beaches** are outside town toward and past Pichilingue and are virtually empty except on weekends. There's a simple museum, the **Museum of Anthropology**, covering the area's early inhabitants. Carnival is celebrated here. It is the week before Ash Wednesday, some time in late February or March. **Ferries** to the mainland cities of Topolobampo and Mazatlán dock at Pichilingue, see the *Ferries* section in the *Details, Details, Details* chapter.

La Paz Campgrounds

🚐 OASIS RV PARK

Address:	Km 15 Carr. Transp. al Norte, La Paz, B.C.S, México
Telephone:	(612) 124-6090
Open:	All Year

GPS Location: N 24° 06' 31", W 110° 25' 00"

This is a very small park located west of La Paz. It is in the small town of El Centenario and is located right on a beach. Unfortunately, the bay is very shallow here, the area out front is really mudflats during lower tides. This campground sustained quite a bit of hurricane damage recently and facilities are very limited, in fact the campground will probably close.

There are 24 back-in spaces, all with 15-amp outlets, sewer, and water. The rest-

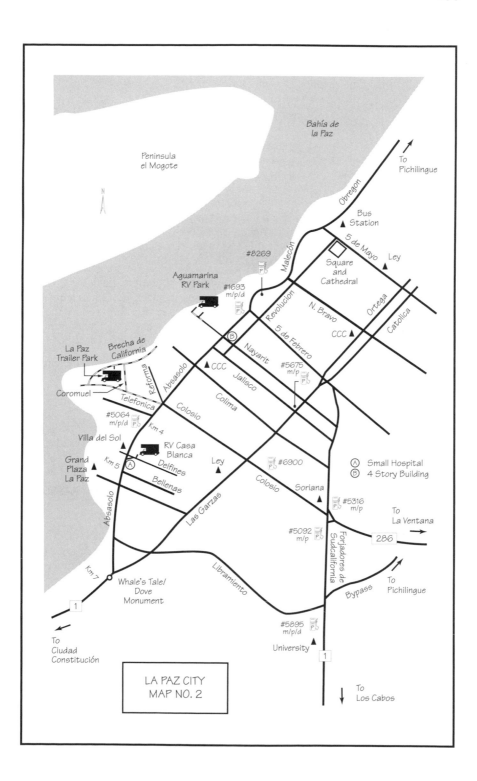

Bahía de
la Paz

Peninsula
el Mogote

To
Pichilingue

Obregon

Bus
Station

#8269

5 de Mayo

Ley

Malecón

Square
and
Cathedral

Aguamarina
RV Park

#1693
m/p/d

Revolución

N. Bravo

Ortega

Catolica

B

Nayarit

5 de Febrero

CCC

La Paz
Trailer Park

Brecha de
California

Jalisco

#5675
m/p

Reforma

Absasolo

CCC

Colima

Coromuel

Telefonica

Colosio

#5064
m/p/d

Km 4

Villa del Sol

RV Casa
Blanca

Ley

#6900

A   Small Hospital

Grand
Plaza
La Paz

Km 5

A

Delfines

Colosio

Soriana

B   4 Story Building

Bellenas

Absasolo

Las Garzas

#5316
m/p

To
La Ventana

#5092
m/p

Forjadores de Sudcalifornia

286

Km 7

Whale's Tale/
Dove
Monument

Libramiento

Bypass

To
Pichilingue

1

#5895
m/p/d

University

1

To
Ciudad
Constitución

LA PAZ CITY
MAP NO. 2

To
Los Cabos

rooms are old, they have tiled floors, white painted walls, and hot water showers.

The campground is on the water side of Mex 1 half way between the Km 14 and Km 15 markers. It is in the town of El Centenario which is just west of La Paz.

CAMPESTRE MARANATHA

Address:	Carr. Al Norte, Km 11, La Paz, B.C.S, México
Telephone and Fax:	(612) 124-6275, (360) 686-6103 (US)
Email:	maranatha@prodigy.net.mx
Open:	All Year

GPS Location: N 24° 05' 48", W 110° 23' 13"

Campestre Maranatha has been in La Paz for many years. It's a camp with facilities to host groups including rooms, a kitchen, restrooms with hot showers, a laundry, and a swimming pool. Now they've added RV sites, these are built for individual RV travelers and are available on a daily or monthly basis.

There are eight full-hookup RV sites large enough for 40 footers. Each has 20 and 30 amp outlets, water, and sewer hookups These are angled back-in sites in a quiet area with parking on dirt. More sites are planned. There's a coffee shop run by the same folks out front along the highway that offers Wi-Fi internet access. The monthly rate here is $320.

The campground is located just east of El Centenario. As you leave El Centenario headed east on Mex 1 watch for the El Exquisito coffee ship on your right, it's at about Km 11.3, turn south on the road to the west of the coffee shop, the camping area entrance is on the left in about 100 yards.

RV CASA BLANCA

Address:	Carret. Al Norte Km 4.5, Esq. Av. Pez Vela, Fracc. Fidepaz, CP 23090 La Paz, B.C.S., México
Telephone and Fax:	(612) 124-2477
Open:	All Year

GPS Location: N 24° 07' 51", W 110° 20' 31"

The Casa Blanca is quite nice, very tidy, easy to find, and usually has lots of room. This may not be true during caravan season since this is probably the most popular place in La Paz for them to stop, sometimes there are two in here at one time.

There are 43 slots with electricity, sewer, and water. Some sites have 50-amp outlets, others are 15 amp. One is a pull-thru, the others are all back-in spaces. The entire area is hard-packed sand and spaces are separated with low concrete curbs. The restrooms are plain but clean and have hot showers. The entire campground is surrounded by a high white concrete wall. There is a swimming pool, a decent tennis court, a palapa meeting/party room, and a coffee shop and internet café out front. The monthly rate here is $380.

The Casa Blanca is right off Abasolo, the entrance highway from the north. Zero your odometer at the dove statue (whale's tale) as you come into town. In about a mile slow down and watch carefully, you want to turn right into a street called Avenida Delfines at 1.2 miles (1.9 km) which is just after a small hospital and before a high white wall. It may have a large sign overhead for Frac. Fidepaz. Immediately after the turn make a left turn into the campground entrance. The coffee shop serves as the office.

🚐 AQUAMARINA RV PARK

Address:	Nayarit Street # 10, Apdo. 133, La Paz,
	B.C.S, México
Telephone:	(612) 122-3761
Fax:	(612) 125-6228
Open:	All Year

GPS Location: N 24° 09'00", W 110° 20'06"

We think this little campground is La Paz's nicest trailer park but you can make up your own mind. This is a well-kept park with flowering plants and lots of shade.

There are 19 back-in slots, all have 50 and 30-amp outlets, sewer, water, a patio and shade. RVs over 35 feet will find this campground a little cramped but will fit with careful driving. In the center of the park is a swimming pool and covered patio. Restrooms are well maintained and clean, they have hot water showers. The same owners have a dock in front of the campground (severely damaged by the 2003 hurricanes) where larger yachts formerly tied up. There is a coin-operated laundry in the building they use as an office for both operations. English is spoken and reservations are recommended. This is the La Paz campground most likely to fill up with individual RVs, it's too small for caravans. The monthly rate here is about $550.

The campground is located at the ocean end of Av. Nayarit, which is a paved street off Absolo as it comes into La Paz. If you zero your odometer at the dove statue (some people see a whale's tail instead) Nayarit goes to the left at 2.5 miles (4 km). There is a small trailer pictogram sign marking the street and a four-story building with balconies on the right opposite the turn. Follow Nayarit about .4 mile (.6 km), you'll see the gate on the right. If it is not unlocked just park in front of it and walk to the end of the road and through the gate to reach the office.

🚐 LA PAZ TRAILER PARK

Address:	Brecha California #1010, PO Box 482,
	La Paz, B.C.S., México
Telephone:	(612) 124-0830
Fax:	(612) 124-0837
Open:	All Year

GPS Location: N 24° 08'42", W 110° 20'29"

This large park is a little off the beaten path which is good, less road noise. Unless it is filled by a caravan you can usually find a place to camp here even without reservations. It's another popular caravan stop.

There are about 40 campsites, both pull-thru and back-in. They have 30-amp outlets, sewer, and water. The sites are completely paved over and the few palms provide little shade but there should be plenty of room for slide-outs. The restrooms are clean and modern and have hot showers. There is a swimming pool and coin-operated laundry. Reservations are accepted.

As you enter La Paz zero your odometer at the dove statue (whale's tail). At 1.7 miles (2.7 km) you'll Pemex #5064 on the left. Continue for another 0.1 mile (0.2 km) to a

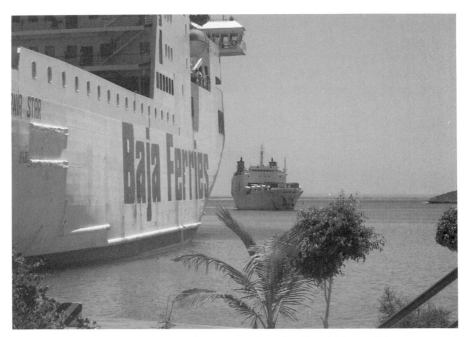

CATCH THE FERRY FROM PICHILINGUE TO MAINLAND MEXICO

stoplight. Turn left here onto a wide dirt road. Make sure that after the turn you bear slightly left, don't take the road that goes off to the right. Now carefully count the streets going right, in 0.3 mile (0.5 km) you want to take the sixth street right. It's not named. Drive three blocks, turn left and enter the park on the left near the end of the block. Don't worry, if you've counted those streets wrong you'll probably still find the campground.

PLAYA TECOLOTE

Open:　All Year

GPS Location: N 24° 20' 09", W 110° 18' 55"

This large open beach is a popular camping location for RVers. This can be an unpleasant windy location when a north wind is blowing as it often does in the winter but when it's not the camping is great. There is no security but normally there are many campers here, for most folks the main concern is theft of things left outside the RV overnight or while they're gone.

As you arrive at the beach you'll see that there are several restaurants ahead and to the left. They have primitive restrooms with cold showers. During the winter they're pretty quiet, only during Easter week and the summer do a lot of people visit the beach. Most campers park along the beach to the right. Watch for soft spots. We recommend that you walk the route first to make sure it's OK. Lots of people get stuck out here. To the left there's a large open area, so large you might think it's a runway. Caravans often park in this area and so do individual RVs.

There is a new bypass that makes it easy to reach the beaches east of La Paz without driving through town. When you arrive at the dove statue (whale's tail) at the entrance to La Paz follow signs for Cabo San Lucas. In 2.7 miles (4.3 km) they'll lead you to a T with a stoplight at Mex 1 south of town. If you went right here you'd be heading for Cabo, instead turn left. In .3 mile (.5 km) take the right turn signed for Pichilingue or Ruta de Camiones. After 12.4 miles (20 km) this bypass road intersects with the Pichilingue road. Turn right, you'll reach the ferry terminal in another 3.8 miles (6.1 km). Continue straight. In another 4.1 mile (6.6 km) the road forks, left is Balandra Bay, right is Tecolote, turn right. You'll reach Tecolote in another 0.9 miles (1.5 km).

BALANDRA BAY

Open: All Year

GPS Location: N 24° 19'20", W 110° 19'28"

Balandra Bay is more protected than Tecolote. That means that it's better when that north wind is blowing. It also means that there are many more biting insects here. Balandra is seldom used by campers but some do stay here. Occasionally the police ask campers to move on but this is unusual. There's lots of flat parking room in the lot. There is no security so we recommend that you do not stay here as a single tent or camping vehicle. The beach itself is pleasant, particularly if you walk around the point to the right. This is where the famous mushroom rock that you see in all the postcards is located. It was knocked over by vandals at one time but has been resurrected.

To reach Balandra Bay just follow the instructions given above for Tecolote, the Balandra Bay turnoff is mentioned in that write-up.

SIDE TRIP TO LA VENTANA
28 Miles (45 Km), .75 Hour

From La Paz you can follow a paved highway (BCS 286) southeast to the farming country in the vicinity of San Juan de los Planes. Just to the north along the coast of Bahía La Ventana is the town of La Ventana, a popular windsurfing destination. Two basic campground located in La Venana are discussed below.

From the boulevard called Calz. Forjadores de Sudcalifornia which is an extension of Mex 1 from the south in eastern La Paz follow the signs for Highway 286. The signs will say Los Planes. The two-lane paved highway climbs as it leaves town, it reaches a summit at 15 miles (24 km). Twenty-three miles (37 km) from La Paz you'll reach an intersection, turn left. This road is marked for La Ventana and El Sargento. You'll reach La Ventana in 5 miles (8 kilometers).

LA VENTANA (LAH VEHN-TAH-NAH)

This is a very small village stretched along the west shore of the bay. Actually, the towns of El Teso and El Sargento, both to the north, tend to merge together with La Ventana to form one town. Facilities in the towns are limited to a small store or two and a few restaurants.

SOUTH TO LA PAZ

PLAYAS MIRAMAR

Open: All Year

GPS Location: N 24° 03' 18", W 109° 59' 24"

This campground is very popular with windsurfers, in fact, that's why it is here. Winter is the season with reliable winds from the north. Expect to find few RVs, it is usually filled with tents and vans.

The campground is a large flat sandy area directly adjoining the beach. You can park not twenty feet from the water. If you watched for soft spots you could park pretty large RVs here since it's just a flat piece of ground. Facilities consist of a couple of toilet blocks with flush toilets and cold water showers. There are a few water faucets and also some scattered trees providing some shade. The entire area is fenced. There's a mini-super and a restaurant across the street.

From the intersection on Highway 286 23 miles (37 km) from La Paz that is marked

WINDSURFERS IN FRONT OF PLAYAS MIRAMAR

for La Vantana and El Sargento drive north for about five miles (8 km). You'll see the camping area and its chain-link fence on the right next to the beach.

YoYo's Campground
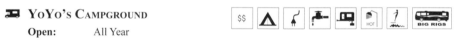

Open: All Year

GPS Location: N 24° 02' 44", W 109° 59' 19"

This campground, also located in La Ventana, is smaller than Playas Miramar, with more amenities, and equally popular with windsurfers. Parking is away from the water behind a building but there's good access to the beach.

There are about 20 parking sites here with low-amp electrical hookups and water available. There's also a dump site. A restroom building has flush toilets and hot showers. Management is very informal here, walk in and ask for the owner to make your arrangements.

This campground is located about 0.6 mile (1 km) south of Playas Mirimar. From the intersection on Highway 286 23 miles (37 km) from La Paz that is marked for La Ventana and El Sargento drive north for about 4.4 miles (7 km). The campground had no sign when we visited but you will probably see several campers parked on the right inside a chain-link fence.

To
Ciudad
Constitución

La Paz

San Antonio

La Paz
to
Los Barriles

La Paz
to
Todos Santos

Los Barriles

Los Barriles

La
Ribera

Cabo
Pulmo

Todos Santos

Todos Santos

Miraflores

Los
Frailes

Todos Santos
to
Cabo San Lucas

Santa
Rosa

San José
del Cabo

Los Barriles
to
San José
del Cabo

Cabo San Lucas

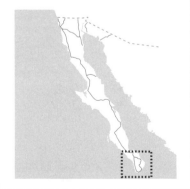

CHAPTER INDEX

Highlights .... Page 173
Roads and Fuel Availability .... Page 173
Sightseeing .... Page 174
Beaches and Water Sports ...... Page 174
Fishing .... Page 175
Backroad Adventures .... Page 175
La Paz to Todos Santos .... Page 176
Todos Santos .... Page 177
Todos Santos to Cabo
  San Lucas .... Page 178
La Paz to Los Barriles .... Page 180
Los Barriles .... Page 182
Los Barriles to San José
  del Cabo .... Page 185

SOUTHERN LOOP

Chapter Nine

Southern Loop

INTRODUCTION

This chapter of the book covers the area of the peninsula between La Paz and the Los Cabos area at the tip. The loop drive accesses both the west and east coasts, there are a good selection of destinations and activities.

Highlights

Todos Santos, near the west coast about half way between La Paz and the cape, has become something of an artist colony and day-trip destination for people who have flown in to Los Cabos. You'll find some good shopping and restaurants in the town.

Fishing fanatics congregate at **Los Barriles**. The combination of a decent campground and great fishing make this a place to stop or even base yourself for an extended stay. It's also a popular wind-surfing destination during the winter.

Cabo Pulmo and **Los Frailes** offer some of the best diving, beach fishing, and seaside boondocking on the whole peninsula.

Roads and Fuel Availability

South of La Paz there is a Y, you have a choice of traveling the west coast on Mex 19 or the eastern side of the peninsula on Mex 1. The Mex 19 route is a shorter and easier route to Los Cabos but the choice is yours, you'll probably drive the whole circle before you head back north.

The distance from La Paz to Cabo San Lucas via the western route is 99 miles (160 km). The kilometer markers on this highway, unlike all kilometers markers on Mex 1 in Baja Sur, run from north to south. They start with zero at the Y on Mex 1 at Km 185 and end with 124 in Cabo San Lucas.

The distance from La Paz to San José del Cabo in the Los Cabos area is 112 miles (181 km) via the eastern Mex 1 route. Mex 1 from La Paz to the Y 16 miles (26 km) south of town is being four-laned. Beyond that it's all two-lane blacktop except the last 6 miles (10 km) of 4-lane after you reach the main airport for the Los Cabos region just north of San José del Cabo. Kilometers on this section begin in Cabo San Lucas, they have reached 30 at San José del Cabo and 185 at the junction with Mex 19 south of La Paz and then 211 at La Paz.

There is a new bypass of the built-up area in San José del Cabo that runs inland from the airport around to a point near where Mex 1 reaches the ocean just west of San José del Cabo. It's a toll road and practically unused at this time, the traffic on the main road just isn't that bad yet. The bypass is a road ahead of it's time.

Driving south on Mex 19 you'll find gas as follows, with types, and distances between stations: **La Paz**, gas and diesel; **Todos Santos**, gas and diesel, 48 miles (77 km); **Cabo San Lucas**, gas and diesel, 45 miles (73 km).

Driving south on Mex 1 you'll find gas as follows, with types and distances between stations: **La Paz**, gas and diesel; **San Antonio**, gas only, 36 miles (58 km); **Los Barriles**, gas and diesel, 28 miles (45 km); **Miraflores**, gas and diesel, 23 miles (37 km); **Santa Rosa**, gas, 22 miles (35 km); **San José del Cabo**, gas and diesel, 2 miles (3 km).

Sightseeing

Don't miss **Todos Santos** for excellent shopping and restaurants.

As you drive between San José del Cabo and Los Barriles you'll see a monument in the form of a big ball along the side of the road. This marks the **Tropic of Cancer**.

On Mex 1 just south of Los Barriles at Km 85 take the spur road about a mile and a half (2 km) out to **Santiago**. Once the site of a mission the little town now has a zoo that is fun to visit. Follow signs through town to find it.

Beaches and Water Sports

There are excellent beaches for surfing along the west side of the peninsula. Access is probably easiest at the Los Cerritos Campground near Todos Santos.

The east coast of the peninsula north of Los Cabos is accessible by dirt road, see the *Backroad Adventures* section below. **Cabo Pulmo** is home to one of the very few coral reefs on the whole west coast of the Americas and an excellent diving spot. There's camping there as well as at nearby Los Frailes.

SEE THE ANIMALS IN THE SANTIAGO ZOO UP CLOSE

Fishing

Some of the best billfish fishing in the world is along the east coast of the peninsula. The reason is that deep water comes right close to shore. The fishing seasons are spring, summer and fall with May to July and October and November the best periods.

The area lacks formal ramps, La Paz and Cabo San Lucas are the closest. Boats are launched over the beach, there is a fairly sophisticated setup for launching boats at Los Barriles using trucks.

Probably the best charter fishing is available at Los Barriles. There are both pangas and cabin boats available, good fishing waters are nearby, and campgrounds are handy.

If you are restricted to fishing from the beach you might want to try Los Frailes. An underwater canyon comes so close to shore here that billfish have actually been caught from the beach!

Backroad Adventures

See the *Backroad Driving* section of *Chapter 2 - Details, Details, Details* for essential information about driving off the main highway on the Baja and for a definition of road type classifications used below.

From Los Barriles - A road goes north along the coast. If you zero your odometer at Martin Verdugo's RV Park and drive north you will reach the small community of **Punta Pescadero** after 9 miles (15 km) and **El Cardonal** after 14 miles (23 km). In El Cardonal the El Cardonal Resort offers RV parking. This is normally a Type 2 road as far as the resort. The road continues north from El Cardonal to connect with the back road to La Paz at San Juan de los Planes, but the road north of El Cardonal is normally a Type 3 road. Note that there is now a paved road running inland from Los Barriles directly to El Cardonal.

From Km 93 Between San José del Cabo and Los Barriles - This is one of the more interesting back roads on the whole peninsula. Also one of the most heavily traveled, at least at the northern and southern ends. It follows the **eastern coastline of the peninsula** near the cape from San José del Cabo all the way north to La Ribera near Los Barriles. The better portion of the road is in the north so we'll describe it from north to south. On Mex 1 at Km 93 a paved road goes east toward La Ribera. Seven miles (11 km) from the junction another paved road goes south. Zero your odometer here at the turn. This road is gradually being upgraded, in May of 2006 the pavement still ended at about 11 miles (17 km) from the turn. The road continues to **Cabo Pulmo** (17 miles (27 km) from the turn), **Los Frailes** (22 miles (35 km) from the turn), and south all the way to San José del Cabo (55 miles (89 km) from the turn). The northern part of the road to Cabo Pulmo is usually Type 1, then it becomes Type 3 in the middle section then improves to a Type 1 near San José del Cabo where it provides access for many impressive homes for miles along the coast. The condition of the central part of this road varies dramatically depending upon how much damage was done by erosion during the last rainy season and how much repair has been done. Many wide arroyos cross the road and there is a section along dirt cliffs that can easily erode making passage very difficult.

From Km 71 Between San José del Cabo and Los Barriles - This is a road that passes across the lower elevations of the southern portion of the **Sierra de la Laguna**. If you are in the Los Cabos region and feel the need to do some exploring in your 4WD this is a possibility. The road is a Type 2 at the eastern end but becomes a Type 3 as it descends to Mex 19 near Km 71.

THE ROUTES, TOWNS, AND CAMPGROUNDS

LA PAZ TO TODOS SANTOS
45 Miles (73 Km), 1.50 Hours

Head out of town toward the south on Mex 1. In 16 miles (26 km) you'll come to a Y. Mex 1 continues straight, Mex 19 cuts off to the right. To get to Todos Santos we'll go right.

The green vegetation that appears as you approach Todos Santos is welcome after crossing miles of dry country. You'll enter the outskirts of town 29 miles (47 km) after turning right at the Y.

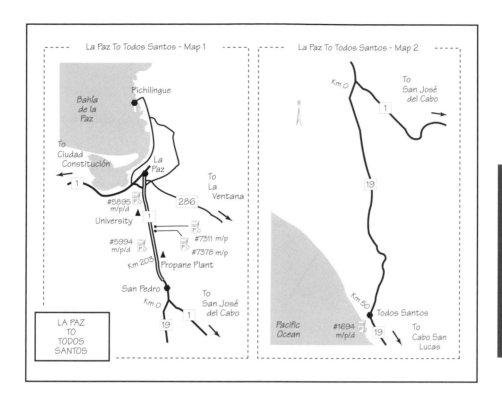

TODOS SANTOS (TOE-DOES SAHN-TOES)
Population 4,000

Todos Santos is the Baja's art colony. This is an old mission and sugar cane town but today it is better known for the many Norteamericanos who have arrived in search of a simple small-town ambiance. There are galleries, crafts stores, and restaurants, as well as a bookstore called El Tecolote. The town is only a mile or so from the coast, there are decent beaches near town but the one at the Los Cerritos park is one of the best in the area. You're just south of the Tropic of Cancer in Todos Santos, that means you're in the Tropics!

Todos Santos Campground

EL LITRO

Telephone: (612) 125-0121
Open: All Year

GPS Location: N 23° 26' 25", W 110° 13' 36"

This is a small campground on a dusty back road in the village of Todos Santos. The entrance road is a little tight but passable, once inside there's room for larger rigs to maneuver but not many come here. There's a definite small village Mexican ambiance to this campground.

SOUTHERN LOOP

The campground has 15 back-in spaces with 15-amp outlets, sewer, and water hook-ups. There are also a few small sites with only electrical hookups and shaded tent sites. Several of the spaces have patios, some are even shaded by palapas. Restrooms are simple but functional with flush toilets and hot water showers. Recently there's been an on-site manager.

To find the campground turn west on Carrillo near the southern entrance to Todos Santos. The turn is marked by a campground sign. The campground is directly ahead 0.2 miles (0.4 km) from the turn.

TODOS SANTOS TO CABO SAN LUCAS
45 Miles (73 Km), 1.25 Hours

Heading south from Todos Santos you'll find yourself much closer to the Pacific Ocean than you have been since San Quintín. Many small roads lead west to the beach. One that you'll see leads to a camping area, it's listed below. Seven miles (11 km) south of Todos Santos is the small farming town of El Pescadero. There's now a small campground here too.

As you get closer to Cabo the road turns inland. Before long you'll find yourself de-scending the last hill in to town. The main road doglegs to the left letting you bypass

THE ARTS TOWN OF TODO SANTOS HAS SOME OF BAJA'S BEST SHOPPING

SOUTHERN LOOP

the chaotic streets of this fast-growing town with you RV. All of the RV parks are accessible from Mex 1 to the east of town, see the following chapter for the details.

Todos Santos to Cabo San Lucas Campgrounds

BAJA SERENA

Address:	Carretera Transpeninsular, Col. Unica, CP 23300 Pescadero, B.C.S, México
Telephone and Fax:	(612) 130-3006
Email:	mayra_pithaya@yahoo.com.mx
Open:	All Year

GPS Location: N 23° 22' 05", W 110° 10' 26"

This campground has been here for two years. It's located in the small town of Pescadero, south of Todos Santos. It sits next to a small Mini Super, the Los Arcos, and is not on the beach.

There are 8 back-in sites. They are suitable for RVs to about 40 feet. Parking is on sand and small plants separate the sites. There are water and sewer hookups, but no electricity. Bathrooms are provided, they have nice bathrooms with hot water showers. The monthly rate is $120.

The Mini Super is easy to spot on the east side of the highway across from Pemex #7513, it's near Km 63. The campground has a good sign.

SOUTHERN LOOP

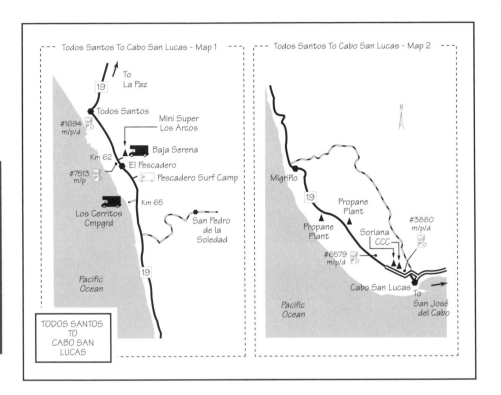

🚐 **LOS CERRITOS CAMPGROUND**

Open: All Year

GPS Location: N 23° 20' 51", W 110° 09' 42"

This is a beautiful beach, it has long been a very popular camping and surfing location. The land back from the sand is now being developed, apparently as house lots and camping is no longer allowed in the old government campground area. However, people are still camping in the front of that area along the beach. It's difficult to say how long this situation will last. Soft sand makes this best for RVs under 30 feet.

There are no facilities other than pit toilets. The road used to reach Los Cerritos leaves the highway near Km 65, about 6 miles (10 km) south of Todos Santos. It's a 1.2 mile (2 km) gravel road in to the beach.

LA PAZ TO LOS BARRILES
61 Miles (98 Km), 2 Hours

Heading south from La Paz you'll come to a Y in the road after 16 miles (26 km). The left fork is Mex 1, that's the one we'll take. Soon the road begins climbing into the northern reaches of the Sierra Laguna.

Two towns soon appear. **El Triunfo**, 13 miles (21 km) from the Y is an old gold and silver mining town. The tall smokestack marks the smelter. A few miles farther on is **San Antonio**, a farming town that fills a valley. There is a gravel road, usually a badly washboarded Type 1, that connects this town with San Juan de los Planes and La Ventana to the north.

Near Km 110 there is a paved cutoff to the left that leads to a coastal road and central Los Barriles.

La Paz to Los Barriles Campground

RANCHO VERDE RV HAVEN

Address:	PO Box 1050, Eureka, Montana 59917 (Reservations)
Telephone:	(406) 889-3030 (U.S.)
Website:	www.rancho-verde.com
Open:	All Year

GPS Location: N 23° 45' 46", W 109° 58' 46"

This is a campground located in the mountains west of Los Barriles. The green high wooded country is a nice change from flat desert and sandy seashore.

There are 29 widely separated back-in spaces. Each one has water and sewer hook-ups, there is no electricity. Most sites are large and can take big rigs, the entry road

SOUTHERN LOOP

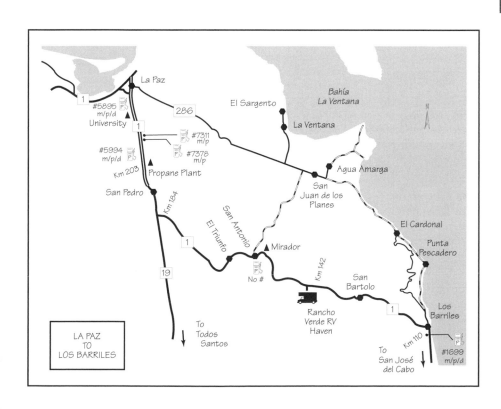

is somewhat tight so take a look, it's easy to walk the road from the highway where there's a pull-off. The restrooms are in a simple palapa roof building but are extremely clean and have hot water for showers. This is ranch country and there are miles of trails for hiking and bird-watching. Lots are for sale but you need not fear high pressure sales tactics. You may fall in love with the owner's open-air living area and RV shelter next to the campground.

Rancho Verde is located in the mountains about 20 miles (33 km) west of Los Barriles near San Bartolo. The entrance road is off Mex 1 near Km 142.

LOS BARRILES (LOES BAR-EEL-ACE)
Population 1,000

Los Barriles and nearby Buena Vista are enjoying a surge of RVer popularity as development overtakes the campgrounds farther south near Cabo. This is an excellent area for windsurfing. You'll find a number of restaurants, some small hotels, trailer parks, an airstrip, and a few shops in Los Barriles. Fishing is quite good because deep water is just offshore, campers keep their car-top boats on the beach. Trucks are used for launching larger boats, there is no ramp.

Los Barriles Campgrounds

MARTIN VERDUGO'S BEACH RESORT

Address:	Apdo 17, CP 23501 Los Barriles, B.C.S., México
Telephone:	(624) 141-0054
Website:	www.verdugosbeachresort.com
Email:	martinverdugo@prodigy.net.mx
Open:	All Year

GPS Location: N 23° 40' 56", W 109° 41' 56"

This old-timer is a very popular place. It's located on a beautiful beach although there are two large motel buildings between the camping area and the water. There is a swimming pool and a palapa bar overlooking the beach. The resort offers fishing expeditions on its own cruisers and room to keep your own small boat on the beach.

The campground has 65 RV spaces with 15 and 30-amp outlets, sewer, and water. You'll see RVs to 45 feet in here. There are also 25 tent spaces with water and electric hookups. Restrooms are clean and modern, they have hot water showers. There is a coin-operated laundry, a library in the office, a restaurant (breakfast only) atop one of the two hotel buildings, and of course the pool and palapa bar overlooking the beach. English is spoken and reservations are recommended. The monthly rate here is $375.

Take the Los Barriles exit from Mex 1 between La Paz and Cabo San Lucas near the Km 110 marker. You'll reach a T in .3 miles (.5 km). Turn left and you'll see the RV park on the right in .2 miles (.3 km).

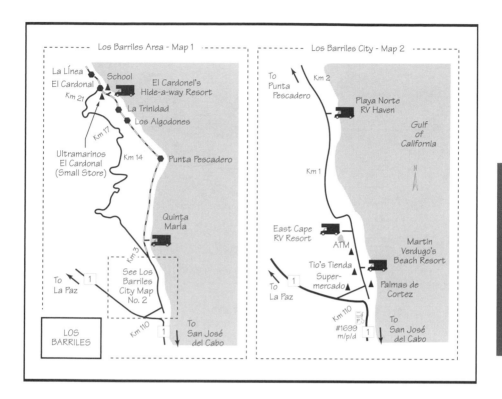

☞ EAST CAPE RV RESORT

Address:	PO Box 75, Los Barriles, B.C.S., México
Telephone:	(624) 141-0231, (208) 726-1955 (US)
Website:	www.eastcaperv.com
Email:	res@eastcaperv.com
Open:	All Year

GPS Location: N 23° 41' 11", W 109° 41' 56"

This is a new campground that has quickly become one of the most popular on the peninsula. It's the place to stay if you have a big rig since there's plenty of room and good 30-amp power.

This is a large campground with both back-in and pull-thru sites. There are about 60 sites. Palm trees provide shade and there are lots of shrubs and flowers. In fact, there are so many different kinds of plants here that a pamphlet has been written to help you identify them. The palapa-style restroom building has some of the nicest and cleanest facilities on the Baja and there are coin-operated washers and dryers. Wi-Fi is available throughout the park. A new spa and a nice swimming pool have just been added, and they're kept at a proper temperature. This is a well-managed park with lots of information provided about things to do in the area. From the park

THE EAST CAPE RV RESORT IS ONE OF BAJA'S NICEST RV PARKS

it's just a short walk for groceries and restaurants. It's also a short walk to the beach. The campground owners/managers operate two popular sport-fishing boats, it's easy to make arrangements for a fishing trip. The monthly rate here is about $405.

Take the Los Barriles exit from Mex 1 between La Paz and Cabo San Lucas near the Km 110 marker. You'll reach a T in .3 miles (.5 km). Turn left and you'll see the RV park on the left in 0.4 miles (0.6 km).

PLAYA NORTE RV HAVEN

Email:	wpaloblanco@comcast.net
Open:	All Year

GPS Location: N 23° 42' 05", W 109° 42' 04"

This campground occupies a large piece of land north of Los Barriles on a good beach. In past years it's been a popular wind-surfing campground with little in the way of facilities, but this is changing. RV slots in the front row are more expensive than those farther back, the rate above is for the back sites. The restrooms have flush toilets and hot showers. There's a dump station and electricity is being installed. The office is some distance away on the far side of the road, Wi-Fi and a telephone are available there.

Take the Los Barriles exit from Mex 1 between La Paz and Cabo San Lucas near the Km 110 marker. You'll reach a T in .3 miles (.5 km). Turn left and drive 1.8 miles (2.9 km), the campground entrance is on the right. There's a manager on-site during the busy winter season.

🚐 QUINTA MARÍA

Address: Km 5.5 Carr. Los Barriles-Cardonal, B.C.S.,
                  México
Telephone: (624) 142-8134
Email: quintamariabungalows@prodigy.net.mx
Open: All Year

GPS Location: N 23° 43'05", W 109° 42'30"

This is a small place with rental bungalows and a nice swimming pool. They have an open lot between the cabins and the ocean, it's a good out of the way place to park your RV and boondock. There are no hookups, but there's enough room for any size RV. Services provided by the Quinta María include the swimming pool and use of one of the rooms for showers. The bluff overlooking the ocean is a high one, but there's a ramp to reach the beach.

The camping area is north of Los Barriles. Take the Los Barriles exit from Mex 1 between La Paz and Cabo San Lucas near the Km 110 marker. You'll reach a T in .3 miles (.5 km). Turn left and drive 2.3 miles (3.7 km) to a Y. Go right. In another .7 mile (1.1 km) turn right into the access road to the Quinta María.

🚐 EL CARDONAL'S HIDE-A-WAY RESORT

Telephone: (612) 100-3382
Website: www.elcardonal.net
Email: info_by_owner@elcardonal.net
Open: All Year

GPS Location: N 23° 50'38", W 109° 44'47"

This is a small hotel and campground. A new paved highway makes it very accessible for any vehicle.

Located in the small village of El Cardonal this motel sits right on a beautiful beach. Camping is possible in a tent out front on the beach or in the formal camping area behind the main building. There are 3 full-hookup sites (30 or 15 amps) and 7 more with electricity only. A few sites will take RVs to 40 feet. Restrooms have flush toilets and hot showers, simple meals are available. The monthly rate is $312.

This campground is located in El Cardonal, north along the coast from Los Barriles. From Los Barriles drive north following the paved road. In 16 miles (26 km) you'll reach the village of El Cardonal. At the T turn right on the dirt road and drive .3 mile (.5 km). Just past the school you'll see the campground entrance on the left.

LOS BARRILES TO SAN JOSÉ DEL CABO
48 Miles (77 Km), 1.5 Hours

The road south from Los Barriles toward San José del Cabo does not follow the coast. To reach the coast you'll want to take the cutoff from Mex 1 to the left at Km 93. It leads northeastward to a small community on the coast known as **La Ribera**. In 6.8 miles (11 km), just before reaching La Ribera, take the road to the right. For more about the road see *Backroad Adventures* above. Two popular camping locations are along this beach road and they are described below.

Continuing south on Mex 1 you'll soon see a cutoff to the right near Km 85 for **San-**

tiago. It's a little over a mile off the road and has a Pemex, as well as a zoo. This was once a mission town but the mission is gone, now it's a ranching and farming town with a town square.

When you cross the **Tropic of Cancer** at latitude N 23° 27' near Km 81 you have entered the tropics. There's a monument in the shape of a globe, stop for a picture.

Miraflores, right from near Km 71, is known for its leather crafts, there's a Pemex on the highway.

The road turns to four lanes near the international airport at Km 44, about 6 miles (10 km) north of San José del Cabo. You're about to enter Baja's tourist zone. See the next chapter for details.

Los Barriles to San José del Cabo Campgrounds

⛺ CABO PULMO CAMPGROUND

Telephone: (612) 125-5583
Open: All Year

GPS Location: N 23° 26' 27", W 109° 25' 39"

The Cabo Pulmo area is known for it's diving. The coral reef here is one of the few on the west coast of the Americas. There are several dive shops in town, a couple of basic restaurants, and this very simple campground. There's a large fenced area next to the beach. In the rear near the road is sand, but parking for RVs overlooks the beach from a mound of gravel with some shrubs near the south end. Other than the mound of gravel the surface is flat, large RVs can maneuver and park but watch for soft spots. The beach here is mostly gravel but there is some sand near the water. There are few amenities. The owner's residence is across the road and up the hill, he advertises showers but their location is a mystery, perhaps at his house. He wasn't around when we visited.

To reach Cabo Pulmo turn east on the paved road near Km 93 south of Los Barriles. Follow the road for 6.8 miles (11 km) until just before La Ribera another paved road goes right. Turn to the right, you'll soon see a sign saying that Cabo Pulmo is 30 km. The road remains paved for only 10.7 miles (17.3 km) then turns to gravel. It's a road that's passable in any vehicle as far as Cabo Pulmo (and also Los Frailes, see below) but it's like driving on a washboard, very unpleasant in an RV. You'll see the campground on your left 5.9 miles (9.5 km) after the road turns to gravel.

⛺ LOS FRAILES

Open: All Year

GPS Location: N 23° 22' 45", W 109° 25' 55"

This remote campground is very popular with folks from the north, even in big RVs. Winter finds dozens of RVs parked in a large area on a gravel arroyo outwash near the beach. You'll find even the largest RVs here, care must be taken to avoid soft spots, there are lots of them. The surface changes each year after the storm season in the fall. The only amenity is a well where water can be drawn by bucket, don't drink it without treating it first. This would be a poor place to camp during storm season, you could get washed away.

Reaching the campground is a bit of a trial due to 10.9 miles (17.6 km) of gravel

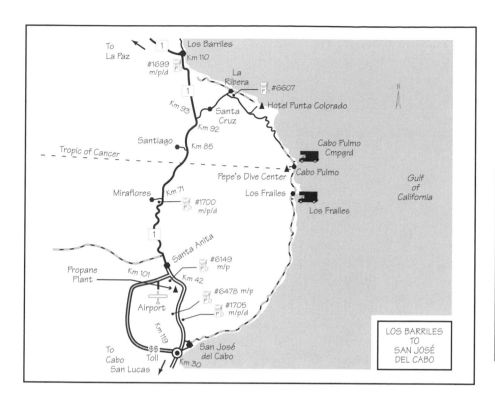

road which often has a washboard surface. From Mex 1 south of Los Barriles turn east on the paved road near Km 93. Follow the road for 6.8 miles (11 km) until just before La Ribera another paved road goes right. Turn to the right, you'll soon see a sign saying that Cabo Pulmo is 30 km. The road remains paved for only 10.7 miles (17.3 km) then turns to gravel. It's a road that's passable in any vehicle as far as Los Frailes. You'll reach the small community of Cabo Pulmo 5.9 miles (9.5 km) after the road turns to gravel, continue on through town. After another 5.0 miles (8.1 km) you'll come to the arroyo and see the RVs parked off to your left.

To
Los
Barriles

N

To
La Candelaria

To
Todos
Santos

19

Cabo San Lucas
to
San José del Cabo

San José
del Cabo

San José
del Cabo

1

Playa Costa Azul

1

Punta
Palmilla

Cabo San
Lucas

Playa Bahía Chileno

Bahía Santa María

1

Playa Barco Varado

Cabo
San
Lucas

Playa Medano

Playa del Amor

Playa Solmar

CHAPTER INDEX

Highlights . . . . Page 190
Roads and Fuel Availability . . . . Page 190
Sightseeing . . . . Page 190
Golf . . . . Page 191
Beaches and Water Sports . . . . Page 191
Fishing . . . . Page 192
Backroad Adventures . . . . Page 192
Cabo San Lucas . . . . Page 193
Cabo San Lucas to San José
  del Cabo . . . . Page 195
San José del Cabo . . . . Page 199

LOS CABOS

Chapter Ten

Los Cabos

INTRODUCTION

For many campers headed down the peninsula for the first time Los Cabos (The Capes) is the end of the rainbow, the ultimate destination. While Los Cabos is a world-class resort and very popular destination for tourists flying out from the U.S. and Canada you will probably find that you've seen a fine selection of much more desirable stops during your trip south. The truth is that Los Cabos is hectic and oriented toward folks looking for a few days of fun in the sun.

Many old-timers decry the growth and avoid Los Cabos at all costs. That reaction to the Los Cabos area is probably a little extreme. Los Cabos has lots to offer and a good number of decent RV parks provide excellent accommodations. The number of RV parks in the Los Cabos area seems to be declining, however, as land values increase.

The Los Cabos area really covers two major towns: Cabo San Lucas and San José del Cabo which is located about 20 miles (33 km) east. San José del Cabo is the older town and is more relaxed and comfortable. Cabo San Lucas, on the other hand, is chock full of hotels, restaurants, shops, and activity. The area between the two is known as the Cabo Corridor. Most campgrounds are located in the Cabo Corridor just to the east of Cabo San Lucas.

Highlights

Los Cabos is probably best known for its **deep-sea fishing**. This is one of the world's premier fly-in resort areas as well as a cruise ship port so it also offers lots of excellent **restaurants**, **shopping**, and **golf**. It's much different than the much quieter country to the north, if you judiciously indulge in the entertainment offerings you'll find the area to be a lot of fun.

Roads and Fuel Availability

The primary road on this section of the peninsula is the four-lane free highway between Cabo San Lucas and the Los Cabos International Airport which is located about six miles (10 km) north of San José del Cabo. The distance between Cabo San Lucas and San José del Cabo is 18 miles (29 km). The road is marked with kilometer posts, they start in Cabo San Lucas and have reached 30 by the time you reach San José del Cabo. This road was upgraded to four lanes less than ten years ago and when this was done the kilometer posts moved, some addresses along the road reflect the old numbers. Our directions to campgrounds use the new mileposts, the ones in place during May 2006.

Recently a new twist has been added. Along the western end of the corridor, from Km 2 to Km 10 there are now lateral roads on both sides of the main highway. They complicate access to several of the RV parks listed here since you must be on the laterals to turn. If you want to turn left you must also do it from a lateral, in other words, you must exit to the lateral, drive to a break in the curbs, and then cross four lanes of traffic. Traffic moves very fast along here so exercise caution.

Fuel is readily available in the area. There is a Pemex station near the intersection of the road that circles Cabo San Lucas and Mex 1. It has gas and diesel. There is another in the northern outskirts of Cabo San Lucas along Mex 19. Eastward along the Cabo Corridor toward San José del Cabo there is a Pemex station on the south side at Km 5 and another on the north side near Km 23. At the north side of San José del Cabo near the intersection with Calle Zaragoza there is a Pemex station and finally, about 2.2 miles (3.5 km) north in the suburb of Santa Rosa there is another on the east side of Mex 1. All of these stations sell both gas and diesel except the one near Km 23 which does not have diesel.

Sightseeing

Probably the most popular excursion from Cabo San Lucas is the boat ride out to see **Los Arcos** at **Finisterra** (Land's End), perhaps with a stop at **Playa del Amor** (Lover's Beach). This trip really does offer the chance for some spectacular photos. You may see sea lions on the rocks.

A popular stop for visitors is the **glass factory** in Cabo San Lucas.

San José del Cabo's **Boulevard Mijares** is a good place to do some shopping for Mexican folk art and souvenirs. It's much quieter than similar places in Cabo San Lucas, and just as good.

There are some spectacular **hotels** in Los Cabos. You might want to visit the **Hotel Presidente Inter-Continental Los Cabos** along the beach in San José del Cabo; **Hotel La Jolla** just west of the Brisa del Mar RV Park; **Hotel Palmilla** near Km 27 along the Cabo Corridor; the **Cabo Real** resort area including the Hotel Westin Regina, the Hotel Melia, and the Hotel Casa del Mar, all between Km 39 and Km 24 of the Cabo Corridor; **Hotel Cabo San Lucas** near Km 15 of the Cabo Corridor; **Hotel Twin Dolphin** near Km 11 of the Cabo Corridor; **Cabo del Sol** resort area near Km 10 of the Cabo Corridor (great views of Land's End); the **Hotel Finisterra** perched on the ridge west of the marina in Cabo San Lucas (the bar is good for whalewatching); or the **Hacienda Beach Resort** or **Melia San Lucas** along Playa El Medano looking out toward Land's End.

If you've been traveling the highway for several weeks you might find that the most interesting attraction in Cabo is its new Costco store. It's on the north side of the Cabo San Lucas to San José del Cabo highway near Km 4.

Golf

Los Cabos now has eight golf courses with more to come. Most of these are world-class, with prices to match. The most economical is the 9-hole Club de Golf **San José del Cabo** located between downtown San José del Cabo and the beach hotel strip. Others are the **Quercia Country Club**, **Palmilla Golf Course**, **Cabo Real Golf Course**, **Eldorado Golf Course**, **Cabo del Sol Golf Course**, **Cabo del Sol Desert Golf Course,** and the **Raven** at **Cabo San Lucas Country Club.**

Beaches and Water Sports

The best known beach in Los Cabos must be Playa del Amor (Lover's Beach). It is a small beach out on the Lands End cape that is hemmed in

PLAYA DEL AMOR

Roy Boorman

by rocks. Snorkeling is excellent here. Access is via water taxis and tour boats from the Cabo San Lucas harbor. Just offshore (to the east) is a 3,000-foot underwater canyon that is the most popular scuba location in the area, unique sandfalls down the underwater cliffs are the attraction.

The most populous swimming beach near Cabo San Lucas is called Playa Medano. It stretches east from the harbor mouth. The beach on the western side of Land's End is called Playa Solmar, the water is considered dangerous and access is difficult so the beach doesn't get much use.

Between Cabo San Lucas and San José del Cabo, along the Cabo Corridor, there are quite a few beaches although many are difficult to access because hotels, condos, and housing developments overlook them. Access routes of one kind or another are usually available since under the law access can not be cut off. Easiest access is to Playa Barco Varado (Shipwreck Beach) near Km 9, Bahía Santa María near Km 13, and Playa Bahía Chileno near Km 15.

The Playa Costa Azul is a long beautiful beach stretching from the lagoon at San José del Cabo westward for several miles. The Brisa del Mar RV Park is located on this beach.

A popular scuba diving spot offshore (also a popular fishing spot) is the Gorda Banks with a depth of 110 feet. The location has lots of fish, sometimes whales, and also black coral.

Fishing

Fishing for large game fish is the thing to do in Los Cabos. The possible catch includes marlin, sailfish, dorado, and tuna. The months for the best fishing are May to July and October to December. Catch-and-release fishing is popular here, no one wants to see the fishing decline as it inevitably would if everyone kept all the fish caught. It is easy to arrange charter fishing trips in cruisers or pangas.

Backroad Adventures

See the *Backroad Driving* section of *Chapter 2 - Details, Details, Details* for essential information about driving off the main highway on the Baja and for a definition of road types used below.

From Km 1.7 of the Cabo San Lucas Ring Road - The small village of **La Candelaria**, located in the foothills of the Sierra Laguna north of Cabo is becoming a popular destination for tours from Cabo. The town is known for its handicrafts (pottery, baskets, and simple furniture) and for its "white magic" witches, actually traditional curanderos or healers with a knowledge of local herbs. You can drive there yourself from a turnoff on the road that runs around the east side of Cabo San Lucas some 1.1 miles (1.7 km) north of its intersection with Mex 1. This road (normally a Type 2) leads about 25 miles (40 km) north to the village. From there a rough normally Type 3 road leads on to Mex 19 north of Cabo.

From very near the central shopping district in San José del Cabo - A dirt road goes east to the beachside village of La Playa. The road continues beyond and leads all the way up the coast to **Los Frailes**, **Cabo Pulmo**, and **La Ribera**. It is described in more detail in the previous chapter under *Backroad Adventures*. This is usually a Type 1 road at both ends but Type 3 in the middle section.

THE ROUTES, TOWNS, AND CAMPGROUNDS

CABO SAN LUCAS (KAH-BOW SAHN LOO-KAHS)
Population 25,000

Cabo San Lucas is the major resort town in the Los Cabos area. It is filled with fly-in visitors and often also with cruise ship passengers wandering the streets during their short visits.

The town is centered around the **harbor**. The harbor itself is surrounded by modern hotels and shops, they almost cut it off from the streets of town which stretch off to the north. These streets become less touristy and more Mexican as you progress northward, there is a large population here attracted in recent years by the tourism industry.

In the harbor area you can arrange for a boat trip. Many people come to Los Cabos primarily for the fishing and this is where most of the charter boats are based. You can also find water taxis or tour boats to take you out to see **Finisterra (Lands End)** or visit **Playa Amor (Lover's Beach)**. There's always a lot of activity in the harbor and you can stroll along taking it in.

Roy Boorman

FINISTERRA - THE TIP OF LOS CABOS

LOS CABOS

A. Marina
B. Hotel Finisterra
C. Plaza las Glorias
D. Plaza Aramburo
E. Restaurant and Shopping Area
F. Sightseeing Boats
G. Town Square/Zocalo
H. Playa del Amor
I. Los Arcos
J. Hacienda Beach Resort
K. Melia San Lucas
L. Glass Factory
M. Faro Viejo Trailer Park

In the streets immediately north of the harbor you'll find most of the **restaurants and tourist-oriented shops** in town. This is actually a pretty good place to shop for Mexican gifts and art. There are also some small supermarkets in the area.

The closest beach to Cabo San Lucas is **Playa Medano**. It is on the far side of the harbor. Driving access is actually best from Mex 1 near the point where Mex 19 joins it just east of town.

Cabo recently acquired several large stores making it just as good a place to re-supply as La Paz. North of town there are a large Soriana and a big CCC. Along the Cabo Corridor, at about Km 4 on the north side of the highway is a Costco.

Cabo San Lucas Campground

CLUB CABO MOTEL AND CAMP RESORT

Address:	Apdo. 463, Cabo San Lucas, B.C.S, México
Telephone and Fax:	(624) 143-3348
Website	www.clubcaboinn.com
Email:	clubcaboinn@hotmail.com
Open:	All Year

GPS Location: N 22° 54' 00", W 109° 53' 41"

This campground is different than the others in Cabo. It somehow seems more European than Mexican. It is a combination motel and campground and is slightly off the beaten track.

There are 10 campsites, most have 15-amp outlets, sewer, and water. These are all back-in sites. There isn't room for really big RVs, 24 feet is about the maximum length motorhome that can easily enter and park. This is definitely the best tent campground in the area. The bathroom and shower building has a flush toilet and good hot shower. There is a very nice pool and spa, there is an extra charge for their use. Laundry service is available and so is breakfast. A shaded outdoor lounge area has a color TV, barbecue, and kitchen clean-up station. It takes about 7 minutes to walk to the beach from here. English is spoken and reservations are recommended.

The Club Cabo is located right behind the Vagabundos campground. To get to it you must take a roundabout route. Start from Mex 1 about two miles (3 km) east of downtown Cabo San Lucas where Mex 19 and Mex 1 intersect. Go south from this intersection for 0.3 miles (0.5 km) until it dead-ends. Turn left and drive 0.2 miles (0.3 km) to a Y, the Villa de Palmas is right, go straight for Club Cabo. You are now on a small dusty road, in 0.6 mile (1 km) you'll see the Club Cabo on the left.

CABO SAN LUCAS TO SAN JOSÉ DEL CABO
20 Miles (32 Km), 0.5 Hour

Mex 1 starts in Cabo San Lucas so kilometer markers count up as you drive eastward and then turn north in San José del Cabo. The area between the two towns is known as the "Cabo Corridor" or simply as "The Corridor". From Cabo San Lucas all the way to the Los Cabos International Airport north of San José del Cabo the highway is four lanes wide and heavily traveled.

Three of the campgrounds in this section are located near the western end of the Cabo Corridor. Vagabundos del Mar is near Km 3 on the south side of the road, El Arco is near Km 5 on the north side of the road, and Villa Serena is near Km 7 on the south side of the road.

As the highway approaches San José del Cabo you'll see the Brisa del Mar RV park on the right side of the highway near Km 30, then it turns north to pass just west of central San José del Cabo. There are several stop lights along this section of the highway. You can turn right along Paseo San José if you are in a tow car or small RV to reach the shopping district south of the central plaza.

Frequent busses run both ways along the Cabo Corridor. They are inexpensive and convenient, and they are the best way to visit the central area of either Cabo San Lucas or San José del Cabo. During the high season it can be difficult to find convenient parking in either of these towns.

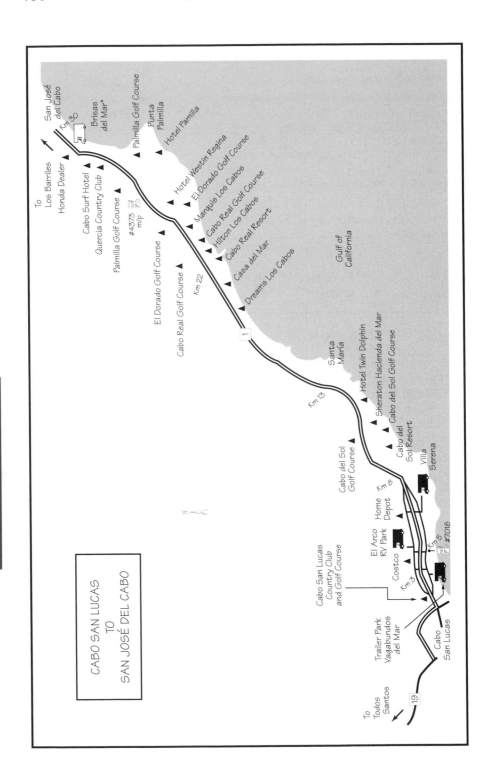

CABO SAN LUCAS
TO
SAN JOSÉ DEL CABO

Cabo San Lucas to San José del Cabo Campgrounds

TRAILER PARK VAGABUNDOS DEL MAR

Address:	Apdo. 197, Cabo San Lucas, B.C.S., México
Telephone:	(624) 143-0290 (Mex), 800 474-Baja or
	(707) 374-5511 (US)
Fax:	(624) 143-0511
Website:	www.vagabundosrv.com
Email:	reserve@vagabundosrv.com
Open:	All Year

GPS Location: N 22° 54'03", W 109° 53'46"

The Vagabundos park probably has the nicest facilities in Cabo. However, it has no view and is not on the beach. It is more convenient to town than most other parks.

There are 85 spaces with 15 or 30-amp outlets, sewer, water, and patios. Many are filled with permanently-located RVs, mostly in the sites along the outside of the park. The roads are paved and the parking spaces are gravel. The restrooms are clean and modern and have hot water showers. There's a swimming pool with a palapa bar and restaurant, a laundry, vehicle washing facilities, a computer for internet access, and free Wi-Fi that can be received by units parked near the office. The bus running from Cabo San Lucas to San José del Cabo stops right out front. English is spoken and reservations are recommended. The monthly rate here is $440.

The campground is right at the Km 3 marker on Mex 1 east of Cabo San Lucas. It is on the south side of the road. Access is from a lateral in this section so be sure to get

A COMFORTABLE RV SITE AT VAGABUNDOS DEL MAR

LOS CABOS

into the lateral as soon as possible eastbound. Westbound traffic will have to travel farther west and find a place to reverse direction.

EL ARCO RV PARK

Address: Km 5.5, Carr. a San Jose del Cabo, Cabo San Lucas,
                 B.C.S., México
Open: All Year

GPS Location: N 22° 54'19", W 109° 52'30"

This is a large park located on a hillside overlooking Cabo San Lucas. The place has been undergoing an ownership or management crisis of some kind for several years. The old office and lounge area were severely damaged years ago and no repairs have been made so when you pull in you'll think the place is abandoned. It's not. Some folks still stay here and workers do show up for a few hours most days. Restrooms are relatively clean, sometimes there is no water, often it is hard to find someone to pay. There's no telling how much longer this park will be around so don't be surprised if you find the gates locked.

There are 90 camping slots, all have 15-amp outlets, sewer, water, and patios. They are arranged around a semi-circular brick driveway or in an area farther up the hill. The upper slots are long and can take any size RV. They are all back-ins.

The campground is located just east of Cabo San Lucas with the entrance road on the north side of Mex 1 at Km 5.2. There is a lateral here so be sure to get into the lateral well before Km 5 if you are westbound. Eastbound traffic will have to enter an eastbound lateral and cross four lanes of traffic to reverse direction onto the westbound lateral. Lots of traffic will be doing this as they head for the Home Depot.

VILLA SERENA

Address: Km 7.5 Carretera Transpeninsular Benito Juárez,
                 CP 23410 Cabo San Lucas, B.C.S., México
Telephone: (624) 145-8165 or (624) 143-1888 or
                 in USA (800) 932-5599
Fax: (408) 778-1513
Website: www.grupobahia.com
Email: grupobahia@aol.com
Open: All Year

GPS Location: N 22° 54'22", W 109° 51'48"

This is a newer campground with lots of room for big RVs. The facilities are good but there is no shade. Some trees have been planted but it will take them a while to grow to the point where they are of some use. The campground sits near the highway which is far from the water at this location. Some of the upper sites have a water view. This has become the most popular campground in the area for caravans.

The campground has 53 very large back-in spaces. Each has electricity, sewer, and water hookups. The outlets are the small 15-amp variety although the breakers are 40 amp. There's a new and very nice facilities building with restrooms with flush toilets and hot showers, a self-service laundry with good washers and dryers, and a lounge area. There's also a spa on the roof. Nearby is the Restaurant Bar Villa Serena, a nice place with a swimming pool that you can use if you don't mind being the center of attention. The monthly rate is $392.

FISHING FROM THE SHORE AT SUNRISE

Los Cabos

The entrance road goes south from near the Km 7 marker between Cabo San Lucas and San José del Cabo. It's just opposite the Home Depot. There is a lateral here so eastbound traffic will need to get onto the lateral before reaching the campground entrance. If you are westbound you will have to enter a westbound lateral and cross four lanes of traffic to reverse direction onto the eastbound lateral.

San José del Cabo (Sahn ho-SAY dell KAH-boh)
Population 25,000

San José is the older of the two Los Cabos towns. A Jesuit mission was founded here in 1730 but the estuary to the east had been used by ships as a watering stop far before that. Today San José is the center of business and government for the cape area.

We find the streets of San José much more pleasant to wander than those of Cabo San Lucas. Boulevard Mijares running south from the plaza is the center of the action for Norteamericanos, there are many restaurants and shops along it. If you walk westward on the streets between the plaza and Mex 1 you'll find a much more authentic Mexican town, and it has been around longer than Cabo San Lucas so it has more character.

South of the downtown area is a golf course built by FONATUR when the Los Cabos scheme was just getting off the ground. South of that are the hotels along Playa Costa Azul. East of town is the Estero San José, a swampy lagoon with a walking path along the western border. You can follow a road across the northern border of the estero to reach the small village of La Playa. On the beach in front of this little place you'll find lots of pangas available for charter, San José doesn't have a marina, this is the substitute.

It's always tough to get RV supplies or to have RV systems work done on RVs in Mexico. San José has a place: Wahoo R.V. Center (Calle Misión de Mulegé #166, Col. Chula Vista, San José del Cabo. BCS, (624) 142-3792; 1wahoorv@prodigy.net. mx). They specialize in gas refrigeration problems, gas heaters and toilets. They also carry an inventory of RV supplies. Give them a call for detailed driving instructions, they speak English.

San José del Cabo Campgrounds

BRISA DEL MAR RV RESORT

Address:	Apdo. 45, CP 23400 San José del Cabo B.C.S., México
Telephone:	(624) 142-3999
Open:	All Year

GPS Location: N 23° 02' 14", W 109° 42' 29"

CAMPING ON THE BEACH AT BRISA DEL MAR

The Brisa del Mar is the only beachfront campground left in the Cape region. This is a large popular campground with decent facilities, it is much closer to San José del Cabo than to Cabo San Lucas. The beach is very nice. The rumors have this park closing soon, but they've said the same thing for several years now.

This is a large campground, the sites along the beach are pull-in or back-in, the others are mostly pull-thrus. Most sites are full hookups with 30-amp outlets. The sites back from the beach also have patios and some shade. Restrooms are OK but not outstanding, they have hot water showers. There is a very nice bar and restaurant, a pool, and a laundry. There are also some game areas and equipment rentals as well as a small store. English is spoken and reservations are accepted and strongly advised during the winter. The price ranges above are for high season which is from December 1 to February 28, low season prices are about $5 per day lower. The Cabo San Lucas to San José del Cabo bus stops right out front.

You'll see the campground just south of Mex 1 between the Km 29 and Km 30 markers just west of San José del Cabo. Access heading east is easy, just turn in. If you are heading west on this divided highway you'll have to go another 1.8 miles west (2.9 km) to an off ramp and overpass just beyond Puente Arroyo Seco and come back to get into the park. Don't try to use the earlier off-ramp and underpass, you probably won't fit under the highway.

Tijuana
Tecate
Mexicali
2D
Mexicali
2D
1D
San
Luis Río
Colorado
USA
2
MEXICO
3
Cañon
Guadalupe
Ensenada
Santo
Tomás
3
Golfo de
Santa Clara
5
Mexicali
to
San Felipe
Punta Colonet
1
San Felipe
Cañon
del Diablo
San Felipe
Vicente Guerrero
Laguna
Percebú
San Quintín
Puertecitos
El Rosario

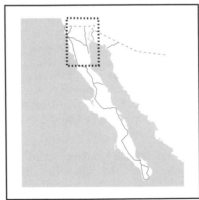

CHAPTER INDEX

Highlights . . . . Page 203
Roads and Fuel Availability . . . . Page 203
Beaches and Water Sports . . . . Page 204
Fishing . . . . Page 204
Backroad Adventures . . . . Page 204
Mexicali . . . . Page 205
Mexicali to San Felipe . . . . Page 206
San Felipe . . . . Page 209

SAN FELIPE

Chapter Eleven

San Felipe

INTRODUCTION

Many folks think San Felipe offers a better combination of easily accessible sand, sun, and laid-back Mexican ambiance than any destination close to the border. It's an excellent choice for your first camping trip into Mexico. A word or warning though. The big-rig RV parks in San Felipe have been closing and new big-rig parks haven't appeared yet so if good hookups and big spaces are what you are looking for, you'll like Puerto Peñasco better.

Highlights

The **drive south to San Felipe** across the driest of Baja's deserts is an experience itself. If you've not been in to Mexico before you'll probably have the chance to experience your first **army checkpoint**, there's usually at least one along this road.

Once you reach San Felipe the prime attraction is beautiful sandy beaches, lots of good places to park your RV, and a friendly little town to enjoy.

Roads and Fuel Availability

The road south from Mexicali to San Felipe is paved all the way. Kilometer markers count up as you drive south. The highway starts as four lanes and then, about 24 miles (39 km) south of Mexicali, narrows to two. It is generally in fine condition and you can easily maintain the speeds shown on the speed-limit signs, usually 80 kph. The distance to San Felipe is 122 miles (197 km).

There are lots of Pemex stations in Mexicali offering both gas and diesel. Between Mexicali and San Felipe, at least once you pass Km 31, there are no Pemexes until you reach San Felipe. In San Felipe there are four Pemexes, not all sell diesel. In the past diesel has also been available at the marina.

Beaches and Water Sports

San Felipe's malecón (waterfront promenade) borders **Playa San Felipe**. Like other beaches in the north end of the Gulf of California when the tide goes out here it *really* goes out. Locals use pickups and special trailers to launch and retrieve their pangas across the wide hard-packed sand flats. When the tide is in, however, this is a great beach.

North of San Felipe is **Playa Las Almejas** (Clam Beach). It's eight miles long and starts about 5 miles (8 km) north of town. Many of the boondocking campgrounds are on this beach.

For many miles south of San Felipe there is a wide sandy beach. Many of the camp-grounds and camps listed here are along this beach.

Another beach south of town is **Laguna Percebú**. It's a great place to collect sand dollars. The beach is located about 18 miles (29 km) south of town and has a small restaurant. Watch for the sign pointing left from the road to Puertecitos.

Fishing

Fishing is not nearly as good here as it once was. Over fishing, much of it by big commercial boats, decimated fishing in the northern gulf during the late sixties. Things have recovered somewhat, charter pangas are available.

Backroad Adventures

See the *Backroad Driving* section of *Chapter 2 - Details, Details, Details* for essential information about driving off the main highways on the Baja and for a definition of road type classifications used below.

The back country around San Felipe is extremely popular with folks who have dune buggies and other vehicles capable of traveling across soft sand. If you have a high-flotation vehicle you'll have a great time following the many tracks in the area. It is best to stay on established tracks to minimize damage to the desert and your tires.

From Km 178 Between San Felipe and Mexicali - One possibility is the road to the **Cañon del Diablo**. Access is via the road that heads for the Sierra San Pedro Mártir past the old El Cachanilla RV Park. This road goes out past the El Dorado home sites and then continues across the dry lakebed of the Laguna Diablo and then right up to the mountains. The canyon is green and has water, an oasis of sorts. It is possible to park and hike up into the Sierra from here. This is real backroad explora-tion on a Type 3 road, take all the precautions we recommend in the *Backroad Driv-ing* section of *Details, Details, Details* and discuss your plans with someone with good local knowledge before attempting this drive.

From San Felipe - The road to **Puertecitos** leads 47 miles (76 km) south from

San Felipe. At one time this road was paved, now the pavement is sometimes so broken up that a dirt road would be faster. Consider it a Type 2 road. In Puertecitos there is a hot springs at the tide line on the outer side of the peninsula. There is sometimes a fee for use. Puertecitos has a launching ramp useable at high water and fishing is better than in San Felipe. A Type 2 road continues south from Puertecitos along the coast to **Ensenada San Francisquito** and then inland to meet Mex 1 south of Cataviña after 81 miles (131 km). The government says that some day this route will be paved so that it will be a second major access route leading south.

From Km 28 on Mex 2D West of Mexicali - While not strictly in the San Felipe area **Cañon Guadalupe** is a popular camping destination also near Mexicali. Access to the canyon and the campground there requires driving a Type 2 road with soft sandy spots 35 miles (56 km) south across the desert to the campground. Once there you will find no hookups but campsites have tubs with hot water fed by springs. You should make reservations, get directions, and check road conditions by calling (949) 673-2670. There is also a website: www.guadalupe-canyon.com.

THE ROUTES, TOWNS, AND CAMPGROUNDS

MEXICALI (MECK-SEE-KAL-EE)
Population 800,000

This large border city is the capital of Baja California. The big business here is farming, the Colorado river irrigates thousands of surrounding acres where produce is grown, primarily for markets north of the border. Mexicali is a sprawling low-rise town. There are two border crossings, one at the center of town and another about 7 miles to the east. Neither crossing is usually particularly busy but the one east of town is much easier.

Most RVers probably think of Mexicali as a barrier to get around rather than as a place to stop. On the outskirts of town you'll find some of the large Mexican supermarkets, if you didn't stock up north of the border these offer a much better selection than anything in San Felipe. There's even a Costco. There are also lots of Pemex stations. See our route log from the east border crossing outlined below, it passes near several of these stores.

Mexicali Campground

DESERT TRAILS RV PARK AND GOLF COURSE

Address:	225 Wake Avenue, El Centro, CA 92243
Telephone:	(760) 352-7275
Fax:	(760) 352-7474
Website:	www.deserttrailsrv.com
Email:	deserttrails@hotmail.com
Open:	All Year

GPS Location: N 32° 46' 13", W 115° 32' 50"

This campground is really in the U.S. In fact, it's a good 10 miles north of the border on the southern edge of El Centro. Still, it's a great place to park the night before heading south.

SAN FELIPE

This is a big campground that is full of snowbird RVers. It's built around a nine-hole golf course and has amenities which include a good pool and a spa. While there are hundreds of nice sites, if you're only staying for a night or two you are most likely to be parked in their gravel lot near the swimming pool. it's very handy with good access to restrooms and the pool area. There are 30-amp electrical and water hookups and a dump station.

You'll find the Desert Trails just south of Interstate 8 on Highway 86. From Interstate 8 take the exit for Highway 86, go south one block, then turn left and you'll soon see the campground entrance on your right.

MEXICALI TO SAN FELIPE
126 Miles (203.2 Km) along route detailed below, 4 Hours
(including border crossing)

Most RVers cross at the eastern border crossing because it's less congested and easier. Here are the directions you'll need to head south on Mex 5.

The crossing is about 7 miles east of Calexico, Mexicali's alter ego on the north side of the border. If you are approaching from the north on Highway 111 you'll want to head east on the northern outskirts of Calexico on Highway 98. The way to the border crossing is well signed, the turn to the south from Highway 98 is 7.2 miles (11.6 km) east of Highway 111. You turn south on Highway 7. Follow the signs for the car crossing, not the truck crossing. In 1.6 mile (2.6 km) you'll pass the U.S. border station and a short distance later arrive at the Mexican station.

Zero your odometer as you pass through the Mexican crossing. In 0.3 mile (0.5 km) the road comes to a T. Turn right here and you will be on a four-lane divided highway. At 2.2 miles (3.5 km) you'll reach a traffic circle or glorieta with an artistic monument in the middle, turn left here onto Morin. At 2.9 miles (4.7 km) you'll pass Pemex #5595, it will be on the right and you'll know you're on the right road. At 4.5 miles (7.3 km) you'll see a large Ley supermarket on the right, continue straight or stop for groceries. At 6.6 miles (10.6 km) you'll see Pemex #5995 on the left. At 7.2 miles (11.6 km) a sign tells you to go left for Mex 2 and San Louis Colorado, don't do it. Finally, at 7.3 miles (11.8 km) turn left for San Felipe. Almost immediately you'll see a Costco off to your left, and Pemex #1803 also on the left. You're on Mex 5, straight ahead to San Felipe.

For the first 24 miles (39 km) the road has four lanes and is bordered by scattered homes and business. There are several Pemex gas stations along here. Watch the speed limit signs, they require you to drive much slower than the speed you will feel is safe.

After the 4-lane ends the highway skirts the western edge of the Rio Hardy, a small river that drains into the Colorado to the east. Soon the highway makes a 12-mile (19 km) crossing of the dry Laguna Salada, at one time this area flooded with Colorado River water.

Once south of the Laguna the highway runs through very dry desert country. Mex 3 from Ensenada joins the highway at a crossroads known as El Crucero at Km 140. Often there are army checkpoints along the highway near El Crucero where soldiers may search your rig. See the *Drugs, Guns, and Roadblocks* section of the *Details, Details, Details* chapter.

Finally, near Km 175 the highway nears the ocean although you really can't see it from the highway. Many small roads lead eastward to campos along the water. Many offer camping, usually little more than boondocking sites. You'll have a selection of these almost all the way in to San Felipe which the road reaches at about Km 189.

Mexicali to San Felipe Campgrounds

CAMPO SONORA

| Location: | Km 52 of Mex 3 |
| Open: | All Year |

GPS Location: N 32° 09' 26", W 115° 18' 05"

As you drive south from Mexicali you'll spot this campground on the left at about Km 52 of Mex 5. It's a basic place, the reason it's here is the Rio Hardy which has some freshwater fishing. We've never seen an RV in here. There are ramadas for shade for tent campers and a small store. Restrooms have flush toilets in poor condition.

SAN FELIPE

CAMPO MOSQUEDA

Telephone: (686) 566-1520
Open: All Year

GPS Location: N 32° 09' 26", W 115° 18' 05"

This is another Rio Hardy campground. It's a more going concern, a resort area for folks from Mexicali. There are campsites for tents and some for RVs to about 35 feet with electricity. The restrooms have flush toilets and cold showers. There is a restaurant. The campground is near the river and has it's own lake which is stocked with fish. There are even peddle boats.

The road to the campground leaves Mex 3 to the east at about Km 54. The rough gravel road leads 2 kilometers to the campground.

EL MAYOR TRAILER PARK

Location: Km 55 of Mex 3
Telephone: (686) 192-6372

GPS Location: N 32° 07' 54", W 115° 16' 55"

El Mayor is the third Rio Hardy campground. It's right along the highway near Km 55, about two miles south of the Campo Sonora. There are 15 no-hookup sites and basic restrooms.

🚐 PETE'S CAMP

Address:	PO Box 516, Temecula, CA 92592
Telephone:	(951) 694-6704 (US)
Website:	www.petescamp.com
Email:	renel@petescamp.com
Open:	All Year

GPS Location: N 31° 08' 04", W 114° 53' 20"

This is an older campground, actually more of a community, located along the beach north of San Felipe. There are many permanently located trailers here but also a large camping area below overlooking the excellent beach.

The camping area has dozens of thatched-roof ramadas (shade shelters) with room for small RVs to squeeze between them. Large RVs park behind the ramadas. There are no hookups but a dump station is available as is drinking water. There are restrooms with flush toilets and hot showers as well as a restaurant.

The campground access road is at about Km 177.5. This is about 7.5 miles (12.1 km) north of the San Felipe entrance monument. There's a 1.1 mile (1.8 km) good oiled road east to the camp.

🚐 PLAYAS DEL SOL

Address:	Apdo. 128, San Felipe, BC, México
Telephone:	(686) 576-0292
Email:	playasol@telnor.net
Open:	All Year

GPS Location: N 31° 05' 26", W 114° 52' 10"

This is a large camping area on the beautiful beach north of San Felipe. Similar to Pete's but even simpler. There are many ramadas near the beach with parking for smaller RVs beside them or larger ones behind if things aren't too crowded. Flush toilets and hot showers are provided.

The campground entrance is near Km 183, about 4 miles (6 km) north of the San Felipe entrance monument. Follow the somewhat grand divided entrance road east a mile to the beach.

SAN FELIPE (SAHN FAY-LEE-PAY)
Population 15,000, Elevation sea level

Although San Felipe is a Baja town, its location in the far northeast portion of the peninsula means that it is not normally part of a visit to the peninsula's destinations farther south. That doesn't mean that this isn't a popular place. Like Puerto Peñasco this town is full of Americans looking for easily accessible sun and sand. The majority of them seem to be RVers.

In many ways San Felipe and Puerto Peñasco are very similar. Both are small towns at the north end of the Gulf of California pretty much devoted to RV tourism. Both are probably on the cusp of a development boom, both have recently opened golf courses although those struggle with limited fresh water for watering the grass.

Most of the action in San Felipe is found along its **malecón** (waterfront promenade) and the street one block inland - Mar de Cortez. Overlooking the malecón and the strip of sandy beach that fronts it is Cerro El Machorro, a tall rock with a shrine to the Virgin de Guadalupe at its top. This is a great place for photos. The bay in front of town goes dry at low tide, the panga fishermen who use the beach launch and retrieve their boats by driving pickups out on the solid sand. Several of the campgrounds are located along the southern extension of Mar de Cortez so strolling in to central San Felipe is very easy. The town has a selection of decent restaurants and small shops as well as four Pemex stations.

Most of the important streets in town are paved and the rest present no driving problems. Watch for stop signs, however. They are in unexpected places. Sometimes the smallest dusty side street has priority over a main arterial.

At this time San Felipe does not have a large supermarket but there are several small ones. A new shopping center going in north of town near the El Dorado Ranch properties (now called La Ventana del Mar) is expected to have a large one, perhaps a Soriana.

It seems like San Felipe always has some kind of celebration in the works. The **San Felipe 250** is a big off-road race at the end of March. Just before the off-road race is the **Mid-Winter West Hobie Cat Regatta**. Like many Mexican ports San Felipe celebrates **Carnival** (Mardi Gras) at the appropriate time in the spring. **Spring Break** is big here, just as on the rest of the peninsula, it happens during the third and fourth weeks of March. **Semana Santa**, the week up to and including Easter, is

SAN FELIPE'S ENTRANCE MONUMENT

SAN FELIPE

a big Mexican beach holiday and San Felipe is very popular as it hosts a number of sporting events. During the summer the town celebrates **Día de la Marina** on June 1. And in November there's the **Shrimp Festival**, one of the biggest celebrations of the year in San Felipe.

In addition to all of the above San Felipe gets lots of visitors from Mexicali and California on weekends and any excuse for a holiday in either the States or Mexico. Many of the campgrounds are really set up for tent campers with ramadas for shade. Expect lots of noise and activity when these visitors are in town.

San Felipe Campgrounds

In the last few years the campsite situation has changed considerably in San Felipe. Virtually every campground with large sites and decent hookups has closed. Recently closed big-RV campgrounds include the San Felipe Marina Resort RV Park and both the main El Dorado Ranch RV park and the El Cachanilla (now closed to non-owners). These parks haven't closed because they weren't doing well, the land was just needed for other projects. Looking at Puerto Peñasco it is apparent that there is an opportunity for several good big-rig parks in San Felipe and it's probably just a matter of time before one is built. Until then you'll find that there are still a few parks in the San Felipe area that can take large RVs, but most are either non-hookup parks or they squeeze big RVs into sites that are really built for smaller rigs.

The prices we have given for the parks in San Felipe are the normal rates for slots back from the water. Expect to pay a bit more for waterfront sites at the campgrounds that offer them and also expect rates to be from $5 to $10 higher on holiday weekends or during special events.

MARCO'S TRAILER PARK

Address:	Av. Golfo de California 788, San Felipe, B.C., México
Telephone:	(686) 577-1875
Open:	All Year

GPS Location: N 31° 02' 08", W 114° 49' 42"

Marco's isn't on the water and all San Felipe campers seem to want to be in a campground next to the beach, even if they're parked so far back that they never see the water. Nonetheless Marco's succeeds in staying relatively full, perhaps because it is *almost* next to the beach.

There are 20 back-in spaces arranged around the perimeter of the campground. There is lots of room in the middle of the campground but large RVs have some difficulty parking because the lot slopes and the leveled parking pads aren't very long. Each space has 15-amp outlets, sewer, water, and a nice little covered patio. There is even a little shrubbery to separate the sites, unusual in San Felipe. The restrooms are old but clean and in good repair, they have hot water showers. There is a small meeting room with a library and a sun deck on top.

From the glorieta (traffic circle) at the entrance to town take the road that leads northeast. This is Mar Caribe Norte and is the road to the left as you come from Mexicali. It will curve to the right at 0.8 miles (1.3 km) and come to a T at 1 mile (1.6 km). Turn left and you'll see the entrance to the campground on the left in one block.

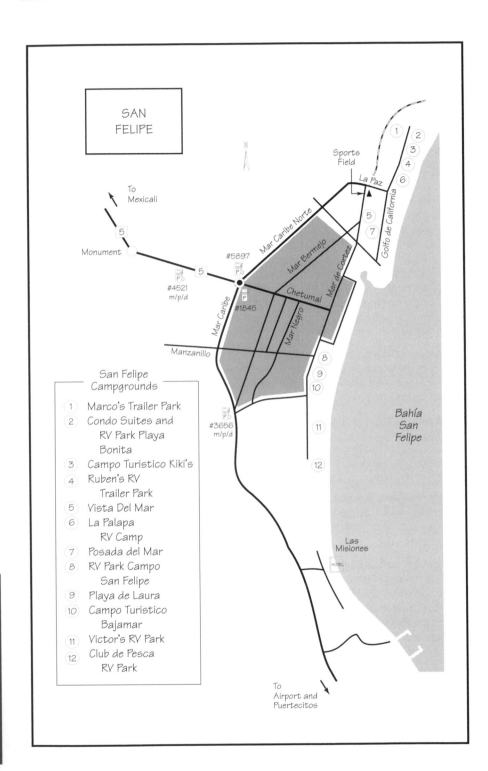

SAN FELIPE

San Felipe
Campgrounds

1. Marco's Trailer Park
2. Condo Suites and
   RV Park Playa
   Bonita
3. Campo Turistico Kiki's
4. Ruben's RV
   Trailer Park
5. Vista Del Mar
6. La Palapa
   RV Camp
7. Posada del Mar
8. RV Park Campo
   San Felipe
9. Playa de Laura
10. Campo Turistico
    Bajamar
11. Victor's RV Park
12. Club de Pesca
    RV Park

⛟ CONDO SUITES AND RV PARK PLAYA BONITA

Address:	475 E. Badillo Street, Covina, Cal. 91723
	U.S.A. (Reservations)
Telephone:	(686) 577-1215 (Mex), (626) 967-8977 (USA)
Website:	www.sanfelipebeachcondos.com
Email:	playabonita@aol.com
Open:	All Year

GPS Location: N 31° 02' 09", W 114° 49' 43"

This is a beachfront campground at the north end of town. Someday the campground may be entirely replaced by condo suites, but there are still small RV and tent sites.

The spaces are suitable only for vans, tents or small trailers. Most of these smaller spaces have 15-amp electricity, sewer, and water. All spaces have paved patios with ramada-style roofs and picnic tables. The restrooms are older and rustic, the showers were barely warm when we visited. There's a nice beach out front.

From the glorieta (traffic circle) at the entrance to town take the road that leads northeast. This is Mar Caribe Norte and is the road to the left as you come from Mexicali. It will curve to the right at 0.8 miles (1.3 km) and come to a T at 1 mile (1.6 km). Turn left and you'll see the entrance to the campground on the right across from Marco's.

⛟ CAMPO TURISTICO KIKI'S

Address:	Golfo de California 703, San Felipe, BC, México
Telephone:	(686) 577-2021
Open:	All Year

GPS Location: N 31° 02' 04", W 114° 49' 43"

This is the northern half of the old Ruben's RV Trailer Park. Now there's a fence between the north and south halves It has the same very small sites that are really for tents with a second level above. Sites have 15-amp outlets, sewer, and water. People also tent camp on the beach out front. Access is very cramped, it's really only suitable for tenters or very small RVs.

From the glorieta (traffic circle) at the entrance to town take the road that leads northeast. This is Mar Caribe Norte and is the road to the left as you come from Mexicali. It will curve to the right at 0.8 miles (1.3 km) and come to a T at 1 mile (1.6 km). Turn left and you'll almost immediately see the entrance to Kiki's on the right.

⛟ RUBEN'S RV TRAILER PARK

Address:	Apdo. 59, CP 21850 San Felipe, B.C., México
Telephone:	(686) 577-1442
Open:	All Year

GPS Location: N 31° 02' 03", W 114° 49' 42"

Ruben's is well known in San Felipe for its two-story patios. These are very popular with tenters during the Mexican holidays, it is easy to enclose the patio below and use the roof for added room. Some people think the two-story patios give the crowded campground the atmosphere of a parking garage but Ruben's remains a popular beach-front campground. There's always a lot of activity at this place, maybe too much.

There are about 20 camping spaces, all with 15-amp outlets, sewer and water. Most

SAN FELIPE

TWO STORY RAMADAS ARE POPULAR IN SAN FELIPE CAMPGROUNDS

spaces are small and maneuvering room is scarce. Like Kiki's above this campground is really for tent campers and perhaps very small RVs. The restrooms are adequate and have hot water showers. There is also a bar/restaurant. Recently the campground has been split in two by a fence, see Campo Turistico Kiki's above.

From the glorieta (traffic circle) at the entrance to town take the road that leads northeast. This is Mar Caribe Norte and is the road to the left as you come from Mexicali. It will curve to the right at 0.8 miles (1.3 km) and come to a T at 1 mile (1.6 km). Turn left and you'll almost immediately see the entrance to Ruben's on the right.

⛽ VISTA DEL MAR

Address:	601 Ave. de Cortez, San Felipe, B.C., México
Open:	All Year

GPS Location: N 31° 01'50", W 114° 49'51"

The Vista del Mar is another campground suffering from a location far from the water. The facility is really very good, but often virtually empty. We find that it sometimes closes during slow periods but opens again when things are likely to be busy.

There are 21 back-in spaces arranged on both sides of a sloping lot with a view of the ocean and hills to the north of town. Each space has 15 and 30-amp outlets, sewer, and water. Large RVs will have trouble parking because the level parking pad is not very long. The entire campground is paved, much of it with attractive reddish bricks. Each campsite has a tile-roofed patio with a table and barbecue. The restrooms are spic-and-span and have hot water showers. At the upper end of the campground is a group barbecue area.

From the glorieta (traffic circle) at the entrance to town take the road that leads northeast. This is Mar Caribe Norte and is the road to the left as you come from Mexicali. It will curve to the right at 0.8 miles (1.3 km). You must take the turn to the right at 0.9 miles (1.4 km) just before the fenced sports field, the campground is a short way up the hill on the left.

LA PALAPA RV CAMP
Open: All Year

GPS Location: N 31° 01' 53", W 114° 49' 42"

This little trailer park is located right next to the much better known Ruben's. At first glance it even looks like Rubens, it has some of the same two-story ramadas. It's much quieter, however.

There are 22 spaces in this park. Six are along the front next to the beach. Most spaces are really van-size or short-trailer-size but a few will take RVs to about 30 feet. The camping slots have 15 or 30-amp outlets, sewer, water, and paved patios with a roof serviced by a ladder. You can use them for the view or pitch a tent up there. The bathrooms are old and need maintenance, they have hot water showers. The park is managed from the small store out front.

From the glorieta (traffic circle) at the entrance to town take the road that leads northeast. This is Mar Caribe Norte and is the road to the left as you come from Mexicali. It will curve to the right at 0.8 miles (1.3 km) and come to a T at 1 mile (1.6 km). Turn left and the campground will be on the right almost immediately, the sign is very small.

POSADA DEL MAR
Address: Av. Golfo de California, 355, San Felipe, México
Telephone: (686) 577-1543 or (686) 555-1457
Open: All Year

GPS Location: N 31° 01' 43", W 114° 49' 47'

The Posada del Mar is an old park with the same two story ramadas that you find at Rubens, Kiki's, and La Palapa. The campground is located a block back from the beach. Sites are best for tent campers or vans although this is a much larger park than the others and there are a few places RVs to about 30 feet could fit. Hookups are limited to low amp two-prong outlets in poor condition as well as water and sewer connections. Restrooms are old and in poor condition but hot water was available when we visited. There are also a few motel rooms here.

From the glorieta (traffic circle) at the entrance to town take the road that leads northeast. This is Mar Caribe Norte and is the road to the left as you come from Mexicali. It will curve to the right at 0.8 miles (1.3 km) and come to a T at 1 mile (1.6 km). Turn right and the campground will be on the right in .3 mile (.5 km).

⛟ RV Park Campo San Felipe

Address: Ave. Mar de Cortez #301, San Felipe, B.C., México
Mail: PO Box 952, Calexico, CA 92232
Telephone: (686) 577-1012
Website: www.camposanfelipe.com
Open: All Year

GPS Location: N 31° 01' 10", W 114° 50' 05"

You'll find the San Felipe to be very much like the Playa de Laura next door but in much better condition. It has the distinction of being the closest campground to central San Felipe.

The campsites are arranged in several rows parallel to the beach, the closer to the beach you are the more you pay. Thirty-four sites have 30-amp outlets, sewer, water, and covered patios with tables. Most are pull-thrus. Another 5 are small and have sewer and water only. RVs to 35 feet can use some of the sites but maneuvering is difficult. The restrooms are clean and in good repair, they have hot water showers. There is a handy telephone next to the office. English is spoken.

As you enter town zero your odometer at the glorieta (traffic circle). Turn right toward the airport and drive 0.8 miles (1.3 km) to the Pemex. Turn left here and drive down the hill toward the beach. You'll come to a T at 1.2 miles (1.9 km). Turn left and almost immediately you'll see the Campo San Felipe on the right in 0.2 miles (0.4 km).

⛟ Playa de Laura

Address: PO Box 686, Calexico, CA 92232 (US)
Telephone: (686) 577-1128 or (686) 554-4712
Fax: (686) 554-4712
Email: hernanh@telnor.net
Open: All Year

GPS Location: N 31° 01' 06", W 114° 50' 07"

This older RV park doesn't seem to have been kept up to quite the same standards as the ones on either side. Still, it has a good location and is quite popular.

Forty-three campsites are arranged in rows running parallel to the beach. The front row is really packed and limits beach access by campers in the rows farther from the beach. Pricing varies with beach slots more expensive than those farther back. Each camping space has 15-amp outlets, water and a covered patio with table and barbecue. Many have sewer hookups. Most of the spaces are pull-thrus but maneuvering space is limited, some sites are good for RVs to about 35 feet. Restrooms are older and need maintenance, they have hot water showers.

As you enter town zero your odometer at the glorieta (traffic circle). Turn right toward the airport and drive 0.8 miles (1.3 km) to the Pemex. Turn left here and drive down the hill toward the beach. You'll come to a T at 1.2 miles (1.9 km). Turn left and almost immediately you'll see the Playa de Laura on the right in 0.2 miles (0.3 km).

SAN FELIPE

⊞ CAMPO TURISTICO BAJAMAR

Address: Av. Mar de Cortez s/n, San Felipe, B.C., México
Reservations: Av. Madero No. 702, Zona Centro, CP 21100
                  Mexicali, B.C., México
Telephone: (686) 552-2363
Email: jf_uriastorres@hotmail.com
Open: All Year

GPS Location: N 31° 01'05", W 114° 50'07"

The Bajamar is the newest of the downtown San Felipe campgrounds. Rather than having rows of sites on sand, this campground has large back-in spaces off paved access roads. It's on a nice beach and you have convenient strolling access to central San Felipe.

There are 60 full-service spaces with 30-amp breakers (15-amp outlets however), sewer, and water. The central access roads are paved with curbs and the parking pads are gravel with patios, some have sun shades. This campground has left the water-front open so that it can be enjoyed by all of the residents, there is a large patio with a palapa there and some small tables with umbrellas on the sand. The Bajamar has a much less crowded feel than the other campgrounds in this area. Restrooms are in very poor condition but do have flush toilets and hot water showers. There is a self-service laundry, and a playground.

As you enter town zero your odometer at the glorieta (traffic circle). Turn right toward the airport and drive 0.8 miles (1.3 km) to the Pemex. Turn left here and drive down the hill toward the beach. You'll come to a T at 1.2 miles (1.9 km). Turn left and almost immediately you'll see the Bajamar on the right.

⊞ VICTOR'S RV PARK

Address: PO Box 1227, Calexico, CA (Res.)
Telephone: (686) 577-1055
Fax: (686) 577-1752
Email: cortezho@telnor.net
Open: All Year

GPS Location: N 31° 00'47", W 114° 50'09"

This 50-space campground is older with a lot of permanently located or long-term RVs. About 20 slots are available for daily rent. It is run by the El Cortez Motel located just next door so the facilities are really pretty good for such a small park.

Victor's parking slots have 30-amp outlets, sewer, and water. Each space has a covered patio. The restrooms are clean and showers have hot water. Some are large enough for RVs to 35 feet. The campground has a meeting room near the front next to the beach and the motel next door has a swimming pool and restaurant for the use of campground residents. There is also a laundry. This campground is fully fenced, even along the beach, and usually has an attendant.

As you enter town zero your odometer at the glorieta (traffic circle). Turn right toward the airport and drive 0.8 miles (1.3 km) to the Pemex. Turn left here and drive down the hill toward the beach. You'll come to a T at 1.2 miles (1.9 km). Turn right and almost immediately you'll see Victor's on your left.

SAN FELIPE

THE BEACH IN FRONT OF VICTOR'S RV PARK

🚐 **CLUB DE PESCA RV PARK**

Reservations: PO Box 3090, Calexico, CA 92232
Telephone: (686) 577-1180
Fax: (686) 577-1888
Email: clbdpaca@telnor.net
Open: All Year

GPS Location: N 31° 00' 45", W 114° 50' 10"

This is an old San Felipe favorite. The campground has many permanents, but also some choice slots for tents and smaller RVs along the ocean and others toward the rear of the park.

There are 32 slots along the beach with ramadas and with 30-amp outlets and water but no sewer hookups. These spaces are paved. We've seen RVs to 34 feet in them but usually only shorter RVs park here. At the rear of the park are 22 slots with 15-amp outlets, sewer, and water. Larger RVs fit here better, there's room for RVs to about 35 feet, some will take 40 footers and even a bit larger. Restrooms are neat and clean and have hot water showers. There is a small grocery store and a room with a ping-pong table next to the beach dividing the beachside sites.

As you enter town zero your odometer at the glorieta (traffic circle). Turn right toward the airport and drive 0.8 miles (1.3 km) to the Pemex. Turn left here and drive down the hill toward the beach. You'll come to a T at 1.2 miles (1.9 km). Turn right and you'll find the Club de Pesca at the end of the road.

South of San Felipe Campgrounds

🚐 CAMPO SAN FERNANDO

$$$	⛺	🔧	🚰	🚐	🚿

Address: PO Box 23, Calexico, CA 92232
Open: Not Known

GPS Location: N 30° 56'36", W 114° 44'05"

When we last visited we found this campground unattended and is very poor condition. Things can change rapidly in Baja, it wouldn't take much to have this place up and operating again. You might want to check it yourself some time. Here's what we found.

This older campground has about 20 sites. The campground sits high on a hill overlooking the water, there are a few permanents here. Although the traveler's sites have electricity, water, and sewer hookups installed, only the sewer appeared to be useable. Several sites were badly eroded. The restrooms have flush toilets and were clean.

The campground is located south of San Felipe. Zero your odometer as you reach the glorieta (traffic circle) at the entrance to town. Turn 90 degrees right toward the airport and head south. At 7.1 miles (11.5 km) the road makes a right angle turn to the left, the airport is straight. Turn left. In another 3.5 miles (5.6 km) you'll see the entrance on your left, there is a nice sign.

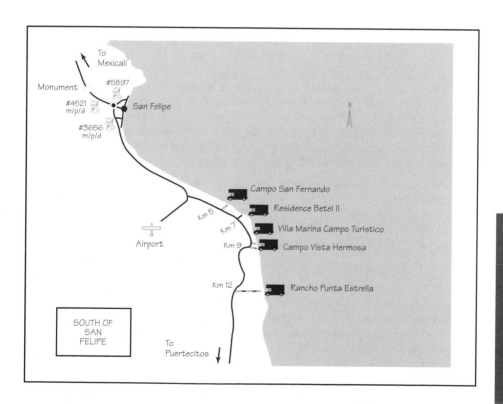

🚐 RESIDENCE BETEL II

Open: All Year

GPS Location: N 30° 56' 15", W 114° 43' 42"

The old El Faro, now called the Residence Betel II, is worth a stop for a look even if you decide not to stay. Actually, the name change indicates that redevelopment into home sites is probably upcoming, but when we recently visited nothing had changed other than the name. This is one of the most elaborate RV resorts in Mexico, yet it's been abandoned to the sand.

The campground occupies a hillside above a beautiful sandy beach. There are many back-in sites as well as a resort complex near the water, all abandoned. A few tenters and smaller RVs occupy some of the sites (with no useable hookups) but big RVs that stay here park on top of the bluff overlooking everything and boondock with no hookups. The restrooms sometimes have flush toilets and showers but don't count on it. There is an attendant watching over things, drive in and take a look.

The campground is located south of San Felipe. Zero your odometer as you reach the glorieta (traffic circle) at the entrance to town. Turn 90 degrees right toward the airport and head south. At 7.1 miles (11.5 km) the road makes a right angle turn to the left, the airport is straight. Turn left. In another 4.2 miles (6.7 km) you'll see the entrance on your left. The paved entrance road will take you to the park.

🚐 VILLA MARINA CAMPO TURISTICO

Telephone: (686) 577-1342 or (686) 590-7663
Open: All year

GPS Location: N 30° 54' 58", W 114° 42' 54"

This is the nicest and most modern campground south of San Felipe. There are 26 full-hookup spaces. They have 15-amp electrical outlets. The camping area is located on a low bluff above a sandy beach. Many sites are covered and have stairways leading to terraces on top with excellent views. Amazingly, sites are long enough, wide enough, and even high enough for most big RVs although you'll have to maneuver with care. Modern clean restrooms have flush toilets and hot showers. There's laundry service and this is a gated and attended campground.

The campground is located south of San Felipe. Zero your odometer as you reach the glorieta (traffic circle) at the entrance to town. Turn 90 degrees right toward the airport and head south. At 7.1 miles (11.5 km) the road makes a right angle turn to the left, the airport is straight. Turn left. In another 5.4 miles (8.7 km) you'll see the entrance on your left. The 0.3 mile (0.5 km) gravel road will take you to the park.

🚐 CAMPO VISTA HERMOSA

Open: All Year

GPS Location: N 30° 54' 53", W 114° 42' 51"

This campground sits on a low bluff above an excellent beach. It's not large, perhaps 15 scattered ramada sun shelters on hard dirt for tenters or RVs to about 25 feet. Erosion threatens several of them. When we recently visited the campground was in use but in very poor condition.

The campground is located south of San Felipe. Zero your odometer as you reach the glorieta (traffic circle) at the entrance to town. Turn 90 degrees right toward the airport and head south. At 7.1 miles (11.5 km) the road makes a right angle turn to the left, the airport is straight. Turn left. In another 5.5 miles (8.9 km) you'll see the entrance on your left. The 0.2 mile (0.3 km) gravel entrance road will take you to the campground.

RANCHO PUNTA ESTRELLA

Address:	Km 13 Carretera San Felipe a Puertecitos
Telephone:	(686) 565-2784 or (USA) (760) 357-6933
Email:	puntaestrella@mexico.com
Open:	All year

GPS Location: N 30° 53'00", W 114° 42'28"

This is a large campground with simple facilities. There are miles of beach and desert behind. The camping sites are a long row of 70 wood-roofed ramadas stretched along the beach. They are intended for tent camping. The sand between the ramadas is soft, probably too soft for any RV parking. An electrical cord with light bulbs hanging from it has been strung along the front of the camping ramadas. Behind the row of ramadas the surface is harder so RVs can boondock there. Simple restrooms have flush toilets and hot showers.

The campground is located south of San Felipe. Zero your odometer as you reach the glorieta (traffic circle) at the entrance to town. Turn 90 degrees right toward the airport and head south. At 7.1 miles (11.5 km) the road makes a right angle turn to the left, the airport is straight. Turn left. In another 7.7 miles (12.4 km) you'll see the entrance on your left. It's 0.9 mile (1.4 km) to the campground.

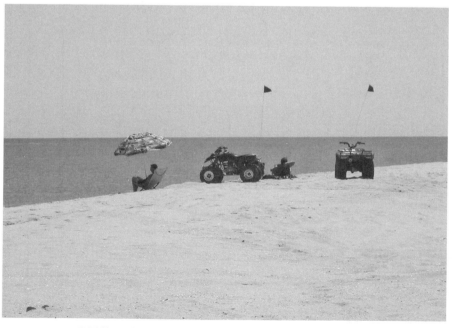

PUNTA ESTRELLA IS FRONTED BY MILES OF EMPTY BEACH

SAN FELIPE

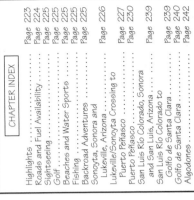

CHAPTER INDEX

Highlights . . . . Page 223
Roads and Fuel Availability . . . . . Page 224
Sightseeing . . . . Page 225
Golf . . . . Page 225
Beaches and Water Sports . . . . . . Page 225
Fishing . . . . Page 225
Backroad Adventures . . . . Page 225
Sonoyta, Sonora and
  Lukeville, Arizona . . . . Page 226
Lukeville/Sonoyta Crossing to
  Puerto Peñasco . . . . Page 227
Puerto Peñasco . . . . Page 230
San Luis Río Colorado, Sonora
  and San Luis, Arizona . . . . Page 239
San Luis Río Colorado to
  Golfo de Santa Clara . . . . Page 239
Golfo de Santa Clara . . . . Page 240
Algodones . . . . Page 242

PUERTO PEÑASCO, GOLFO, AND ALGODONES

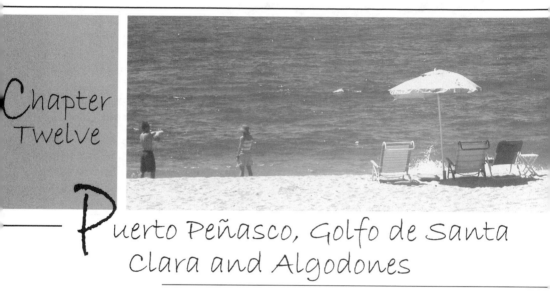

Puerto Peñasco, Golfo de Santa Clara and Algodones

INTRODUCTION

Three of the easiest places for RVers to visit in Mexico are Puerto Peñasco (Rocky Point), Golfo de Santa Clara, and Algodones. The first two are easy drives from easy border crossings on quiet roads. Of the two, Puerto Peñasco (often called Rocky Point), has the most to offer. There are hundreds of campsites and services designed for folks from north of the border. Golfo de Santa Clara on the other hand has only a handful of camping sites and virtually no services. Golfo is an authentic little Mexican fishing town.

Algodones is well known as the place residents of Arizona and southeast California go to visit doctors, dentists, and pharmacies in Mexico. The town now has an RV park.

Highlights

The attraction of Puerto Peñasco and Golfo de Santa Clara is that they are the only beach towns easily available to residents of Arizona. Here you can camp just a few feet from the water. The quality of some of these parks compares favorable with those north of the border. You don't need to worry at all about being able to speak Spanish and dollars are accepted for virtually everyting. It's almost like you're still in the U.S.

THE BEACH AT ROCKY POINT

Roads and Fuel Availability

The road from the Lukeville/Sonoyta crossing leads 62 miles (100 km) south to Puerto Peñasco. The route passes through the outskirts of Sonoyta, but this is a quiet little town and driving through is no problem. You can wait until you reach Puerto Peñasco if you want to change money or shop.

From the junction in Sonoyta where Mex 8 intersects Mex 2 the road is marked with kilometer posts, they count up from 0 at the junction to 95 as you enter Puerto Peñasco.

Gas is available in Lukeville if you wish to gas up before heading south. However, there is a Pemex station along the road as you drive through Sonoyta and fuel prices in Mexico are sometimes lower than in the US. After Sonoyta there is not another station until you reach Puerto Peñasco.

If you are bound for Golfo de Santa Clara you will want to cross in San Luis Río Colorado. This crossing is about 26 miles (42 km) south of Yuma, AZ. Follow signs for Golfo de Santa Clara once you cross the border, they'll lead you through the small border town and onto Hwy. 40, a two-lane paved highway. The distance to Golfo is about 71 miles (114 km). Both gas and diesel are available north of the border, in San Luis, and at a Pemex station in Golfo.

Sightseeing

You will want to visit **Puerto Peñasco's old town on Rocky Point**. You'll find a selection of restaurants and several stores selling Mexican handicrafts.

Another interesting place to visit while visiting Puerto Peñasco is **CEDO**, also known as the **Desert and Ocean Studies Center**. It's located a few miles east of town in the Las Conchas housing development. It's a learning and research center with the skeleton of a fin whale and other exhibits.

Golf

Puerto Peñasco has at least three golf courses under development. Apparently only one course, the one at the Mayan Palace some 21 miles (34 km) east of town is truly open for business at this time.

Beaches and Water Sports

Puerto Peñasco has beaches both northwest and east of the rocky point that gives the town its name. The sandy beaches near town are sometimes interrupted by outcrops of the basalt lava rock that makes up the point.

East of the point is **Las Conchas**. It is rocky at the western end but sandy to the east. Many of the campgrounds line this beach, there are boat-launching ramps at some of them.

Northwest of the point is a long sandy beach that begins as **Playa Bonita** and then becomes **Sandy Beach** as it curves westward. There are also campgrounds along this beach. ATV use is popular on Sandy Beach and in the dunes to the north.

In Golfo de Santa Clara the good beach is about a mile south of town. That is where the out-of-town campgrounds are located. Access is via a mile-long sand road that is a continuation of the main road through town. Tides in this section of the Gulf of California can have as much as 25 feet between high and low water. When the tide is in there is a nice sand beach, when the tide is out there are miles of mud flats.

Fishing

While the fishing in the far northern Gulf of California can't compare with the fishing farther south in the gulf, Puerto Peñasco does have a healthy sports fishing fleet. You can easily charter a panga or cruiser for a day of fishing. These aren't really big fish waters but there is something to catch all year long.

Backroad Adventures

See the *Backroad Driving* section of *Chapter 2 - Details, Details, Details* for essential information about driving off the main highways and for a definition of road types used below.

Km 73 Between Sonoyta and Puerto Peñasco - Riserva De La Biosfera De El Pinacate y Gran Desierto De Altar is an infrequently visited but interesting destination located west of the highway. It's an austere desert region filled with volcanic craters, lava fields, and sand dunes. The last eruption was in 1935. Permits are required to visit the park, you can get them at the ranger station near the entrance. There are also entrances from Mex 2 between Sonoyta and San Luis Río Colorado. Some of the roads in the park are Type 2, others Type 3. The reserve has two very basic camping areas with no hookups.

THE ROUTES, TOWNS, AND CAMPGROUNDS

SONOYTA, SONORA AND LUKEVILLE, ARIZONA

These small towns are located on opposite sides of the border about a mile from each other. During the week the crossing here is a pleasant experience because it tends to be very quiet. Sometimes, but not always, weekends are much busier. Lukeville has a gas station and a motel with a good RV park in the back. Organ Pipe National Monument with another good campground is located just a few miles to the north. The crossing here is open 24 hours. Insurance is available in Lukeville.

After crossing the border the route curves through the edge of quiet Sonoyta and Mex 8 heads southwest toward Puerto Peñasco. Gas and diesel are available at the Pemex here but most folks have already gassed up in the U.S. and don't even stop.

Sonoyta and Lukeville Campgrounds

ORGAN PIPE N.M.

Open: All Year

GPS Location: N 31° 56' 28", W 112° 48' 40"

This national monument campground is an excellent place to stay on the U.S. side of the border before or after your crossing. It is only a few miles north of the border crossing at Sonoyta, the desert flora here is spectacular. This is the north end of the range for the organ pipe cactus, known as the pithahaya dulce on the Baja.

The campground has over 200 sites. They are all pull-thrus but due to their length are only suitable for rigs to 35 feet. There are no hookups. The restrooms have flush toilets but no showers. There is a dump station and water fill. The entrance road for the campground passes an information center, when we visited the fees were being collected there although there is also a fee station at the campground for busier seasons. There are excellent hiking trails from the campground and nearby, also some interesting drives.

The turn-off for this campground is at Mile 75 of Highway 85, about 6 miles (10 km) north of the crossing at Lukeville/Sonoyta.

GRINGO PASS MOTEL AND RV PARK

Address: PO Box 266, Hwy. 85, Lukeville, AZ 85341
Telephone: (602) 254-9284
Open: All Year

GPS Location: N 31° 52' 54", W 112° 49' 04"

If you find that you have reached the border crossing at Lukeville/Sonoyta too late in the day to drive on to Puerto Peñasco before dark you can stay in this conveniently located RV park and go on in the morning.

The Gringo Pass Motel has a large number of sites out back. There are a variety of site types, some back-in and some pull-thru. The sites have full hookups with 50 and 15-amp outlets. Sites have picnic tables and there is a swimming pool. Restrooms have hot showers and some sites have shade.

The motel is located just north of the border crossing on the east side of the road. There's a Chevron station, a grocery store, an insurance office, and a restaurant on the west side.

LUKEVILLE/SONOYTA CROSSING TO PUERTO PEÑASCO
62 Miles (100 Km), 1.25 Hours

After crossing the border the road leads to an intersection with Mex 2 just 2 miles (3 km) from the crossing. Turn left, drive past the Pemex, and turn right in just a quarter-mile to follow Mex 8 south toward Puerto Peñasco.

Within a minute or so you'll be driving across the desert. There is little traffic other than folks headed to or returning from Puerto Peñasco.

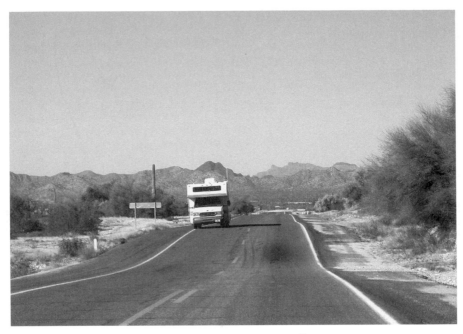

THE ROAD SOUTH TO PUERTO PEÑASCO

As you approach Puerto Peñasco you'll begin to see a few scattered RV parks. A major new intersection is near Km 90, the road to Caborca is to the left, the new Laguna del Mar land development to the right, Puerto Peñasco is straight ahead. At Km 95 you'll pass under the "Welcome to Rocky Point" sign.

Lukeville/Sonoyta Crossing to Puerto Peñasco Campgrounds

HACIENDA DE MARCOS

Reservations: PO Box 379, Lukeville, AZ 85341
Telephone: (638) 385-1030
Open: All Year

GPS Location: N 31° 25' 36", W 113° 28' 09"

This campground is located north of town on the road to Sonoyta. If you are looking for a small friendly place you should stop in here. Each time we visit the place is even nicer.

The campground has 20 back-in spaces with full hookups (50 and 30-amp outlets). Big rigs will find lots of room to park and maneuver. There's a laundry and restrooms are modern and clean with flush toilets and hot water showers. The swimming pool is very nice, there's also a restaurant. The owner/managers are from north of the border.

The Hacienda De Marcos is located on the east side of Mex 8 near Km 83, some 7.5 miles (12 km) north of Puerto Peñasco.

🚍 Quality Star RV Park

Address: PO Box 560 PMBZ2, Lukeville, AZ 85341
Telephone: (638) 102-0062
Fax: (638) 102-0063
Open: All Year

GPS Location: N 31° 22'08", W 113° 30'21"

This is the most unusual campground in Puerto Peñasco, perhaps in Mexico. When you drive in the first thing you see is a furniture gallery, that's where the office is located. Then you notice that the sites look a little like a storage yard. Some rigs here really are in storage, but most are not. The unusual look derives from the high surrounding fence and the very high metal shade structures over every site in the park. Then, in the rear of the campground, you'll find a mini water park with pools and spa.

The campground offers 34 sites. All are covered back-in sites suitable for any size rig and have full hookups including 30-amp outlets. The restrooms are modern and very nice with hot showers. There's a coin operated laundry and out back are swimming pools, they're open to the public and closed for part of the winter.

The campground is located east of the highway near Km 90. This is just outside Puerto Peñasco to the north.

DESERT OASIS RESORT

Address:	Carr. Sonoyta Km 91, Puerto Peñasco, Son., México
Telephone:	(638) 102-0222
Open:	All Year

GPS Location: N 31° 21'52", W 113° 30'28"

This is a modern motel and campground with a nice bar/restaurant.

The campground has about 40 spaces with full hookups, a few are pull-thrus. Good maneuvering room and large sites make it suitable for any rig. Power outlets are 30-amp and parking is on gravel. The restrooms have hot showers and flush toilets. There's also a coin-operated laundry. There is no shade in the RV park.

The park is located at Km 91 which is 2.5 miles (4 km) north of Puerto Peñasco.

MAR Y SOL TRAILER PARK

Address:	Carr. Sonoyta Km 94, CP 83350 Puerto Peñasco, Sonora, México
Telephone:	(638) 383-3190
Fax:	(638) 383-3188
Open:	All Year

GPS Location: N 31° 20'22", W 113° 31'28"

This trailer park adjoins the Mar y Sol Hotel on the south side. There are about 20 back-in spaces suitable for rigs to 35 feet. All spaces have full hookups with 30-amp outlets, there is no shade. Restrooms have hot water showers. The hotel has a restaurant.

The campground is on the east side of the highway near Km 94 just as you arrive in Puerto Peñasco.

PUERTO PEÑASCO (PWEHR-TOE PEN-YAHS-KOE)
Population 13,000

Many Mexico travel guides ignore Puerto Peñasco as if it weren't even part of Mexico. This attitude is understandable, the town really does have a great deal of American influence. To ignore Puerto Peñasco in a camping guide to Mexico would be something of a crime, however. RVers virtually own this town, hordes of them fill RV parks and boondock in the vicinity. On weekends and holidays Puerto Peñasco is even more popular. After all, it is only a little over an hour's driving time south of the Arizona border, it is located in a free zone requiring no governmental paperwork, and there are beaches, desert, fishing, and Mexican crafts and food. Don't forget to pick up Mexican auto insurance, however.

Americans often call the town Rocky Point, you'll see why when you see the location of the old town. The road to Rocky Point was built by the American government during World War II when it was thought that it might be necessary to bring in supplies this way if the west coast was blockaded by Japanese submarines. That never happened, but the road, now paved and in good shape, makes the town easy to reach. Puerto Peñasco is also a fishing port, not everything here is tourist oriented. Campgrounds are located in three areas. Some campgrounds are starting to appear along the main highway north of town. These are the least expensive but their desert location away from the beach makes them the least popular. Several are along the beach to the west of town. And finally, most of the older parks and some newer ones are along the beach to the east of the old town. There is lots of major tourist development in Rocky Point now, including condos and golf courses. Supplies of all kinds are available, the latest addition is a modern Ley supermarket that makes it unnecessary to bring supplies from the States.

Puerto Peñasco Campgrounds

BONITA RV PARK

Address: PO Box 254, Lukeville, AZ 85341-0254 (USA) or
                 Paseo Balboa #100 (Apdo 34), CP 83550 Puerto
                 Peñasco, Sonora, México
Telephone: (638) 383-1400
Website: www.playabonitaresort.com
Email: bonitarv@playabonitaresort.com
Open: All Year

GPS Location: N 31° 18' 41", W 113° 32' 48"

This is one of the newer parks in town. It's conveniently located near the beach and the tourist area of town. Unfortunately, the park itself is uninviting due to the surrounding wall.

The campground has 96 full-hookup sites. These are back-ins with 30-amp power.

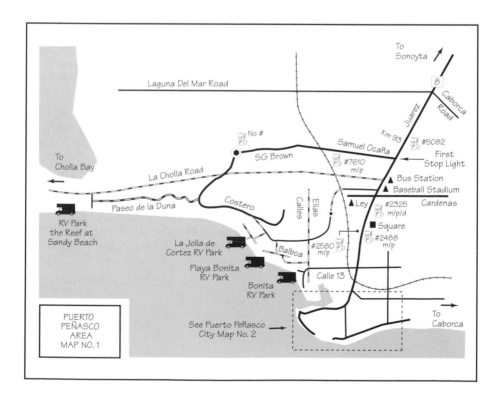

There's lots of room here for big rigs, particularly as the campground is seldom even partly full. Restrooms are modern and offer hot showers, there's a lounge room with television, but no television at the sites.

As you enter town you will pass four Pemexes, two on the left, then one on the right, then another on the left (Pemex #2488). A half mile (.8 km) after the fourth Pemex is a cross road marked with many large green signs on a pedestrian bridge over the road. Turn right here on Calle 13. Proceed across the railroad tracks and drive 0.4 mile (0.7 km). The campground entrance is on the right.

🚐 PLAYA BONITA RV PARK

Address:	Paseo Balboa #100., Apdo. 34, CP 83550 Puerto Peñasco, Son., México
Telephone:	(638) 383-2596
Website:	www.playabonitaresort.com
Email:	playabonitarvpark@hotmail.com
Open:	All Year

GPS Location: N 31° 19' 06", W 113° 33' 16"

This is a large campground located northwest of town on Playa Bonita. The Playa Bonita RV Park is affiliated with a nice hotel next door, as well as with the Bonita RV Park listed above. This campground has good access to lots of four-wheeling so it's full of off-road folks and their equipment most weekends.

There are 300 spaces in this huge campground. All are back-in slots with 30-amp outlets, sewer, and water. Some sites have TV hookups. Many big rigs use this campground although the sites aren't really quite long enough and maneuvering room is restricted. Restrooms are clean and have hot water. The campground has a small recreation room with a TV, a self-service laundry, limited groceries, and the affiliated hotel next door has a restaurant. The campground has free Wi-Fi too. The beach out front is beautiful. One nice feature is the malecón (walkway) that fronts the entire park, a great place to walk and watch the beach action. There's also a spa. Evening fireworks displays are a tradition at this campground.

As you enter town you will pass four Pemexes, two on the left, then one on the right, then another on the left (Pemex #2488). A half mile (.8 km) after the fourth Pemex is a cross road marked with many large green signs on a pedestrian bridge over the road. Turn right here on Armada de Mexico, also called Calle 13. Proceed across the railroad tracks and drive for about 0.3 mile (0.5 km)., turn right on a dirt road named Elias Calles. The turn is marked with a sign for the Playa Bonita RV Park. Drive north for 0.2 miles (0.3 km) and turn left on Oscar Palacio. Follow the road around to the right, pass through a stop sign and in 0.3 mile (0.5 km) you'll come to another stop, a subdivision arch is directly ahead. Now turn left before the arch and follow the road (Balboa) as it leads 0.3 mile (0.5 km) west to the campground.

🚐 LA JOLLA DE CORTEZ RV PARK

Address:	PO Box 1285, Lukeville, AZ 85341
Telephone:	(638) 383-7111
Fax:	(638) 383-7112
Email:	jimc802003@yahoo.com
Open:	All Year

GPS Location: N 31° 19' 14", W 113° 33' 46"

La Jolla is a newer park located beyond the Playa Bonita but on the same beach to the west. This campground has 60 large back-in spaces with full hookups, half have 50-amp power, the rest 30-amp. Sites are large and there's lots of maneuvering room, the campground is suitable for large rigs. New restrooms are modern and tiled with hot showers

Now that access past the Playa Bonita has been cut off access is somewhat convoluted to this park. As you enter town you will pass four Pemexes, two on the left, then one on the right, then another on the left (Pemex #2488). A half mile (.8 km) after the fourth Pemex is a cross road marked with many large green signs on a pedestrian bridge over the road. Turn right here on Armada de Mexico, also called Calle 13. Proceed across the railroad tracks and drive for about 0.3 mile (0.5 km). Turn right on a dirt road named Elias Calles. The turn is marked with a sign for the Playa Bonita RV Park. Drive north for 0.2 miles (0.3 km) and turn left on Oscar Palacio. Follow the road around to the right, pass through a stop sign and in 0.3 mile (0.5 km) you'll come to another stop, a subdivision arch is directly ahead. Now turn left before the arch and go west to the first road to the right, turn right here. To this point you've been following instructions to the Playa Bonita, now the route is different. Go north for 0.3 mile (0.5 km) to a T. Turn left and drive 0.5 mile (0.8 km) to a road to the left that is signed for the La Jolla. Turn left here and drive 0.3 mile (0.5 km) to a T. Turn right and you'll see the La Jolla on the left in 0.1 mile. Wasn't that fun?

RV PARK THE REEF AT SANDY BEACH

Address:	PO Box 742, Lukeville, AZ 85341
Telephone:	(638) 383-5790
Fax:	(638) 383-6530
Website:	www.thereefrvpark.com
Email:	thereefrvpark@prodigy.net.mx
Open:	All Year

GPS Location: 31° 19' 38", W 113° 36' 12"

This used to be a popular boondocking spot. Now it's a large RV park offering full hookups above beautiful Sandy Beach.

This is a large RV park with 52 waterfront sites and over a hundred behind. These are all really big back-in sites with lots of room for big rigs. The parking surface is almost white crushed gravel, there isn't a bit of shade. About half the sites have full hookups with 50 and 30-amp outlets. Restroom facilities don't measure up to the sites, they're old and in poor condition but have hot showers for a fee. There's a popular bar/restaurant adjacent. Future improvements are planned for this park. There is also a boondocking area controlled by this campground that is along the beach on the town side of the park. There are no hookups, just a flat, well-packed area overlooking the beach. The price for boondocking is in the $$ category.

This campground is located a long distance west of town in an area that is being developed. Roads are bound to change but here's how you get to the campground at this time. As you arrive in Puerto Penasco from the direction of Sonoyta you'll spot Pemex #5082 on the left. In another half mile (.8 km) you'll spot Blvd. Samuel Ocaña going right, it should be signed for both La Cholla and The Reef RV Park. This is a new paved road, turn right onto it and follow it west. You'll pass another Pemex (#7610) on the left in 1.1 mile (1.8 km) and then come to a large traffic circle

P. PEÑASCO, GOLFO, ALGODONES

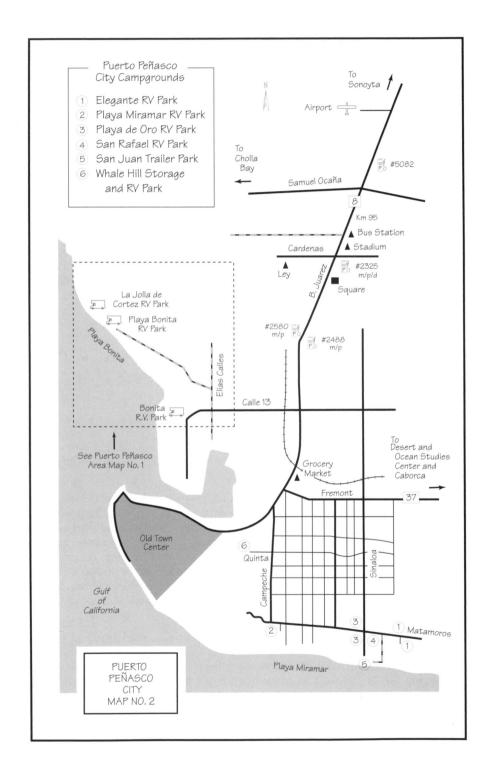

Puerto Peñasco
City Campgrounds

1 Elegante RV Park
2 Playa Miramar RV Park
3 Playa de Oro RV Park
4 San Rafael RV Park
5 San Juan Trailer Park
6 Whale Hill Storage
    and RV Park

To Sonoyta

Airport

To Cholla Bay

#5082

Samuel Ocaña

8

Km 95

Bus Station

Cardenas   Stadium

Ley   B. Juarez   #2325
                              m/p/d

                              Square

#2580
m/p   #2488
            m/p

La Jolla de
Cortez RV Park

Playa Bonita
RV Park

Playa Bonita

Elias Calles

Calle 13

Bonita
R.V. Park

See Puerto Peñasco
Area Map No. 1

Grocery
Market

To
Desert and
Ocean Studies
Center and
Caborca

Fremont   37

Old Town
Center

6

Quinta

Campeche   Sinaloa

Gulf
of
California

2

3

1 Matamoros

3 4

1

5

Playa Miramar

PUERTO
PEÑASCO
CITY
MAP NO. 2

(glorieta) in another 1.3 mile (2.1 km). Turn left here and soon you'll reach a wide dirt road. This is the old Cholla Bay Road. Turn right onto the road and watch for the signed road for The Reef on the left. Turn here and in 0.5 mile (0.8 km) you'll reach the campground gates.

ELEGANTE RV PARK

Address:	91 Matamoros Ave., Puerto Peñasco, Son., México
Reservations:	PO Box 56, Lukeville, AZ 85341
Telephone:	(638) 383-3712
Fax:	(638) 383-6071
Website:	www.elegantervpark.com
Email:	playaele@prodigy.com
Open:	All Year

GPS Location: N 31° 17' 46", W 113° 31' 54"

The Playa Elegante is the farthest-east trailer park in the look-alike group clustered along Calle Matamoros on the oceanfront east of the old town. It is a large beach-fronting campground with easy access. There is another section of the campground located a short distance away, not along the water.

The campground has 350 spaces. They are all back-in slots with 30-amp outlets, sewer, water, and satellite TV hookups. The largest rigs park here although no space is wasted. None of the spaces has a patio or shade, they all have a gravel parking surface. The bathrooms are in the main building which also houses a self-service laundry and meeting room. The bathrooms are modern and clean and have metered

MANY OF THE CAMPGROUNDS IN PUERTO PEÑASCO ARE ON THE BEACH

hot showers, they cost a quarter. There is a sun deck on the top of the main building, the beach is better for sun but the deck offers a good view. This campground also has a boat ramp.

To reach the campground when approaching Puerto Peñasco from the north on Mex 8 zero your odometer as you pass the airport. At 1.3 miles (2.1 km) you'll enter Puerto Peñasco, at 2 miles (3.2 km) you'll see the town square on the left, at 3.1 miles (5 km) you'll pass under a pedestrian overpass with a cluster of green overhead signs. At a stoplight at 3.5 miles (5.6 km) Fremont Boulevard cuts off to the left, this is Son. 37 to Caborca. Continuing straight and bear left at the Y at 3.6 miles (5.8 km) and at 4.1 miles (6.6 km) you'll reach Matamoros Ave. which runs east and west along the beach. Turn left here and pass a series of campgrounds and finally reach the right turn for the Playa Elegante at 4.7 miles (7.6 km). The campground is just down the road toward the water and to the left, the entrance is obvious.

If you are approaching from Caborca on Son. 37 watch carefully as you enter town. You'll see a paved road with wide shoulders on the left that is well marked with campground signs. This is Sinaloa, if you turn here you'll soon reach the beach and can make a left and then a right to reach the Playa Elegante. The other Calle Matamoros campgrounds are to the right stretching westward along the beach.

PLAYA MIRAMAR RV PARK

Address:	27 Matamoros Ave., Apdo. 2, CP 83550	
	Puerto Peñasco, Sonora, México	
Reservations:	PO Box 456, Lukeville, AZ 85341	
Telephone:	(638) 383-2587	
Fax:	(638) 383-2351	
Open:	All Year	

GPS Location: N 31° 17' 52", W 113° 32' 25"

This is the last (or first) of the three big RV parks between Ave. Matamoros (Calle 1) and the beach. It's the farthest west. The Playa Miramar has 90 spaces, all are back-in with 30-amp electricity, sewer, water and satellite TV. This park seems to find room for the largest rigs although it sometimes appears to be a struggle. The restrooms are very clean and have hot water for showers that are metered and cost a quarter. There is a recreation room, a laundry, and a boat ramp. Check the rates on the public phone here before you use it. This campground is close to the base of the big rock that gives Rocky Point it's name, as a result the sandy beach is fronted next to the water by bowling ball-sized black rocks. English is spoken.

If you follow the instructions given above for reaching the Playa Elegante Trailer Park the Playa Miramar is the first trailer park you'll see after turning onto Matamoros. It is on the right.

PLAYA DE ORO RV PARK

Address:	60 Matamoros Ave., Apdo. 76, CP	
	83550 Puerto Peñasco, Son., México	
Reservations:	PO Box 583, Lukeville, AZ 85341	
Telephone:	(638) 383-2668	
Website:	www.playadeoro-rv.com	
Open:	All Year	

GPS Location: N 31° 17' 48", W 113° 32' 07"

This huge campground is one of the oldest ones in Puerto Peñasco. It bills itself as the only full service RV park in Rocky Point. Quiet a bit of the park has been recently redone, particularly the service buildings. It's looking pretty good.

There are now 325 spaces at the Playa de Oro. They are located south of Matamoros Ave. along and back from the beach and also extending well inland to the north of Matamoros. The sites have 30-amp (some 50-amp) electricity, sewer, and water. They have gravel surfaces, no shade, and no patios. The bathrooms are remodeled, the showers require a quarter for 4 to 5 minutes. The campground has a small, simple restaurant, a mini-mart, a self-service laundry, and a boat ramp. There is also a large long-term storage yard for those wishing to leave a trailer or boat when they go back north.

To find the campground follow the instructions given for the Playa Elegante above. After turning left onto Matamoros proceed 0.4 miles (0.6 km), you'll see the Playa de Oro entrance on the right.

⊞ SAN RAFAEL RV PARK

Address:	Apdo. 58, CP 83550 Puerto Peñasco, Son., México
Telephone:	(638) 383-5044, (638) 383-2681
Open:	All Year

GPS Location: N 31° 17' 49", W 113° 31' 58"

This is a smaller campground with no beachfront sites even though it is south of Calle Matamoros.

The campground has 31 slots for visiters, all have 30-amp outlets, sewer, and water. These are gravel-surfaced back-in spaces without patios or shade. These are long sites suitable for big rigs. Permanent resident rigs occupy two sides of the park. The campground has clean modern restrooms with hot showers, a TV room, a self-service laundry, and English is spoken.

To find the campground follow the instructions given for the Playa Elegante above. After turning left onto Matamoros proceed 0.5 miles (0.8 km), you'll see the San Rafael entrance on the right.

⊞ SAN JUAN TRAILER PARK

Telephone:	(602) 344-4175 (US), (638) 388-0516
Open:	All Year

GPS Location: N 31° 17' 42", W 113° 31' 52"

This is a new campground on the beach side of the San Rafael RV Park. There are about 20 back-in sites, half are waterfront. A few have 50-amp outlets, most have 30-amp. All spaces also have water and sewer outlets. Restrooms have hot water showers.

To find the campground follow the instructions given for the Playa Elegante above. After turning left onto Matamoros proceed 0.5 miles (0.8 km), you'll see the San Rafael entrance on the right. Turn right down the street just after the San Rafael, the San Juan Trailer Park is at the end of the street next to the water.

WHALE HILL STORAGE AND RV PARK

Address:	PO Box 1704, Lukeville, AZ 85341
Location:	Campeche y Primo de Verdad, CP 82550 Pto. Peñasco, Sonora, México
Telephone:	(638) 383-6066
Open:	All Year

GPS Location: N 31° 18'07", W 113° 32'35"

Whale Hill RV park nestles up to the east side of the Rocky Point rock. It offers a central location but is not on the beach. Despite this it is generally almost full of long-term campers, the price is right.

The campground has 24 sites inside a walled compound and another 8 outside. These are full-hookup back-in sites with 30-amp outlets. Inside the compound there is one restroom, it has a hot shower.

To reach the campground when approaching Puerto Peñasco from the north on Mex 8 zero your odometer as you pass the airport. At 1.3 miles (2.1 km) you'll enter Puerto Peñasco, at 2 miles (3.2 km) you'll see the town square on the left, at 3.1 miles (5 km) you'll pass under a pedestrian overpass with a cluster of green overhead signs. At a stoplight at 3.5 miles (5.6 km) Fremont Boulevard cuts off to the left, this is Son. 37 to Caborca. Continuing straight and bear left at the Y at 3.6 miles (5.8 km). Now watch on the right for the sign for the Whale Hill RV park, you'll turn to the right on Calle Quinta and find the campground at the end of the road.

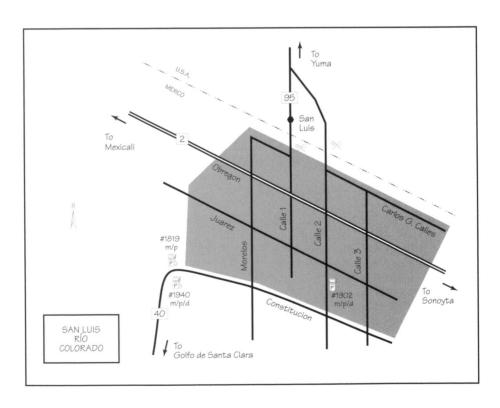

SAN LUIS RÍO COLORADO, SONORA AND SAN LUIS, ARIZONA

This small town, tucked right up against the line directly south of Yuma, is the best place to cross if you are headed toward Golfo de Santa Clara. The crossing is open 24 hours and has a much better reputation with RVers than Algodones, the crossing nearest to Yuma. Besides, the route to Golfo is much shorter and quicker than if you cross in Algodones.

Yuma probably has more campgrounds than any similar sized city anywhere in the U.S. so we won't pick one as the best place to stay before heading south. You should be aware that most of these campgrounds are filled with snowbirds for the entire season so get a reservation ahead of time if you plan to spend the night.

SAN LUIS RÍO COLORADO TO GOLFO DE SANTA CLARA
71 Miles (114 Km), 2 Hours

The road to Golfo de Santa Clara is Highway 40. Watch for signs in San Luis Río Colorado, the way is well-signed. This it a two-lane paved road, much of it through farming country. You may share the road with a few tractors and overloaded trucks during the first half of your drive.

If you cross the border at San Luis it's easy to find your way out of town to the south. Go straight for 0.2 miles (0.3 km), then turn left on Juarez. Almost immediately turn right on Calle 2. In 0.5 mile (0.8 km) turn right following the sign to Golfo. In 1.8 mile (2.9 km) you'll see Pemex #1940 on the left, it's a sign that you're on the right road. From here it's just a matter of following the highway.

GOLFO DE SANTA CLARA (GOLF-OH DAY SAHN-TAW CLAW-RAH)
Population 1,500

If you are looking for a piece of the real outback Mexico with no tourist glitz Golfo de Santa Clara is the place for you. This is a small fishing village surrounded by miles and miles of sand. Most tourist guides don't even mention the town but it is becoming something of a popular camping destination. A camping club operates the only decent RV campground in town, however, so your choices of places to stay are limited if you are not a member. See *Other Camping Possibilities* below for more about this club campground. Non-member choices are largely beachfront restaurants with San Felipe-style ramadas, perhaps with an electric light bulb. During holidays this town really fills with Mexicali residents seeking a little beach time. The beach south of town stretches for miles and ATVs are welcome.

The busiest day of the year for Golfo is June 1, Día de la Marina, lots of people come down from Mexicali and San Luis for the party.

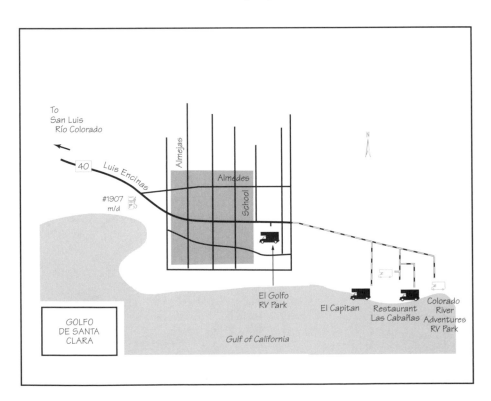

Golfo de Santa Clara Campgrounds

🚐 EL GOLFO RV PARK

Open: All Year

GPS Location: N 31° 41' 08", W 114° 29' 53"

This little campground is very basic. People from the club campground often stay here for a period so they can qualify to go back to the campground on the beach.

There are 12 back-in slots with 30-amp outlets, sewer, and water on a dirt lot. Some sites will take big rigs but it would be crowded if all 12 sites were full. That's uncommon from what we hear. There are no restroom facilities. A manager usually lives on site.

To find the RV park zero your odometer as you come to Pemex # 1907 at the entrance to town. Continue straight on the pavement for 0.2 miles (0.3 km), the park is on the right side of the road and you reach it just before you reach the end of the pavement.

🚐 EL CAPITAN

Open: All Year

GPS Location: N 31° 40' 43", W 114° 29' 25"

The El Capitan is a palapa-style restaurant and bar near the beach. It advertises that it has the best shrimp in town – cheap. The restaurant also has a row of ramadas for

GOLFO DE SANTA CLARA IS POPULAR FOR OFF ROAD VEHICLES

tent campers out front, you can park an RV here too if you want. There are bathrooms with flush toilets but no showers. Expect this place to be pretty busy during any holidays.

To find the El Capitan watch for Pemex # 1907 as you come in to town. Zero your odometer and keep going straight. You'll reach the end of the pavement at 0.4 miles (0.6 km), the road turns to (hopefully) packed sand and you'll see the El Capitan on the right at 1.1 miles (1.8 km).

RESTAURANT LAS CABAÑAS

Open: All Year

GPS Location: N 31° 40' 35", W 114° 29' 22"

This is another palapa-style beach restaurant which also has motel rooms. It sits right next to the club campground. It too has connected ramadas for tent camping and will allow RVs to park on the grounds. There are flush toilets but no showers. Some of the ramadas have an electric light and outlet. To find this campground just follow the El Capitan directions above. You'll find the Las Cabañas about a block beyond the El Capitan.

Other Camping Possibilities

There is an RV park about a mile south of town on the beach. We stayed there several years ago, it had a great location but terrible facilities. The new operator has improved the facilities so this is probably the best place in Golfo. It is operated by Colorado River Adventures, a camping club with several campgrounds along the lower Colorado River. You must be a member to stay there. They are affiliated with Coast to Coast so members of that organization may also find a spot. Call (760) 663-4941 to check.

The El Capitan and the las Cabañas are just two of the places out near the Colorado River Adventures campground. Many more offer ramadas along the beach, you could probably arrange to stay at many of them. Be aware of security, however, it's best to be at a place that offers an on-site manager and night watchman.

ALGODONES
Population 15,000

Algodones is a very popular border town. People from the Yuma area usually come over on foot to visit reasonably-priced pharmacies, doctors and dentists. There are also lots of curio shops and restaurants. Now there's even an RV park.

Algodones Campground

VALENCIA OUT LOOK RV PARK

Telephone: (686) 554-0848 or
                 (928) 246-9489 (U.S. cell phone)
Open: All Year

GPS Location: N 32° 42' 30", W 114° 43' 50"

The Valencia Outlook is a newer park located near the south edge of Algodones.

Many people stay here for a week or a month but there are daily rates too. The park has 20 back-in full-hookup spaces with 30-amp power. There's plenty of parking room for big rigs. The park is fully fenced and gated so security is good. Restrooms are good with flush toilets and hot showers. This is a very tidy park.

When you cross the border drive one block to Ave A, turn right and drive 4 blocks to a 4-way stop. Turn left here on Av. Sexta and follow the signs for San Luis Río Colorado for about .7 mile (1.1 km). You'll pass through several stop signs and the road curves to the left and then the right. Just after the right bend you'll see a sign pointing right down Calle Morelos, a dirt street. The campground is about .1 mile (.2 km) block down the street on the left.

APPENDIX - BAJA ROAD SIGNS

Speed Bump
(Tope)

**CAMINO SINUOSO
PROXIMOS 38 km**

Winding Road
Next 38 Kilometers

**DESVIACION
A 500 MTS**

Detour
In 400 Meters

**ESTA CARRETERA NO
ES DE ALTA VELOCIDAD**

This Is Not A High
Speed Road

Stay Right

**CON NIEBLA ENCIENDA
SUS   LUCES**

In Fog Turn On Lights

DISMINUYA SU VELOCIDAD

Reduce Your Speed

**GRACIAS POR USAR EL
CINTURON DE SEGURIDAD**

Thanks For Using
Your Seat Belt

Yield

**CONCEDA CAMBIO
DE LUCES**

Dim Your Lights
For Oncoming Traffic

**DISMINUYA SU VELOCIDAD
CURVA PELIGROSA**

Reduce Your Speed
Dangerous Curve

**MANEJE CON
PRECAUCION**

Drive With Caution

Falling Rocks
(Derumbe)

**CURVA PELIGROSA
A 400 m**

Dangerous Curve
In 400 Meters

**EN B.C.S. ES OBLIGATORIO EL
CINTURON DE SEGURIDAD**

In Baja California South
Seat Belts Are
Mandatory

**MAS VALE TARDE
QUE NUNCA**

Better Late
Than Never

No Passing

DESPACIO

Slow

**ENTRADA Y SALIDA
DE CAMIONES**

Truck Entrance
And Exit

**MIRADOR DE
MOLINERO**

Viewpoint Of Mill

No Right
Turn

Livestock On
The Road

Stop

Speed Bump
(Tope)

NO MALTRATE LAS SEÑALES

Do Not Mistreat
The Signs

PRECAUCION ENTRADA Y SALIDA DE MAQUINARIA

Precaution Entrance
And Exit of Machinery

TERMINA B.C. PRINCIPIA B.C.S.

Leaving Baja California
Entering Baja California South

NO FRENE CON MOTOR

No Braking With Engine

PRECAUCION ZONA DE GANADO

Precaution Livestock Zone

TOPES A 100m

Speed Bumps In 100 Meters

NO DEJE PIEDRAS SOBRE EL PAVIMENTO

Do Not Leave Rocks
On The Road

PRINCIPIA TRAMO EN REPARACION A 500 m

Main Highway Under
Repair in 500 Meters

TRANSITO LENTO CARRIL DERECHO

Slow Traffic Right Lane

NO REBASE CON RAYA CONTINUA

No Passing When
Contineous Line

PROHIBIDO GRAFFITEAR

Graffiti Prohibited

TROPICO DE CANCER

Tropic Of Cancer

OBEDEZCA LAS SEÑALES

Obey The Signs

PROHIBIDO TIRAR BASURA

Throwing Garbage Prohibited

VADO A 300 m

Gully (Ford) In 300 Meters

PRECAUCION CRUCE DE PEATONES

Caution
Pedestrian Crossing

REDUCTOR DE VELOCIDAD A 400 m

Speed Bump (Tope)
In 400 Meters

ZONA URBANA MODERE VELOCIDAD

Urban Zone
Slow Down

PRECAUCION CURVA PELIGROSA A 300MTS

Caution Dangerous
Curve In 300 Meters

RESPETE LIMITE DE VELOCIDAD

Respect the Speed
Limit

Water Over
Road (Vado)

SI TOMA NO MANEJE

If You Drink Don't
Drive

km 1 0 7

Kilometer
Marker

Level Of Water
Over Road

Index

28th Parallel, 99, 108

Accidents, 35
Agua Verde, 153
Air conditioner use, 21
Algodones border crossing, 27
Algodones, 242
Altamara Beach, 100
Aquamarina RV Park, 167

Backroad Adventures
 Central Baja, 101
 Central Gulf of California Coast, 125
 Los Cabos, 192
 Puerto Peñasco, 225
 San Felipe, 204
 South to Ensenada, 51
 South to La Paz, 153
 Southern Loop, 175
 Southern Northwest Coast, 82
Backroad Driving, 18
Bahía Asunción, 102
Bahía Concepción, 123, 125, 136
Bahía de los Angeles, 97, 100, 112
Bahía de Sueños, 154
Bahía Falsa, 83
Bahía La Ventana, 153
Bahía Las Animas, 102
Bahía Magdalena, 152, 161
Bahía San Francisquito, 102
Bahía San Quintín, 80
Bahía San Rafael, 102
Bahía Santa María, 192
Bahía Tordillo, 140
Bahía Tortugas, 102
Baja Ferries, 30
Baja Fiesta Restaurant, 88
Baja Serena, 179
Balandra Bay, 169
Balneario El Palomar, 86
Bay of Dreams, , 154
Beaches and Water Sports
 Central Baja, 99
 Central Gulf of California Coast, 124

Los Cabos, 191
Puerto Peñasco, 225
San Felipe, 204
South to Ensenada, 51
South to La Paz, 152
Southern Loop, 174
Southern Northwest Coast,, 81
Benito Juárez Trailer Park, 108
Boat permit, 26
Boat ramp, 82, 112, 114, 115, 124, 125,
 135, 148, 161, 175, 182, 205, 225,
 236, 237,
Bonita RV Park, 231
Books, 37
Border crossings, 24, 26
Boulevard Mijares, 190
Breakdowns, 39
Brisa del Mar RV Resort, 200
Brisa Marina RV Park, 116
Buenaventura Resort & Restaurant
 Bar, 141
Butane, 33

Cabo del Sol Desert Golf Course, 191
Cabo del Sol Golf Course, 191
Cabo Pulmo Campground, 186
Cabo Pulmo, 173, 174, 176, 192
Cabo Real Golf Course, 191
Cabo San Lucas, 193
Cactus, 98
Caleta San Lucas, 129
Calexico, 207
California gray whales, 97, 98
Camalú, 84
Camp Archelon, 116
Camp Gecko, 115
Camp San Fernando, 219
Campestre La Pila Balneario and
 Trailer Park, 156
Campestre Maranatha, 166
Campground bathroom facilities, 19
Campground hookups, 19
Campgrounds, 19
Campgrounds

Algodones, 242
Bahía Concepción, 137
Bahía de los Angeles, 114
Cabo San Lucas to San José del
    Cabo, 197
Cabo San Lucas, 194
Cataviña to Guerrero Negro, 107
Cataviña, 105
El Rosario to Cataviña, 103
El Rosario, 95
Ensenada to San Quintín, 84
Guerrero Negro to San Ignacio, 118
Guerrero Negro, 107
La Paz, 164
Lopez Mateos, 160
Loreto to Puerto Escondido, 147
Loreto, 144
Los Barriles to San José del Cabo, 186
Los Barriles, 182
Lukeville to Puerto Peñasco, 228
Mexicali to San Felipe, 207
Mexicali, 205
Mulegé, 133
Puerto Peñasco, 231
Puerto San Carlos, 162
San Felipe, 211
San Ignacio, 119
San José del Cabo, 200
San Quintín, 90
Santa Rosalía, 128
Sonoyta and Lukeville, 226
South of San Felipe, 219
Todos Santos to Cabo San Lucas, 179
Todos Santos, 177
Camping Petates, 121
Camping Uruapan, 84
Campo Mosqueda, 208
Campo Sonora, 207
Campo Turistico Bajamar, 217
Campo Turistico Kiki's, 213
Campo Vista Hermosa, 220
Cañon del Diablo, 204
Cañon Guadalupe, 205
Caravan company list, 22
Caravans, 21
Carnival, 151
Casa Diaz, 115
Cash machines, 23
Cash, 22
Cataviña, 97, 104

CEDO, 225
Cerro Pedregoso, 106
Checkpoint, 107
Cielito Lindo Motel and RV Park, 90
Ciudad Constitución, 155
Club Cabo Motel and Camp Resort, 194
Club de Golf San José del Cabo, 191
Club de Pesca RV Park, 218
Condo Suites and RV Park Playa
    Bonita, 213
Credit cards, 22
Crossing the Border, 24
Cuesta del Infierno, 127
Cueva Ratón, 102, 118

Daggett's Beach Camping, 116
Datilillo, 118
Desert and Ocean Studies Center, 225
Desert Oasis Resort, 230
Desert trails RV Park and Golf
    Course, 205
Día de la Marina, 211, 240
Distance Table, 20
Distances, 19
Diving, 132, 186, 192
Dominican missions, 81
Drinking water, 28
Driving in Mexico, 33
Drugs, 28

Eagle statue, 107
East Cape RV Resort, 183
Eiffel church, 128
Ejidos, 21
El Arco RV Park, 198
El Arco, 102
El Capitan, 241
El Cardonal, 176
El Cardonal's Hide-a-Way Resort, 185
El Conejo, 154San Juan de la Costa, 154
El Golfo RV Park, 241
El Litro, 177
El Mármol, 98, 101
El Mayor Trailer Park, 208
El Pabellón Palapas Alvinos, 93
El Pabellón RV Park, 92
El Pescadero, 178
El Pinacate, 225
El Requesón, 141
El Rosario de Abajo, 94

El Rosario de Arriba, 94
El Rosario, 80, 94
El Sombrerito, 132
El Tomatal, 101
El Triunfo, 181
Eldorado Golf Course, 191
Elegante RV Park, 235
English cemetery, 89
Ensenada Los Muertos, 153, 154
Ensenada San Francisquito, 205
Eréndira, 82
Espinosa's Place, 94
ESSA, 108
Evaristo, 154
Exportadadora de Sal, 108
Ferries, 29

Ferry Santa Rosalía, 30
Finisterra, 190, 193
Fishing license, 26
Fishing, 30
Fishing
    Central Baja,, 100
    Central Gulf of California Coast, 125
    Los Cabos, 192
    Puerto Peñasco, 225
    San Felipe, 204
    South to Ensenada, 51
    South to La Paz, 152
    Southern Loop, 175
    Southern Northwest Coast, 81
    Southern Northwest Coast, 89
Fonatur, 143, 148, 199
Fuel, 30

Gas prices, 31
Gas stations, 30
Glass factory, 190
Golf
    Central Gulf of California Coast, 124
    Los Cabos, 191
    Puerto Peñasco, 225
    South to Ensenada, 51
Golfo de Santa Clara, 240
Gorda Banks, 192
Government campgrounds, 21
GPS, 47
Gran Desierto De Altar, 225
Gray whales, 97, 152, 159, 161
Green Angels, 31

Gringo Pass Motel and RV park, 226
Grist mill, 81
Groceries, 31
Guerrero Negro, 108
Guillermo's Hotel and RV Park, 114
Guns, 28
Gypsy's Beach Camp, 91

Hacienda de la Habana, 133
Hacienda de Marcos, 228
Highlights
    Central Baja, 97
    Central Gulf of California Coast, 123
    Los Cabos, 190
    Puerto Peñasco, 223
    San Felipe, 203
    South to Ensenada, 49
    South to La Paz, 151
    Southern Loop, 173
Hookup voltage, 19
Hotel Cuesta Real, 134
Hotel Serenidad, 135
Hunting, 89

Insurance broker list, 25
Insurance, 25
Internet, 32
Isla Angel de la Guarda, 112
Isla Carmen, 144
Isla San Marcos, 130
Itinerary, 14

Juncalito Beach, 147

Kayaking, 100, 112, 116, 125, 131, 132,
    140, 144, 148, 153, 161
Key to symbols, 46

L.A. Bay Junction, 107
La Bocana, 82
La Bufadora, 83
La Espinita Motel and Restaurant, 108
La Jolla de Cortez RV Park, 232
La Palapa RV Camp, 215
La Paz Trailer Park, 167
La Paz, 163
La Posada de Don Vicente, 110
La Purísima, 154
La Ribera, 185, 192
La Ventana del Mar, 210

La Ventana, 169
Laguna Chapala, 106
Laguna Manuela, 100, 101, 107
Laguna Percebú, 204
Laguna San Ignacio, 97, 102, 119
Lakeside RV Park, 121
Land's End, 190
Las Canadas Campamento, 84
Las Conchas, 225
Las Palmas, 128
Las Tres Virgines, 127
Lázaro Cárdenas, 84
Ligui Beach, 149
Lopez Mateos, 159
Loreto Shores Villas and RV Park, 144
Loreto, 123, 143
Los Arcos at Finisterra, 190
Los Barriles, 173, 182
Los Cerritos, 180
Los Flores, 102
Los Frailes, 173, 174, 176, 186, 192
Los Naranjos Beach, 137
Lover's Beach, 191, 193
Lukeville, 224
Lukeville/Sonoyta Crossing, 224

Magdalena Bay, 153
Malarrimo RV Park, 111
Malecón, 164
Malibu Beach Sur RV Park, 86
Maneadero, 83
Manfred's RV Trailer Park, 156
Map legend, 45
Map
    Algodones, 243
    Bahía Concepción to Loreto, 143
    Bahía Concepción, 138
    Cabo San Lucas to San José del Cabo, 196
    Cabo San Lucas, 194
    Cataviña to Guerrero Negro, 106
    Cataviña, 104
    Central Baja, 96
    Central Gulf Coast, 122
    Ciudad Constitución to La Paz, 162
    Ciudad Constitución, 157
    El Rosario to Cataviña, 103
    El Rosario, 95
    Ensenada to San Quintín, 85
    Golfo de Santa Clara, 240

Guerrero Negro to San Ignacio, 117
Guerrero Negro, 109
La Paz Area, No. 1, 164
La Paz Area, No. 2, 165
La Paz to Los Barriles, 181
La Paz to Todos Santos, 177
Loreto to Puerto Escondido, 147
Loreto, 145
Los Barriles to San José del Cabo, 187
Los Barriles, 183
Los Cabos, 188
Mexicali to San Felipe, 208
Mexicali, 206
Mulegé to Bahía Concepción, 136
Mulegé, 133
Puerto Escondido to Ciudad
    Constitución, 155
Puerto Escondido, 149
Puerto Peñasco Area, No. 1, 231
Puerto Peñasco City, No. 2, 234
Puerto Peñasco, Golfo, and
    Algodones, 222
San Felipe, 202, 212
San Ignacio to Santa Rosalía, 126
San Ignacio, 120
San José del Cabo, 200
San Luis Río Colorado to Golfo
    de Santa Clara, 239
San Luis Río Colorado, 238
San Quintín to El Rosario, 93
San Quintín, 90
Santa Rosalía to Mulegé, 130
Santa Rosalía, 128
Side Trip to Bahía de los Angeles, 113
Side Trip to La Ventana, 170
Side Trip to Lopez Mateos, 160
Side Trip to Puerto San Carlos, 161
Side Trip to San Juanico, 158
Sonoyta and Lukeville, 227
Sonoyta to Puerto Peñasco, 229
South of San Felipe, 219
South to La Paz, 150
Southern Loop, 172
Todos Santos to Cabo San Lucas, 180
Todos Santos, 178
Mar y Sol Trailer Park, 230
Marco's Trailer Park, 211
Marine Staircase, 114
Mario's Tours and Restaurant, 110
Martin Verdugo's Beach Resort, 182

MasterCard, 23
Meling Ranch, 83
Mesón Don Pepe, 88
Mexicali border crossings, 27
Mexicali, 205
Mid-Winter West Hobie Cat Regatta, 210
Miraflores, 186
Misión el Rosario, 81, 83
Misión Nuestra Señora de
    Loreto, 124, 143
Misión San Borja, 99, 101, 107
Misión San Fernando Velicatá, 99, 101
Misión San Francisco Javier, 146
Misión San Ignacio, 119
Misión San Javier, 124
Misión San Vicente Ferrer, 81
Misión Santa Gertrudis, 102
Misión Santa Maria, 99
Misión Santa Rosalía de Mulegé, 124, 132
Misión Santo Domingo, 81
Misión Santo Tomás de Aquino, 78, 81
Molino Viejo, 89
Motel and RV Park El Moro, 146
Motel Brisa Salina, 111
Motel Kadekaman, 118
Motel Sinahi RV Park, 95
Muelle Viejo, 89
Mulegé, 124, 132
Museo de los Misiones, 143
Museum of Anthropology, 164

Nopoló, 124

Oasis RV Park, 164
Ojo de Liebre Lagoon Campground, 112
Ojo de Liebre, 97, 108, 118
Old English Cemetary, 81
Old Mill Trailer Park, 92
Old pier, 81
Organ Pipe N.M., 226
Otay Mesa, 26

Palapa 206 RV Park, 156
Palmilla Golf Course, 191
Parque Nacional Sierra San Pedro
    Mártir, 80, 81, 83, 87
Parque Natural Desierto Central Trailer
Park, 105
Pemex sign key, 44
Peso, 22

Pete's Camp, 209
Pets, 33
Picacho Diablo, 81
Playa Armenta, 142
Playa Bahía Chileno, 192
Playa Balandra, 153
Playa Barco Varado, 192
Playa Bonita RV Park, 232
Playa Bonita, 225
Playa Caimancito, 153
Playa Costa Azul, 192
Playa de Laura, 216
Playa de Oro RV Park, 236
Playa del Amor, 190, 191, 193
Playa Dos Amigos, 131
Playa El Corumuel, 153
Playa El Coyote, 141
Playa El Tesoro, 153
Playa Ensenada el Burro, 140
Playa Escondida, 140
Playa La Gringa, 117
Playa La Perla, 142
Playa Las Almejas, 204
Playa Las Conchas, 225
Playa Los Cocos, 140
Playa Medano, 192, 194
Playa Miramar RV Park, 236
Playa Norte RV Haven, 184
Playa Pabellón, 81
Playa Pacheco, 100
Playa Palmira, 153
Playa Pichilingue, 153
Playa San Felipe, 204
Playa Santa María, 81
Playa Santispac, 139
Playa Tecolote, 153, 167
Playas del Sol, 209
Playas Miramar, 170
Posada Concepción, 140
Posada del Mar, 215
Posada Don Diego Trailer Park, 89
Price icon key, 45
Propane, 33
Puertecitos, 204
Puerto Escondido, 148
Puerto Lopez Mateos, 152
Puerto Peñasco, 230
Puerto San Carlos, 161
Puerto San Isidro, 82
Puerto Santo Tomás, 82

Punta Arena, 137
Punta Chivato, 124, 130, 131
Punta Conejo, 163
Punta Eugenia, 102
Punta Pescadero, 176
Punta Prieta RV Park at the L.A. Bay
    Junction, 107
Punta San Jacinto Campground, 87
Punta Santa Rosalillita, 100, 101

Quality Star RV Park, 229
Quercia Country Club, 191
Quinta María, 185

Rancho La Trinidad, 125
Rancho Los Manzanos, 88
Rancho Punta Estrella, 221
Rancho Santa Inez, 105
Rancho Verde RV Haven, 181
Raven at Cabo San Lucas Country
    Club, 191
Residence Betel II, 220
Resort-Hotel San Buenaventura, 141
Restaurant Las Cabañas, 242
Restaurant, Mikasa, 121
Rice and Beans Oasis, 119
Rio Hardy, 207
Río Santa María, 94
Riserva De La Biosfera de El
    Pinacate, 225
Rivera Del Mar RV Park and
    Camping, 145
Roadblocks, 28
Roads and Fuel Availability
    Central Baja, 98
    Central Gulf of California Coast, 123
    Los Cabos, 190
    Puerto Peñasco, 224
    San Felipe, 203
    South to Ensenada, 49
    South to La Paz, 151
    Southern Loop, 173
    Southern Northwest Coast, 80
Roads, 33
Rock art museum, 119
Rock art, 66, 124
Rocky Point, 225
Route, Bahía Concepción to Loreto, 142

Route
    Cabo San Lucas to San José del
        Cabo, 195
    Cataviña to Guerrero Negro, 106
    Ciudad Constitución to La Paz, 162
    El Rosario to Cataviña, 102
    Ensenada to San Quintín, 83
    Guerrero Negro to San Ignacio, 117
    La Paz to Los Barriles, 180
    La Paz to Todos Santos, 176
    Loreto to Puerto Escondido, 146
    Los Barriles to San José del Cabo, 185
    Lukeville to Puerto Peñasco, 227
    Mexicali to San Felipe, 206
    Mulegé to Bahía Concepción, 136
    Puerto Escondido to Ciudad
        Constitución, 154
    San Ignacio to Santa Rosalía, 126
    San Luis Río Colorado to Golfo de
        Santa Clara, 239
    San Quintín to El Rosario, 93
    Santa Rosalía to Mulegé, 129
    Side Trip to Bahía de los Angeles, 112
    Side Trip to La Ventana, 169
    Side Trip to Lopez Mateos, 159
    Side Trip to Puerto San Carlos, 160
    Side Trip to San Juanico, 157
    Todos Santos to Cabo San Lucas, 178
Ruben's RV Trailer Park, 213
Rupestrian art, 99, 124
RV Camacho, 130
RV Casa Blanca, 166
RV Park Campo San Felipe, 216
RV Park El Padrino, 120
RV Park San Lucas Cove, 131
RV Park the Reef at Sandy Beach, 233

Safety, 35
Salt, 108
San Antonio, 181
San Evaristo, 153
San Felipe, 209, 210 250
San Francisco de la Sierra, 118
San Francisco, 102
San Ignacio, 119
San Isidro, 154
San José Comondú, 152
San José de Magdalena, 125
San José del Cabo, 199
San Juan de los Planes, 169

San Juan Trailer Park, 237
San Juanico, 154, 157, 158
San Lucas, 129
San Luis Río border crossing, 27
San Luis Río Colorado, 224, 239
San Miguel Comondú, 152, 154
San Nicolas, 126
San Quintín, 84, 89
San Rafael RV Park, 237
San Sebastian, 125
San Ysidro, 26
Sandy Beach, 225
Sandy Point, 100
Santa Rosalía Church, 128
Santa Rosalía, 127
Santa Rosalillita, 100, 107
Santiago, 174, 185
Santo Tomás Valley, 79
Scammon's Lagoon, 108
Scorpion Bay, 158
Semana Santa, 210
Sematur Transbordadores, 30
Shipwreck Beach, 192
Shrimp Festival, 211
Sierra de la Giganta, 143
Sierra de la Laguna, 176
Sierra San Francisco, 102, 118
Sightseeing
    Central Baja, 98
    Central Gulf of California Coast, 124
    Los Cabos, 190
    Puerto Peñasco, 225
    South to Ensenada, 50
    South to La Paz, 152
    Southern Loop, Southern Loop, 174
    Southern Northwest Coast, 81
Snorkeling, 186, 192
Sonora Free Zone, 24
Sonora RV Camping (Loncheria
    Sonora), 103
Sonoyta border crossing, 27
Sonoyta, Sonora, and Lukeville,
    Arizona, 226
Spanish language, 36
Spring Break, 210
Symbol key, 46

Tecate border crossing, 27
Telephones, 36
Temporary vehicle permits, 24, 25

The Wall, 100
Tijuana border crossings, 26
Todos Santos, 177
Toilet paper, 19
Tour itinerary, 14
Tourist card, 24
Trailer Park Martin Quezada Ruíz, 121
Transpeninsular Highway, 33
Transportación Maritima de California, 30
Travel library, 37
Travelers checks, 23
Tripui Hotel-RV Park, 148
Tropic of Cancer, 174, 186
Turtles, 112
Type 1 Road, 18
Type 2 Road, 19
Type 3 Road, 19

Units of Measurement, 39
Using telephones, 36

Vegetable treatment, 28
Vehicle insurance, 25
Vehicle preparation, 39
Vicente Guerrero, 84
Victor's RV Park, 217
Villa Maria Isabel Recreational Park, 135
Villa Marina Campo Turistico, 220
Villa Serena, 198
Villa Vitta Hotel Resort, 114
Visa, 23
Vista del Mark, 214
Vizcaíno Desert, 118
Volcanos, 89
Voltage, 19

Wahoo RV Center, 200
Weather, 41
Whale Hill Storage and RV Park, 238
When to go, 41
Wi-Fi, 47
Windsurfing, 161, 169, 182

Yo Yo's Campground, 171

TERRI AND MIKE

ABOUT THE AUTHORS

For the last fourteen years Terri and Mike Church have traveled in the western U.S., Alaska, Canada, Mexico, and Europe. Most of this travel has been in RVs, a form of travel they love. It's affordable and comfortable; the perfect way to see interesting places.

Over the years they discovered that few guidebooks were available with the essential day-to-day information that camping travelers need when they are in unfamiliar surroundings. *Traveler's Guide to Camping Mexico's Baja, Traveler's Guide to Mexican Camping, Southwest Camping Destinations, Pacific Northwest Camping Destinations, Traveler's Guide To Alaskan Camping, Traveler's Guide to European Camping, RV* and *Car Camping Vacations in Europe,* are designed to be the guidebooks that the authors tried to find when they first traveled to these places.

Terri and Mike live full-time in an RV – traveling, writing new books, and working to keep these guidebooks as up to date as possible. The books are written and prepared for printing using laptop computers while on the road.

Traveler's Guide To Mexican Camping
6" x 9" Paperback, 480 Pages, Over 250 Maps
ISBN 0-9749471-2-1

Third Edition - Copyright 2005

Mexico, one of the world's most interesting travel destinations, is just across the southern U.S. border. It offers warm sunny weather all winter long, beautiful beaches, colonial cities, and excellent food. Best of all, you can easily and economically visit Mexico in your own car or RV.

The third edition of *Traveler's Guide To Mexican Camping* is now even better! It has become the bible for Mexican campers. With this book you will cross the border and travel Mexico like a veteran. It is designed to make your trip as simple and trouble-free as possible. Maps show the exact location of campgrounds and the text gives written driving instructions as well as information regarding the size of RV suitable for each campground. In addition to camping and campground information the guide also includes information about cities, roads and driving, trip preparation, border crossing, vehicle care, shopping, and entertainment.

Pacific Northwest Camping Destinations
6" x 9" Paperback, 416 Pages, Over 115 Maps
ISBN 0-9749471-3-X

First Edition - Copyright 2006

Seashores, snow-capped mountains and visitor friendly cities have made the Pacific Northwest one of the most popular RV and tent camping destinations in North America, and this guide takes you to more than 100 destinations and 700 campgrounds throughout Oregon, Washington, and British Columbia.

Combining the functions of a campground directory and a sightseeing guide, each entry describes a vacation spot and its attractions and recommends good camping locations in the area, including privately owned, federal, state, and county campgrounds. Each campground is described in detail including a recommendation for the maximum size RV suitable for the campground. Written driving instructions as well as a map are provided showing the exact location. Tourist destinations are described and several itineraries are provided for driving on scenic routes throughout the region.

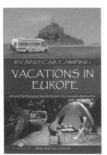

RV and Car Camping Vacations in Europe
6" x 9" Paperback, 320 Pages, Over 140 Maps
ISBN 0-9652968-9-X

First Edition - Copyright 2004

People from North America love to visit Europe on their vacations. One great way to travel in Europe is by RV or car, spending the night in convenient and inexpensive campgrounds. It's a way to travel economically and get off the beaten tourist trail. It's also a great way to meet Europeans. Many of them travel the same way!

Most of us lead busy lives with little time to spend on planning an unusual vacation trip. With this book a camping vacation in Europe is easy. It tells how to arrange a rental RV or car from home, when to go and what to take with you. It explains the process of picking up the rental vehicle and turning it back in when you're ready to head for home. There's also information about shopping, driving, roads, and other things that you should know before you arrive. Then it describes a series of tours, each taking from a week to two weeks. The ten tours cover much of Western Europe and even the capitals of the Central European countries. The book has details about the routes and roads, the campgrounds to use, and what to do and see while you are there.

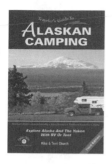

Traveler's Guide To Alaskan Camping
6" x 9" Paperback, 448 Pages, Over 100 Maps
ISBN 0-9749471-1-3

Third Edition - Copyright 2005

Alaska, the dream trip of a lifetime! Be prepared for something spectacular. Alaska is one fifth the size of the entire United States, it has 17 of the 20 highest peaks in the U.S., 33,904 miles of shoreline, and has more active glaciers and ice fields than the rest of the inhabited world. In addition to some of the most magnificent scenery the world has to offer, Alaska is chock full of an amazing variety of wildlife. Fishing, hiking, kayaking, rafting, hunting, and wildlife viewing are only a few of the many activities which will keep you outside during the long summer days.

Traveler's Guide To Alaskan Camping makes this dream trip to Alaska as easy as camping in the "Lower 48". It includes almost 500 campgrounds throughout Alaska and on the roads north in Canada with full campground descriptions, appropriate RV size for each campground, and maps showing exact locations. It also is filled with suggested things to do and see including fishing holes, hiking trails, canoe trips, wildlife viewing opportunities, and much more.

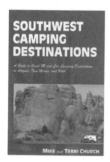

Southwest Camping Destinations
6" x 9" Paperback, 416 Pages, Over 100 Maps
ISBN 0-9749471-4-8

First Edition - Available September 2006

Bryce Canyon, Carlsbad Caverns, the Grand Canyon, and Mesa Verde are among the 100 destinations covered in this travel guide for RVers and car campers. Native American sites and desert habitats are also of interest in this region, making it a great vacation destination for families with children. Maps are provided for each destination along with descriptions of tourist attractions and listings for more than 500 traveler campgrounds.

For those who want to escape to a warm climate in the winter there is a special "snowbird" chapter which gives details on top snowbird destinations in the southwest. Over 350 campgrounds are compared in destination like Palm Springs, Las Vegas, Lake Havasu and Parker, Needles and Laughlin, Yuma, Quartzsite, Phoenix, Mesa, Apache Junction, Casa Grande, and Tucson. This analysis is accompanied by maps showing the exact locations of campgrounds in these favorite destinations.

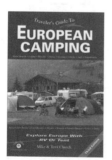

Traveler's Guide To European Camping
6" x 9" Paperback, 640 Pages, Over 400 Maps
ISBN 0-9652968-8-1

Third Edition - Copyright 2004

Over 350 campgrounds including the best choice in every important European city are described in detail and directions are given for finding them. In many cases information about convenient shopping, entertainment and sports opportunities is included.

This guide will tell you how to rent, lease, or buy a rig in Europe or ship your own from home. It contains the answers to questions about the myriad details of living, driving, and camping in Europe. In addition to camping and campground information *Traveler's Guide To European Camping* gives you invaluable details about the history and sights you will encounter. This information will help you plan your itinerary and enjoy yourself more when you are on the road. Use the information in this book to travel Europe like a native. Enjoy the food, sights, and people of Europe. Go for a week, a month, a year. Europe can fill your RV or camping vacation seasons for many years to come!

To order complete the following and send to:

Rolling Homes Press
161 Rainbow Dr., #6157
Livingston, TX 77399-1061

Name_____

Address_____

City_____State_____Zip_____

Telephone_____

Description	Qty	Price	Subtotal
Pacific Northwest Camping Destinations	———	$19.95	———
Southwest Camping Destinations	———	$19.95	———
Traveler's Guide To Alaskan Camping	———	$21.95	———
Traveler's Guide To Mexican Camping	———	$21.95	———
Traveler's Guide To Camping Mexico's Baja	———	$14.95	———
Traveler's Guide To European Camping	———	$24.95	———
RV and Car Camping Vacations in Europe	———	$16.95	———

Subtract - Multiple Title Discounts

3 Book Set (Any 3 Different Titles Shown Above)	**-10.00**	———
4 Book Set (Any 4 Different Titles Shown Above)	**-15.00**	———
5 Book Set (Any 5 Different Titles Shown Above)	**-20.00**	———
6 Book Set (Any 6 Different Titles Shown Above)	**-25.00**	———
7 Book Set (All 7 Titles)	**-30.00**	———

Method of Payment
❑ Check
❑ Visa
❑ Mastercard

Order total ———
Shipping: 5.00 *
Total: ———

Credit Card # _____ Exp. date _____

Signature _____

To order by phone call (425) 822-7846
Have your VISA or MC ready
U.S. Dollars or MC/VISA only for non-U.S. orders
Rolling Homes Press is not responsible for taxes or duty on books shipped outside the U.S.

*$5 shipping regardless of quantity ordered for all orders sent to the same address in the U.S. or Canada. Actual cost for multiple books shipped to other destinations.

Visit our web site at **www.rollinghomes.com**

For mail orders allow approximately 1 month for delivery, for phone orders allow 2 weeks for delivery